Land Rights, Biodiversity Conservation and Justice

In the context of sustainable development, recent land debates tend to construct two porous camps. On the one side, norms of land justice and their advocates dictate that people's rights to tenure security are tantamount and even sometimes key to successful conservation practice. On the other hand, biodiversity protection and conservation advocates, supported by global environmental organizations and states, remain committed to conservation strategies, steeped in genetics and biological sciences, working on behalf of a "global" mandate for biodiversity and climate change mitigation.

Land Rights, Biodiversity Conservation and Justice seeks to illuminate struggles for land and territory in the context of biodiversity conservation. This edited volume explores the particular ideologies, narratives and practices that are mobilized when the agendas of biodiversity conservation practice meet, clash, and blend with the demands for land and access and control of resources from people living in, and in close proximity to, parks.

The book maintains that, while biodiversity conservation is an important goal in a time where climate change is a real threat to human existence, the successful and just future of biodiversity conservation is contingent upon land tenure security for local people. The original research gathered together in this volume will be of considerable interest to researchers of development studies, political ecology, land rights, and conservation.

Sharlene Mollett is an assistant professor in the Centre for Critical Development Studies and the Department of Human Geography Department at the University of Toronto, Canada.

Thembela Kepe is a professor in the Department of Geography, and the Centre for Critical Development Studies at the University of Toronto, Canada.

Routledge Studies in Sustainable Development

This series uniquely brings together original and cutting-edge research on sustainable development. The books in this series tackle difficult and important issues in sustainable development including: values and ethics; sustainability in higher education; climate compatible development; resilience; capitalism and de-growth; sustainable urban development; gender and participation; and well-being.

Drawing on a wide range of disciplines, the series promotes interdisciplinary research for an international readership. The series was recommended in the *Guardian*'s suggested reads on development and the environment.

Universities and Global Human Development
Theoretical and Empirical Insights for Social Change
Alejandra Boni and Melanie Walker

Sustainable Development Policy
A European Perspective
Michael von Hauff and Claudia Kuhnke

Creative Practice and Socioeconomic Crisis in the Caribbean
A Path to Sustainable Growth
Kent J. Wessinger

Engineering Education for Sustainable Development
A Capabilities Approach
Mikateko Mathebula

Sustainable Pathways for our Cities and Regions
Planning within Planetary Boundaries
Barbara Norman

Land Rights, Biodiversity Conservation and Justice
Rethinking Parks and People
Edited by Sharlene Mollett and Thembela Kepe

Land Rights, Biodiversity Conservation and Justice

Rethinking Parks and People

Edited by Sharlene Mollett and Thembela Kepe

Routledge
Taylor & Francis Group
LONDON AND NEW YORK

First published 2018
by Routledge

2 Park Square, Milton Park, Abingdon, Oxfordshire OX14 4RN
52 Vanderbilt Avenue, New York, NY 10017

Routledge is an imprint of the Taylor & Francis Group, an informa business

First issued in paperback 2019

British Library Cataloguing-in-Publication Data
A catalogue record for this book is available from the British Library

Library of Congress Cataloging-in-Publication Data
A catalog record has been requested for this book

ISBN: 978-1-138-21772-0 (hbk)
ISBN: 978-0-367-82086-2 (pbk)

Typeset in Times New Roman
by Wearset Ltd, Boldon, Tyne and Wear

Contents

Contributors

Brock Bersaglio is a postdoctoral fellow in the Department of Geography at the University of Sheffield and an Affiliated Researcher in the East African Institute at Aga Khan University. Focusing on East and Southern Africa, his work investigates the interplay between biodiversity conservation, rural society, and ideologies of nature.

Khairul Chowdhury is Associate Professor in the Department of Sociology, University of Dhaka, Bangladesh. His work examines indigenous peoples in Bangladesh and their relations to colonial and postcolonial states and ideologies of nations, development, and conservation. His research interests include frontiers, forests, climate change, and social transformation in South Asia, and contemporary social theories and Marxism.

María Camila González is an independent researcher based in Bogota, Columbia. Her research focuses on political anthropology and is particularly interested in the ways in which rural populations rework complex relations with nature and diverse spaces of the countryside in Colombia.

Shubhra Gururani is Associate Professor of Social Anthropology at York University, Canada. Her current research focuses on the politics of land acquisition, planning, and city-making in peri-urban India, with a focus on the Millennial City, Gurgaon. Her recent work has appeared in *Urban Geography* and *Economic and Political Weekly*.

Thembela Kepe is a professor in the Department of Geography and the Centre for Critical Development Studies, University of Toronto. He is also a visiting professor in Geography at Rhodes University, South Africa. He works on land rights, people–environment interactions, and rural livelihoods.

Vanessa Lamb is a lecturer in the School of Geography at the University of Melbourne. Dr. Lamb is a human-environment geographer and political ecologist whose work also includes policy analysis and research into the social dimensions of environmental change.

Elizabeth Lunstrum is an associate professor in the Department of Geography at York University in Toronto, Canada. Her research interests include green militarization, conservation-induced displacement, Indigenous conservation and wildlife management, and the political ecology of international borders. Her work focuses on southern Africa and North America.

Katherine MacDonald is a research associate with CERLAC at York University, Toronto, Canada. She is a human-environment geographer interested in the reconciliation of conservation and development across the Amazon biome.

Sharlene Mollett is an assistant professor in the Department of Human Geography and the Centre for Critical Development Studies at the University of Toronto, Canada. Her work interrogates the multiple ways racial and gendered ideologies and logics shape natural resource conflict and protected area management in Latin America.

Diana Ojeda is an associate professor at Instituto Pensar, Pontificia Universidad Javeriana. Her research bridges political ecology and feminist geopolitics in the study of everyday forms of dispossession in Colombia.

Maano Ramutsindela is Professor in the Department of Environmental and Geographical Science at the University of Cape Town, South Africa. His current research focuses on the political ecology of peace parks, land claims in protected areas, and the emergent narratives of African borders and local economic development in southern Africa.

Robin Roth is an associate professor in the Department of Geography at the University of Guelph. Dr. Roth is a trained human-environment geographer with expertise in conservation governance and conflict, political ecology, livelihood change, and aboriginal approaches to conservation.

Medupi Shabangu is a rural development manager in the Agriculture Sector Education and Training Authority in South Africa. He worked as Chief Planner and Deputy Manager in the Regional Land Claims Commission (Limpopo). His research is on the contested resolutions of land claims in the Kruger National Park, South Africa.

Megan Ybarra is an assistant professor in the Department of Geography at the University of Washington. She is author of *Green Wars: Conservation and Decolonization in Guatemala's Maya Forest*. Her research interests include conservation, racialized security, and transnational migrations.

Acknowledgments

Thembela Kepe would like to thank his co-editor, Sharlene Mollett, for her commitment and hard work in this volume. He is grateful to the Social Sciences and Humanities Research Council of Canada for financially supporting his contribution to this volume.

Sharlene Mollett would like to thank her co-editor, Thembela Kepe, for inviting her to collaborate on this volume. Thanks to the Honduran Miskito and Garifuna communities for sharing their stories of struggle, resilience, and joy. Sharlene is also appreciative for the financial assistance from the Social Sciences and Humanities Research Council of Canada and extends special thanks to her undergraduate research assistant Keisha Maloney for her reliable and diligent editorial assistance.

1 Introduction

Land rights, biodiversity conservation and justice—rethinking parks and people

Sharlene Mollett and Thembela Kepe

> In all these matters I would suggest *a little more reverence for life*, a little less straitjacketing of the future, a little more allowance for the unexpected—and a little less wishful thinking.
>
> (Hirschmann 1971, 338, authors' emphasis)

In the context of sustainable development, recent land debates tend to construct two porous camps. On the one side, norms of land justice and their advocates dictate that people's rights to tenure security are tantamount and even sometimes key to successful conservation practice. On the other hand, biodiversity conservation advocates, supported by global environmental organizations and states, remain committed to conservation strategies, steeped in genetics and biological sciences, working on behalf of a "global" mandate for biodiversity and climate change mitigation (Redford 2011; Sandbrook et al. 2012). While we see these positions with different priorities, they are also entangled and complex (Mollett 2016; Igoe 2011). In this book we seek to illuminate struggles for land and territory inside and in close proximity to protected areas, or "parks." Our use of the word "parks" reflects the myriad of protected area designs promoted by the International Union for Conservation of Nature and the different kinds of enclosures that exist beyond protected areas, such as carbon forests, payment for ecosystem programs, etc. Building on an array of insights from scholarship in political ecology, including green grabbing and land grabbing literatures, our interest lies in the kinds of power that are mobilized when biodiversity conservation practices meet, clash, and blend with the demands for land and access to and control of resources from people living in and close to "parks." The chapters in this edited collection maintain that, while biodiversity conservation is an important goal in a time where climate change is a real threat to human existence, we can no longer ignore the underlying power relations that displace people and that re-entrench severe social inequalities unfolding in the context, and in the name of biodiversity conservation. We write with Hirschmann's urging in mind and with "a little more reverence for life" (Hirschmann 1971, 338).

In this volume we acknowledge the role of global capitalism in the marginalization of people affected by biodiversity enclosures. However, our goal is to make visible other kinds of power that become mechanisms of land dispossession. We are particularly interested in how *difference* shapes the various justifications for land governance before, during, and after conservation. In this work we understand the notion of difference in terms of spatial imaginings and signifiers with their concomitant boundaries in the making, and as positionality, in reference to how race, gender, culture, class and national hierarchical differentiation mutually inform (in)justice vis-à-vis local people's land tenure and control (Gupta and Ferguson 1992; Sundberg 2004). Combined, these chapters are attentive to multiple logics of class, race, culture, gender, and colonialism embedded in the practices and processes of biodiversity conservation and land rights distribution and the active mobilization and resistance against them. In light of these spatial struggles, this edited volume offers an urgent reminder about who is made to sacrifice in the name of sustainable development and biodiversity conservation. We argue that the practice of biodiversity conservation facilitates how elites, states, and inadvertently transnational corporations seize control of land from many communities whose racial and cultural identities and land use practices are already subjugated in national and international development priorities. We counter by proposing that climate change mitigation and biodiversity conservation strategies are doomed to fail without respect, autonomy, and enforceable legal protections for the heterogeneous communities reliant on biodiverse landscapes, without which biodiverse "hot-spots" would not exist.

Political ecology of biodiversity conservation

In this volume we employ a political ecology approach to examine the logics, impacts, and practices of conservation and environmental protection. Our collective concern is with the way biodiversity conservation, supposedly designed to improve global conditions, is too often employed as a mechanism for elite control of resources and natures (Peet et al. 2010). Our insights draw from a genealogy of biodiversity conservation that is linked to international development's concern with biological diversity and the rise of the concept vis-à-vis the 1992 United Nations Conference on Environment and Development, held in Rio de Janeiro, and its accompanying Convention on Biological Diversity. The aim, overwhelmingly emerging from scientific and policy circles, focused on transforming peoples' attitudes so as to halt how *some* humans treat nature as a treasure of conquest as opposed to a collective responsibility for care (Escobar 2008). As Escobar maintains,

> under this realization, the conservation of biodiversity became a tireless task, a mission to be carried out in and on behalf of the magic, sacrosanct kingdom of wilderness.... By putting a scientific spin on the crisis, conservation biologists purported to become the authoritative spokesperson for an entire movement to save nature, having as its fundamental goal the "preservation of intact ecosystems and biotic processes."
>
> (Takacs 1996, 79, cited in Escobar 2008, 139)

Indeed, as Redford (2011) agrees, conservation organizations largely ignore the politics and power embedded in conservation and the places where environmental protection takes place. Such organizations are seemingly more concerned with "science driven approaches" "based on biocentric values and assumptions, privileging natural science views of both problems and solutions" (Redford 2011, 325; Chapin 2004). While there has been more attention to politics from conservation organizations more recently, conservation policy still operates as though humans are fundamentally menaces to the other kinds of nature.

While Redford and others suggest this has opened up space to think of "humans as legitimate elements in nature and explicitly part of the solutions to the conservation problems," many of the chapters argue that only *certain* humans get to play a role in conservation. Said differently, even in the designs of biodiversity conservation that claim to offer a more humanized form of protection—i.e., biosphere reserves, carbon markets, payments for ecosystem services—the overwhelming fact remains that local people are meant to sacrifice land control, food security, cultural traditions, and relations to nature on behalf of a global, affluent community that continues to rely on the "merchandising of biodiversity" "green developmentalism," and market conservation "that leaves intact the underlying framework of economics and the market that is inimical to nature in the first place" (Escobar 2008, 143; Martinez Alier 1996; McAfee 1999).

In this volume we are not concerned with finding fault with biodiversity conservationists, but rather we seek to disclose the chains of explanations for the re-entrenchment of precarious social inequalities that are reproduced by biodiversity conservation *mechanisms* complicit in local peoples' dispossession, dehumanization, and ongoing subjugation by states and elites. Nor do we assert that environmental protection is homogenous and always harmful. Rather, we insist that the consequences of protected area management relates to particular historical, cultural and political contingencies (Igoe 2011; West et al. 2006). While some of us in this volume are more concerned with the disclosure of these revelations and the multiple logics of power that inform them, others work toward some kind of "solution." We as editors, however, adhere to the postcolonial political ecological mantra that any "solution" that does not name power in its multiple, intersecting and more than economic iterations and leaves colonial processes intact engenders "a facile dishonesty by suggesting that an easy way out of our immense difficulties lies right around the corner" (Wainwright 2008, 284). We suggest that *change starts with thinking differently* and thus, in this vein, we rethink the relations between *parks and people*.

For clarity

The case studies in this volume disclose the underlying ways difference informs justice around land and land tenure (in)security in the context of sustainable development and biodiversity protection strategies in the Global South. Seemingly the successful and *just* future of biodiversity conservation is contingent upon land tenure security for the people living therein. In the following section we briefly explain the book's main themes as they punctuate *political ecologies of conservation: justice, history, race, and land rights*.

Justice

Justice is one of the most basic values determining the direction of daily human life, particularly how human beings relate to one another (Khakhulina 2015). Many struggles dealing with the plight of the poor and the marginalized tend to focus on justice as a social value that should be central to any positive social change. However, justice as a concept is elusive, often with multiple and contradictory meanings. At the most basic level, there are three conceptions of justice, which are not mutually exclusive. These include procedural justice, which is the application of the law according to prescribed principles and due process; redistributive and social justice, which focuses on fairness in the distribution of rewards, opportunities, and burdens in life; and retributive justice, which is about what is considered appropriate sanctions and punishments for violating certain agreed rules and regulations (Jary and Jary 1995; Rawls 1999; Robertson 2004). In the context of rethinking parks and people *procedural justice* reflects how transparency and fairness inform the processes through which land and natural resources are allocated, and how conflicts are resolved. A colonial legacy has meant that for many marginalized people procedural justice is elusive, and favors a select few. This of course often sets the stage for other kinds of injustices.

Our understanding of redistributive or social justice is informed by John Rawls's (1999) framework of justice as fairness, instrumental in most contemporary notions of justice. Rawls's major contribution is the principle of difference, where he argues that inequalities are justifiable if they are arranged to benefit the most disadvantaged people in a society. As a strong believer in equity, Rawls believes that justice needs to unfold in three stages, in a particular order: to secure equal basic liberties; then to secure fair equality of opportunity; and, finally, for social and economic inequalities to be arranged to benefit the most disadvantaged people. Even though we acknowledge that Rawls's views are not necessarily widely accepted, we wish to point out again that many tensions that exist between land rights and biodiversity conservation are fundamentally about the failure of states, past and present, to uphold the principle of fairness without discriminating based on social difference.

The ways in which contemporary states fail to remedy injustices of the past to the satisfaction of the victims of those injustices is key to land conflicts. Atuahene (2007), for example, has argued for recognition of what she calls property-induced invisibility, in thinking about land justice, emphasizing the socially embedded nature of land, and that the loss of land during colonialism had dehumanizing effect on the victims, which brought about their invisibility, or what she also calls social death. In agreement with others (e.g., Andrews 2006), Atuahene believes that any restorative processes that fails to return the victim's dignity in turn fails to advance true justice. Restoring land as a natural resource alone, she argues, is not enough; recognizing historical roots of those injustices must remain central (Osmani 2010).

History

The overlapping struggles over place and natures have histories. The colonial and nation-building histories from which these struggles emerge continue to shape their formations however contested (Stoler 2016). A focus on history in this volume means not taking for granted "the connectivities joining colonial pasts to 'postcolonial' presents" (Stoler 2016, 4) but being attentive to their mechanisms. Within political ecology, scholars make clear the salience of history. For Offen, historical analysis is significant to a political ecology of conservation in how " 'pristine' landscapes are, in fact, anthropomorphized landscapes that often (politically) conceal their own human history—a history of violence, disease, demographic collapse, colonialism, migration and conceptual transformation" (Offen 2004, 26). Indeed. A historicization of place discloses the way parks are significant to the "formation of a national identity for the dominant settler culture, an identity forged through a mythologized encounter with nature" (Neumann 1998, 32). History helps disclose for some what others seek to conceal, particularly when such histories are "situated" (Peluso 2012, 80). To rethink parks and people, many chapters in this volume make visible how "history making practices often disguise exploitation and oppressive associations" (Peluso 2012, 80). Similarly, the way scholars draw upon histories both contemporary and long past is to "attend to the evasive history of empire that disappears so easily into other appellations and other, more available, contemporary terms" (Stoler 2013, 23). The social landscape upon which colonial power and mechanisms materially and imaginatively influence space are arranged by the "racial ontologies they called in to being, and by the cumulative historical deficiencies certain populations are seen to embody—and the ongoing threats to the body politic associated with them" (Stoler 2013, 23). To reveal these processes engenders possibilities for change.

Race and the politics of difference

History informs race and racial meanings. The chapters in the volume have taken on race in various ways ranging from acknowledgment of past inequalities that shape the present and showing race as an actively producing social formation in the context of land struggles and biodiversity conservation. While not all authors attend to race explicitly, a politics of difference is always present in their colorful discussions. For us, race is a "contingent historical phenomenon that has varied over time and space" (Appelbaum et al. 2003, 2). While it may seem like everyday common sense that race is a social construction without biological foundation (Bonnett and Nayak 2003), the "materiality of race cannot and should not be eclipsed in favor of thinking about its apparent mobility and malleability" (Mahtani 2014, 360). Indeed, racial meanings and characteristics speak to more than skin color; racial ideologies are also embedded in labor power and intersect with other forms of power like gender, caste, nation, religion, sexuality, existing in "intimate, reciprocal and contradictory relations" (McClintock 1995, 5; Goldberg 1993). Notwithstanding the multiple masks that race sports, racial ideologies and racial meanings inform the structures and representations of our social natural world (Bonnett 2000; Goldberg 1993; Kobayashi and Peake 2000).

Racialization is also an important aspect in the construction of difference. Racialization, "the process of marking differences to hierarchical discourses grounded in colonial encounters and their national legacies" (Appelbaum 2003, 2) is key to understanding how some communities both enclosed in protected areas and outside their boundaries become rendered "unimaginable" (Nixon 2011). In borrowing from Nixon, we are alluding to people located inside the nation-state but "whose vigorously unimagined condition becomes indispensable to maintaining a highly selective discourse of national development" (Nixon 2011, 151). Key to rethinking parks and people we reject the way "racial differences are stubbornly held up as natural" (Mollett and Faria 2013, 117) or how "[r]ace serves to naturalize the groupings it identifies in its own name" (Goldberg 1993, 81, cited in Mollett and Faria 2013). To move against this, we acknowledge how the case studies in our volume are a theater for multiple racial projects, such projects do the ideological labor that entangles structure and representation (Omi and Winant 2000). A critical examination of the relationship between parks and people engenders multiple racial projects such as European colonialism and conquest and settler colonialism, a land-centered project where "settler colonizers come to stay" (Wolfe 2006; Kauanui 2016). In addition, a "coloniality of power," where race serves as a genre to distinguish between humans and those human beings deemed less than human is also instrumentalized through conservation practice (Mignolo 2015; McKittrick 2006; Weheliye 2014). As Pulido notes, "we can never overlook the fact that racial ideology (along with guns) enabled colonization," and classifications of "indigenous peoples as less than fully human was entirely necessary for the colonial project" (Pulido 2017, 527).

Land rights

Rethinking parks and people centers the way biodiversity conservation relies on the enclosure of land. For us this exemplifies the way protected area management is imbued in colonial ideologies and exists as a colonial practice, as colonialism is a structure and not simply an event (Wolfe 2006; Quijano 2007). Thus our understanding of land rights in this volume acknowledges that land is an assemblage of power relations with "an especially rich and diverse array of 'affordances'—uses and values it affords to us, including the capacity to sustain *human* life" (Li 2014, 39). The materiality and form matter, as do the "devices" employed into making land a resource for some. For others, land's "buried epistemologies" and unburied ontologies link land relations to other kinds of natures including human beings (Li 2014; Willems-Braun 1997; Escobar 2015). Land

and land control are significant for conservation. For many parts of the world, customary and de facto rights to land were sufficient for long-term tenure security. The cases in our volume show the lack of formal land rights not only makes Indigenous, Afro-descendants, women, and the poor more susceptible to large-scale land transactions, which are not only facilitated via neoliberal hegemonic land titling programs, both legal and extra-legal, but green grabs as well (Fairhead and Leach 2012).

Land legislation does not always satisfy the needs and desires of the world's informal landholders. Land rights in the shape of single users and individual land plots are welcomed by many rural peoples. In fact, according to the World Bank, only 30 percent of the world's population has legal ownership to their land (World Bank 2017). But individuated land titles do not reflect the social relations to land, water, and other natures common to many Indigenous, Afro-descendant and various other rural populations. Rather, land rights, as designed by development institutions and sanctioned by states, often only treat land as a natural resource, without recognizing that the meanings of land and water take shape in collective ways that are always unfinished (Agnew and Oslender 2010; Bryan 2012; Offen 2003).

The book

We bring together an eclectic group of scholars who have ongoing and empirically grounded research projects across the globe in such places as Mozambique, South Africa, Guatemala, Guyana, Honduras, Colombia, Thailand, Bangladesh, Kenya, and India, and who are located in universities in both the Global North and Global South. The chapters in this volume employ a variety of analytical frameworks. They may be read as a collection or as stand-alone pieces.

Justice

There is growing agreement that justice in land requires *intuitive justice*, whereby the collective voices of the people provide material for mitigating circumstances or create space for deviating from formal and legalistic conceptions of justice (Gibson 2008; Kepe, Fukuda, Hicks, Shortly, and Brode 2017). "Intuitive justice" is about a relational and affective approach to the land that could produce justice by acknowledging and respecting local contexts and the power relations at work. *Recognition* and *participation* are key to intuitive justice (Schlosberg 2004).

Intuitive justice is a central theme in Kepe's chapter. With a focus on South Africa, Kepe draws insights from conflicts over land in the context of conservation. Kepe argues that it is the hegemonic alliances between private businesses and conservation, or those between powerful international environmental NGOs and biodiversity conservation projects, that impede justice for local people. Such powerful alliances silence their claims. Ramutsindela and Shabangu also use the case of South Africa's land claim process within conservation areas to explain the tensions between land rights and conservation. They suggest that this tension persists partly because land rights issues are generally seen by the elite as inimical to nature conservation efforts. Through *environmental justice* framework, these scholars examine land claims in the Kruger National Park, and argue that land restitution does not necessarily guarantee environmental justice. Such environmental justice, they suggest, instead hinges on the manner in which land claims are settled.

Violence

> Violence is a habitus … at once structured and structuring: structured because the idea of violence results from historical events, stored as memory of past deeds, of past encounters, of past frustrations; and structuring because the idea of violence informs human actions, determines the acceptability, even the banality of violence, if not the ability to erase the scandal of its occurrence.
>
> (Dumont 1992, 277, cited in Peluso and Watts 2001, 6)

Violence is embedded in environmental struggle (Peluso and Watts 2001). The geographic imaginaries that inform the imperative of protected area enclosures in the Global South often originate from affluent, urban, Global North residents who treat their perspectives as universal and protected areas and their inhabitants, as problematic, read as insecure (Kelly and Ybarra 2016). This has led to the practices of "green security," what Kelly and Ybarra (2016) explain as "the overt use of policing and militarization of protected areas' vast territories (land or maritime) in the name of security" (2016, 171). Such militarization polices borders both seen and unseen and thus such "borders contribute back to the political projects that made them possible" (Valdivia et al. 2014, 687).

As Dumont's definition of violence asserts, we include in our meanings for violence the acts and conditions of displacement. In the context of conservation, development-induced displacement often refers to "the removal of a thing from its place, putting out of place" (Agrawal and Redford 2009, cited in Mollett 2014, 30). While in this context land loss is often enacted through eviction from parks, conservation-induced land loss may also look more like displacement-in-place. For Mollett (2014, 30) this concept acknowledges that displacement is inherent to international development writ large, so that a community may become displaced but remain in place but through "green security," law, or threats of violence, they become dispossessed from access and control of their lands, but without removal (see also Katz 2004; Nixon 2011; Vandergeest et al. 2006). In this volume, displacement exemplifies the way violence is more than simply extreme acts such as war and murder, but violence occurs when people's relations to nature are "irrevocably altered in ways that foreclose or otherwise impede possibilities for habitation" (Lunstrum et al. 2016, 130).

In this vein the co-authored chapter by Lunstrum and Ybarra flesh out the ways state actors in Africa and Central America treat Mozambique's Limpopo

National Park and Guatemala's Maya Biosphere Reserve, and the people therein, as sites and sources of insecurity and threats. To do so, residents in each of these spaces are rendered trespassers and become defined as a "racialized enemy." The cases together are indicative of the entanglement between conservation, race, security, and displacement. In a similar way, Bersaglio's chapter builds on the concept of "green violence" to make visible the increase in violent conflict on private wildlife conservancies. The white settlers who own these large-scale wildlife landscapes in Laikipia Kenya employ "green violence" as way to protect privately owned pasture from pastoralist-livestock invasions. Bersaglio argues that the conflicts that occur as a result of this tension is in fact a "delayed effect of settler colonialism ... rooted in racialized dispossession" (Bersaglio this volume). In similar ways, Ojeda and González combine paramilitary state-sanctioned violence and sustainable development projects to show the ways in which peasants work to define themselves as *green subjects*. In Colombia, peasants are commonly excluded from the benefits of development programs aimed at land titling and biodiversity protection, unable to instrumentalize a political language of ethnicity that has tended to open space and resources, however insecure, to Indigenous and Afro-descendant communities. Ojeda and González argue that peasant space—or, rather, their territorialities—become *elusive* in the increasing landscapes of enclosure and dispossession in the Colombian Caribbean.

Enclosure and exclusion is also the theme in Gururani's chapter. Unique to the volume, Gururani examines the political ecology of the commons perched between rural and urban governance of land and property in Gurgaon, India. This chapter complicates the tensions between and among agro-pastoralists and environmentalists in the making of a park on the urban periphery. As a way to advance "critical ecological praxis," Gururani attends to the ways in which conservation practices are implicated in the "double edge of exclusions" within urban space.

Indigenous territorial struggles

As mentioned above, land rights do not always reflect community claims and their ontological foundations. These active relationships to land are better represented in territorial claims. Territorial claims seek to invoke different ontological meanings from land claims. A territorial claim in essence contests the meanings of territory as "natural," and instead is understood as an "order [that] has been historically constituted through practices of exclusion frequently justified in racial terms" (Bryan 2012, 216; Escobar 2008). While Indigenous and Afro-descendant peoples' territorial claims are recognized in international law and within a number of biodiversity conservation protocols, as our volume shows, neither customary nor statutory rights to territory guarantee territorial security for Indigenous and Afro-descendant peoples. Rather, their tenure (in)security relies on their historical (mis)recognition that places them outside the citizenry and sometimes outside humanity vis-à-vis national elites and dominant ethnic groups.

This volume acknowledges how land and territorial rights are not granted by benevolent states, but won by tenacious Indigenous communities who know their rights and who are willing to fight to defend them. For instance, in his chapter Chowdury illuminates how cultural logics interplay with the growing limits in common property forestry conservation in Chittagong Hills, Bangladesh. Similar to green grabbing critiques, Indigenous peoples in Bangladesh are finding themselves less able to resist against state- and corporate-led conservation and development projects and as a result face threats of displacement. In this chapter, struggles over common property forest are not simply over resources but are also reflected in ethnic contests.

Like Chowdury, MacDonald highlights how Indigenous territorial struggles are at once ontological struggles. In this chapter, MacDonald examines how the Low Carbon Development Strategy taken on by the Guyanese government underpins the newly created Kanuku Mountains Protected Area. Highlighted in the tensions between the park administration and the Wapishana peoples who live in South Rupununi is the way the Wapishana mobilize Indigenous world views as part of a conscientization movement aimed as an anti-colonial struggle for self-determination. Drawing on a history of territorial struggle, MacDonald discloses the contradictions in the politics of state conservation in Guyana.

Like Guyana and Bangladesh, Karen territoriality in Thailand emerges as a result of struggle. In Lamb and Roth's chapter, they argue that history illuminates significant changes in the relationship between science, Indigenous and local knowledge, and place-based movements. The authors make visible the changing landscape of natural resource struggles where the use of "technologies of humility" bring nature claims based on "science" and claims based on local knowledge together in complementary and overlapping ways. The authors also reflect on how "technologies of humility" have led to their own successful collaborations unsettling, for better or worse, past claims to expertise and legitimacy in Thailand.

In the final chapter, Mollett rethinks the relations between "parks and people" by illuminating the limits to territorial formalization inside the Honduran Rio Plátano Biosphere Reserve. In this chapter Mollett reflects on the how a history of colonial power in the Honduran Mosquitia is not erased by territorial legislation, however significant. But, in fact, the forms of violence in the reserve, complicated by protected area policies, have similar logics and justifications to the violence perpetrated against the bodies of Indigenous women mobilizing in defense of Indigenous lands and territories *outside* the reserve. In this chapter Mollett thinks through the ways protected area practice and the state's extractivist development agenda are linked through a shared logic of Indigenous peoples' dehumanization.

Together these chapters serve as a reminder—in a time when more-than-human natures become instrumentalized by conservation practice as a mechanism to ignore local people's needs in parks—that at the heart of these struggles and tensions between conservation and land rights are people, namely, human beings.

References

Agnew, John and Ulrich Oslender. 2010. Overlapping Territorialities, Sovereignty in Dispute: Empirical Lessons in Latin America. *Tabula Rasa*, 13: 191–213.

Agrawal, Arun and Kent Redford. 2009. Place, Conservation, and Displacement. *Conservation and Society*, 7(1): 56.

Andrews, M. 2006. Struggling for a Life in Dignity. In *The Land Question in South Africa: The Challenge of Transformation and Reconciliation*, edited by L. Ntsebeza and R. Hall. Cape Town: HSRC Press.

Appelbaum, Nancy P. 2003. *Muddied Waters: Race, Region, and Local History in Columbia, 1846–1948*. Durham, NC: Duke University Press.

Appelbaum, Nancy P., Anne S. Macpherson, and Karin Alejandra Rosemblatt. 2003. *Race and Nation in Modern Latin America*. Chapel Hill, NC, and London: University of North Carolina Press, 2003.

Atuahene, Bernadette. 2007. From Reparation to Restoration: Moving Beyond Property Rights to Restoring Political and Economic Visibility. *SMU Law Review*, 60: 1419–1470.

Bonnett, Alastair. 2000. *White Identities: Historical and International Perspectives*. Upper Saddle River, NJ: Prentice-Hall.

Bonnett, Alastair and Anoop Nayak. 2003. Cultural Geographies of Racialization – The Territory of Race. In *Handbook of Cultural Geography*, edited by Kay Anderson, Mona Domosh, Steve Pile and Nigel Thrift. London: Sage.

Bryan, Joe. 2012. Rethinking Territory: Social Justice and Neoliberalism in Latin America's Territorial Turn. *Geography Compass*, 63(12): 215–226.

Chapin, Mac. *A Challenge to Conservationists*. WorldWatch Institute. www.worldwatch.org/system/files/EP176A.pdf.

Escobar, Arturo. 2008. *Territories of Difference: Place, Movements, Life, Redes*. Durham, NC: Duke University Press.

Fairhead, James and Melissa Leach. 2012. Green Grabbing: A New Appropriation of Nature? *The Journal of Peasant Studies*, 39(2): 237–261.

Escobar, Arturo. 2015. Degrowth, Postdevelopment, and Transitions: A Preliminary Conversation. *Sustainablilty Science*, 10(3): 451–462.

Gibson, J. L. 2008. "Group Identities and Theories of Justice: An Experimental Investigation into the Justice and Injustice of Land Squatting in South Africa". *The Journal of Politics*, 70(3): 700–716.

Goldberg, David Theo. 1993. *Racist Culture: Philosophy and the Politics of Meaning*. Hoboken, NJ: Wiley Blackwell.

Gupta, Akhil and James Ferguson. 1992. Beyond "Culture": Space, Identity, and the Politics of Difference. *Cultural Anthropology*, 7(1): 6–23.

Hirschmann, Albert. 1971. *A Bias for Hope: Essays on Development and Latin America*. New Haven, CT: Yale University Press.

Igoe, James. 2011. Re-reading Conservation Critique: A Response to Redford. *Oryx*, 45(3): 333–334.

Jary, D. and Jary, J. 1995. Justice. In *Collins Dictionary of Sociology*. Glasgow: HarperCollins.

Katz, C. 2004. *Growing Up Global: Economic Restructuring and Children's Everyday Lives*. Minneapolis, MN: University of Minnesota Press.

Kauanui, J. K. 2016. "A Structure Not an Event": Settler Colonialism and Enduring Indigeneity. *Lateral*, 5(1).

Kelly, Alice B. and Megan Ybarra. 2016. Introduction to Themed Issue: "Green Security in Protected Areas". *Geoforum*, 69: 17–175.

Kepe, T., Fukuda, K., Hicks, M., Shortly, A and Brode, L. 2017. *Unlimiting Land Justice: The Importance of Acknowledging Multiplicity and Complexity of Meanings of Land and Justice*. Unpublished paper, University of Toronto.

Khakhulina, Liudmila. 2015. The Persistence of Mass Conceptions of Justice. *Sociological Research*, 54(2): 71–90.

Kobayashi, Audrey and Linda Peake. 2000. Racism Out of Place: Thoughts on Whiteness and an Antiracist Geography in the New Millennium. *Annals of the Association of American Geographers*, 90(2): 392–403.

Li, Tania Murray. 2014. What Is Land? Assembling a Resource for Global Investment. *Transactions of the Institute of British Geographers*, 39: 589–602.

Lunstrum, Elizabeth, Pablo Bose and Anna Zalik. 2016. Environmental Displacement: The Common Ground of Climate Change, Extraction, and Conservation. *Area*, 48(2): 130–133.

McAfee, Katherine. 1999. Setting Nature to Save It? Biodiversity and Green Developmentalism. *Environmental Planning D: Society and Space*, 17: 133–154.

McClintock, Anne. 1995. *Imperial Leather: Race, Gender and Sexuality in the Colonial Contest*. New York: Routledge.

McKittrick, Katherine. 2006. *Demonic Grounds: Black Women in the Cartographies of Struggle*. Minneapolis, MN: University of Minnesota Press.

Mahtani, Minelle. 2014. Toxic Geographies: Absences in Critical Race Thought and Practice in Social and Cultural Geography. *Social and Cultural Geography*, 15(4): 359–367.

Martinez Alier, Joan. 2002. 1996. Merchandising Biodiversity. *Capitalism, Nature, Socialism*, 7(1): 37–54.

Mignolo, Walter. 2015. Huntington's Fears: "Latinidad" in the Horizon of the Modern/Colonial World. In *Latino/as in the World-System: Decolonization Struggles in the 21st Century U.S. Empire*, edited by Ramon Grosfoguel, Nelson Maldonado-Torres and José David Saldívar. New York: Routledge.

Mollett, Sharlene and Caroline Faria. 2013. Messing with Gender in Feminist Political Ecology. *Geoforum*, 45: 116–125.

Mollett, Sharlene. 2014. A "Modern" Paradise: Land, Labor, and Displacement-in-Place on the Honduran North Coast. *Latin American Perspectives*, 41(6): 27–45.

Mollett, Sharlene. 2016. The Power of Plunder: Rethinking Land Grabbing in Latin America. *Antipode*, 48(2): 412–432.

Neumann, Roderick P. 1998. Imposing Wilderness: Struggles over Livelihood and Nature Preservation in Africa. Los Angeles and Berkeley, CA: University of California Press.

Nixon, Rob. 2011. *Slow Violence and the Environmentalism of the Poor*. Cambridge, MA: Harvard University Press.

Offen, Karl. 2003. Narrating Place and Identity, or Mapping Miskitu Land Claims in Northeastern Nicaragua. *Human Organization*, 62(4): 382–392.

Offen, Karl. 2003. The Territorial Turn: Making Black Territories in Pacific Colombia. *Journal of Latin American Geography*, 2(1): 43–73.

Offen, Karl. 2004. Historical Political Ecology: An Introduction. *Historical Geography*, 32: 19–42.

Omi, Michael and Howard Winant. 2000. Racial Formation. In *Race Critical Theories: Text and Context*, edited by Philomena Essed and David Theo Goldberg. Hoboken, NJ: Wiley-Blackwell.

Peet, R., Robbins, P. and Watts, M. eds., 2010. *Global Political Ecology*. Routledge.
Peluso, Nancy Lee. 2012. What's Nature Got to Do with It? A Situated Historical Perspective on Socio-natural Commodities. *Development and Change*, 43(1): 79–104.
Peluso, Nancy, and Michael Watts. 2001. *Violent Environments*. Ithaca, NY: Cornell University Press.
Pulido, Laura. 2017. Geographies of Race and Ethnicity II: Environmental Racism, Racial Capitalism and State-Sanctioned Violence. *Progress in Human Geography*, 41(4): 524–533.
Osmani, S. R. 2010. Theory of Justice for an Imperfect World: Exploring Amartya Sen's Idea of Justice. *Journal of Human Development Capabilities*, 11(4): 599–607.
Quijano, Anibal. 2007. Coloniality and Modernity/Rationality. *Cultural Studies*, 21(2–3): 168–178.
Rawls, John. 1999. A Theory of Justice: Revised Edition. Cambridge MA: Harvard University Press.
Redford, Kent. H. 2011. Misreading the Conservation Landscape. *Oryx*, 45(30): 324–330.
Robertson, Robbie. 2004. The Historical Context and Significance of Globalization. *Development and Change*, 35(3): 557–565.
Sandbrook, Chris, William, M. Adams, Bram Büscher and Bhaskar Vira. 2012. Social Research and Biodiversity Conservation. *Conservation Biology*, 27(6): 1487–1490.
Schlosberg, D. 2014. "Reconceiving Environmental Justice: Global Movements and Political Theories." *Environmental Politics*, 13(3): 517–540.
Stoler, Ann Laura. 2013. *Imperial Debris: On Ruins and Ruination*. Durham, NC: Duke University Press.
Stoler, Ann Laura. 2016. *Duress: Imperial Durabilities in Our Times*. Durham, NC: Duke University Press.
Sundberg, Juanita. 2004. Identities-in-the-Making: Conservation, Gender, and Race in the Maya Biosphere Reserve, Guatemala. *Gender, Place and Culture*, 11(1): 44–66.
Takacs, David. 1996. The Idea of Biodiversity. Baltimore, MD: Johns Hopkins University Press.
Valdivia, Gabriela, Wendy Wolford and Flora Lu. 2014. Border Crossings: New Geographies of Protection and Production in the Galápagos Islands. *Annals of the Association of American Geographers*, 104(3): 686–701.
Vandergeest, Peter, Pablo Idahosa and Pablo S. Bose. 2006. Development's Displacements: Ecologies, Economies and Cultures at Risk. Vancouver, BC: UBC Press.
Wainwright, Joel. 2008. *Decolonizing Development: Colonial Power and the Maya*. Blackwell Publishing.
Weheliye, Alexander. 2014. *Habeas Viscus: Racializing Assemblages, Biopolitics and Black Feminist Theories of the Human*. Durham, NC: Duke University Press.
West, Paige, James Igoe and Dan Brockington. 2006. Parks and Peoples: The Social Impact of Protected Areas. *Annual Review of Anthropology*, 35: 251–277.
Willems-Braun, Bruce. 1997. Buried Epistemologies: The Politics of Nature in (Post) Colonial British Columbia. *Annals of the Association of American Geographers*, 87(1): 3–31.
Wolfe, Patrick. 2006. Settler Colonialism and the Elimination of the Native. *Journal of Genocide Research*, 8(4): 387–409.
World Bank. 2017. *Land: Brief*. Washington, DC: The World Bank IRBD-IDA.

Part I

Justice

2 Meanings, alliances and the state in tensions over land rights and conservation in South Africa

Thembela Kepe

Introduction

Just like many other countries, South Africa has had a very challenging time mitigating the tensions between the goal of biodiversity conservation and other socio-political goals such as ensuring justice and equity for designated groups that have legitimate claims to spaces affected by conservation. Throughout colonial and apartheid eras these tensions in South Africa were characterized by racial and class divisions that enhanced the marginalization and disenfranchisement of the black population. A large body of literature has shown how, even after the official end of apartheid during the early 1990s and despite progressive policies on conservation (Wynberg 2002) and land rights, at least on paper, biodiversity conservation in South Africa still reflects the relations of power and privilege that have shaped this society (Cock and Fig 2000; Ramutsindela 2004; Kepe 2008; Walker 2008; Butler and Richardson 2015). In particular, there is increasing consensus among scholars that biodiversity conservation in South Africa has not sufficiently broken away from its historical ties with racist policies of colonial and apartheid dispensations (Kepe 2009). The post-apartheid land reform program, which seeks to redress racially based land injustices wrought by apartheid, has helped cast a spotlight on biodiversity conservation. This is because many existing protected areas were established on lands that were dispossessed from black people, meaning that they are now subject to land claims under the land reform program. Resolving land claims on protected areas in South Africa has been controversial at best, for a number of reasons, including the implementation of a policy that forbids any change in land use from conservation to other uses (The Memorandum of Understanding between the Minister of Agriculture and Land Affairs and the Minister of Environmental Affairs and Tourism, signed on 2 May 2007) (Government of South Africa 2007); the continuing mistrust by the conservation lobby (state officials and conservation activists) of poor black people's interest; and management abilities in biodiversity conservation (Kepe 2009, 2014). Kepe (2012) has argued that the role of the state in reconciling land rights and biodiversity conservation is ambiguous, therefore questionable. In addition to the issues discussed above, much of the analysis of this tension has increasingly included a critique of neoliberal conservation

(Büscher 2010), as well as the state's focus on creating post-apartheid policies and legislation that impress on paper but yield no tangible success in practice (Paterson 2007; Ntshona, Kraai, Kepe and Saliwa 2010).

While these angles of analysis of the tension between biodiversity conservation and the land and natural resource rights of the marginalized people are useful in raising awareness of injustices, as well as the prevailing challenges, there is a need to extend the analysis. This chapter, therefore, seeks to explore different lenses through which the tension can be viewed, with the hope of opening up new ways of exploring biodiversity conservation–land rights conflicts in South Africa, and elsewhere, where the broader goal is that of social justice for all. Thus, drawing from the literature, and using examples from selected South African cases, this chapter proposes that there are several issues currently escaping the debate on this subject. The first one is the issue of alliances that form around either biodiversity conservation on the one hand or the land or resource rights of the marginalized people on the other hand. The strength of an alliance around each of these disparate goals is rooted on the perceived meanings of both land (and land rights) and biodiversity conservation to those who support each of these. The dominant view is that conservation can yield tangible benefits for all people, including the local poor (e.g., claimants). Thus biodiversity conservation is increasingly seen as a commodity; with quantifiable aspects (e.g., economic valuation of flora and fauna; the size of the protected area, number of species under threat etc.). But deeper meanings of land to local people (claimants) include intangible aspects that are less appreciated by outsiders. The second issue is about the ambiguous role of the state in the tension in question. In South Africa the state is responsible for land claims on conservation land. Yet, as a signatory to many environmental conventions, and having enshrined biodiversity conservation in the Constitution (Section 24 of the Bill of Rights), the state is duty-bound to maintain biodiversity conservation, including through neoliberal approaches. The state's bias for biodiversity conservation often contradicts local people's land justice goals, thus exacerbating the tension.

In attempting to analyze biodiversity-land rights tensions in South Africa through understanding the alliances on both side of the conflict, as well as the ambiguous role of the state, it is important to reflect on whether or not, as well as how, justice manifests as an outcome of processes that all the stake holders mentioned above engage in. Justice should be a central goal in all attempts to decolonize biodiversity conservation, as well as for dealing with land injustices in countries that were colonized.

This chapter draws on examples from South Africa to explore the challenges mentioned above. The examples are not drawn from one particular study. Rather, they are based on long-term research by the author of this chapter, as well as on other secondary literature. Following this introduction, the next section presents a brief overview of debates on the form and dynamics of justice in the conservation–land rights nexus in South Africa. This is followed by a discussion of selected examples that show the importance of alliances in both the biodiversity conservation and land rights sectors. The last section before the discussion and conclusion reflects on the role on the ambiguous role of the state in the conservation–land rights tension in the country.

Land and justice in biodiversity conservation

Political changes that swept through South Africa during the late 1980s and early 1990s, which ushered in the post-apartheid dispensation, did not spare biodiversity conservation. The documented links between African conservation and colonialism, and apartheid in the case of South Africa (Beinart 2000; Ramutsindela 2004; Kepe 2009), where conservation areas owed their existence to violent, racially motivated exclusions of black people from their land to make way for conservation, have necessitated contemporary debates about land, conservation and justice. In South Africa, for the most part land justice in biodiversity conservation revolves around redressing past injustices that denied marginalized people their land and resource rights on land that is, or later became, conservation areas. These models of redress have taken many forms, including restoration of land rights to the victims of injustice following a land claim (Ramutsindela 2003; Carruthers 2007; Walker 2008), or different versions of co-management arrangements between the state and the victims (Kepe 2009; Ntshona, Kraai, Kepe and Saliwa 2010; Cock and Fig 2000; Thondhlana, Cundill and Kepe 2016) or through projects that purport to increase material benefit to local people (e.g., tourism revenues), which are sometimes used in combination with the other models (Kepe 2009; Spencely and Meyer 2012). However, there is clear evidence that all of these models fall short in terms of dealing with the question of justice, as well as in simply improving the livelihoods of the people who are targeted through these models (see Ntshona, Kraai, Kepe and Saliwa 2010). I suggest that these models of justice are likely based on understandings of justice that are not consistent with those of the local people who are supposed to be the focus of the said justice.

Researchers have increasingly acknowledged the need for conceptions of justice that accommodate political, economic, cultural and geographical differences, while also recognizing the historical roots of injustices (Osmani 2010). Yet, as Kepe, Fukuda, Hicks, Shortly and Brode (2017) argue, more often than not there continues to be a strong preference by the state and others in power for the most commonly understood and simplistic forms of justice that tend to be hegemonic, and linear. These authors suggest that there is a need to move toward taking seriously *intuitive justice*, whereby the collective voices of the people concerned provide material for mitigating circumstances or create space for deviating from formal and legalistic conceptions of justice (Gibson 2008). Here I am proposing the use of the term "intuitive justice" as a relational and affective approach to the land that could produce justice by focusing on local contexts and the power relations at work. This idea draws from Gibson's (2008) idea of "common sense justice" that concept is meant to invoke. However, as Kepe, Fukuda, Hicks, Shortly and Brode (2017) note, it is important to acknowledge that "common sense" is a deeply gendered and could possibly assume a common experience; something that is not consistent with the arguments of multiplicity of justice.

The point about intuitive justice in terms of land rights and protected areas is based on the belief, in agreement with other voices, that multiple meanings of land exist (Kepe, Hall and Cousins 2008; Li 2014) and that these meanings, in their diversity, are dynamic and can be in conflict with one another at any one point in time. Thus, in the case of South Africa, and most likely in many other places with similar conditions, dealing with land injustice that focuses on only one meaning of land risks continuing discontent among those affected by land injustice. Therefore, by highlighting the loss of land as a form of identity and power, for example, seekers of land justice do not necessarily mean to ignore other meanings of the land, which may include land as an important natural resource that is crucial in their livelihoods (Kepe and Tessaro 2014). I suggest that models of addressing land injustice in protected areas in South Africa have thus far narrowly focused on some meanings of land to people, while excluding many other understandings. This, I believe, is an opportunity for learning and further research.

Alliances and advocacy in conservation and land rights

The intensity of tensions that can be observed between biodiversity conservation and land rights is often not only dependent on what happens at a particular locality, at a particular point in time. It can be argued that what manifests at local level is partly directly or indirectly influenced by the alliances that exist on both side of the conflict. Here alliances are understood as relationships that people, groups or states form around a common goal, where there is an assumption of mutual benefit. Observations within biodiversity conservation and land rights show that alliances can form around taking a common stand on an issue, often with one or more powerful members of the alliance supporting weaker ones, as advocates, financially and ideologically. Weaker members of an alliance, being aware of their limitations, often subscribe to visions of more powerful institutions for their mere survival (Kepe 2014). As in many other places around the world, in South Africa these patterns exist in the biodiversity conservation–land rights tension. Below I review dynamics around these alliances, and present some examples from South Africa, for both the conservation and land rights sides of the tension.

Conservation alliances

It can be argued that biodiversity conservation has greatly benefited from being closely tied to the broader sentiment of “environmental concerns” that has dominated debates about the impact of human beings on the Earth. Action around these global environmental concerns have manifested through a focus on environmental governance to deal with the threats facing biodiversity, as well as for mitigating issues such as climate change and over-exploitation of natural resources (Adger, Benjaminsen, Brown and Svarstad 2001; Steiner, Kimball and Scanlon 2003). Biodiversity conservation had already taken root by the time the global initiatives and meetings that focused on climate change and sustainable development took place between the 1970s and 2010s. Modern biodiversity conservation is seen to have established itself during colonial expansion in the seventeenth century (Grove 1995). The United Nations Conference on the Human Environment held in Stockholm in 1972, the World Conservation Strategy developed by the United Nations Environment Program, and the subsequent World Commission on Environment and Development (1987), the Earth Summit in Brazil in 1992, the World Summit on Sustainable Development in South Africa in 2002 (or Rio+10), and the United Nations Conference on Sustainable Development (or Rio+20) in 2012 (Kepe 2010; Scoones 2007; Springett 2013) can be seen as a catalyst for many conservation alliances globally. From these initiatives conservation alliances emerged, including international agencies supporting national states, or NGOs within countries; international NGOs collaborating with national, provincial and local departments and NGOs; and national, provincial and local departments collaborating with locally based environmental organizations. Additionally, academic research has also been used to provide evidence for or against particular conservation initiatives (e.g., research institutes or conservation programs attached to universities).

With power differences always evident in conservation alliances, it is to be expected that some conservation discourses are hegemonic, with views and values of local Indigenous people marginalized for the most part. Writing about Australia, Lee (2016) has even labeled the International Union for the Conservation of Nature's (IUCN) protected area guidelines as a form of tyranny against Indigenous people, as they do not recognize the relational values of these local people. This scenario appears to be a pattern in most other similar situations globally, where local Indigenous people appear on the losing end of relationships with outsiders in regard to how they relate to their natural environment. For example, IUCN's Protected Area Categories, particularly categories 1a (strict nature reserve) and 1b (wilderness area), leave little or no room for alternative uses of the areas by local people, irrespective of the history of land and resource rights (Lee 2016). Similarly, mission statements of many other international conservation NGOs that purport to support community-based conservation strategies, such as the WWF's mission "to conserve nature and reduce the most pressing threats to the diversity of life on Earth" (WWF 2017) and the African Wildlife Foundation's mission "to ensure wildlife and wild lands thrive in modern Africa" (AWF 2017), appear to primarily privilege nonhuman entities, while seeing local people as a threat.

Over the last decade or two, scholars have highlighted an increasing, yet troubling pattern of business–conservation alliances, under the broad umbrella of neoliberal conservation. Even though the common justification for neoliberal conservation is framed as saving conservation through making it pay for itself (Büscher 2008), Brockington and Duffy (2010) highlight how this is not a new phenomenon. They point out that rich elites have long protected particular species for their own enjoyment, and that these capitalist interests were evident in the formation of the first national parks in North America. Business–conservation alliances manifest in many different ways, often rooted in having a shared eco-philosophy, whether this is based on sincere intentions or not (Comi, Lurati and Zamparini 2015). However, Shah (2011) has argued that the success of any these alliances hinges on the perception of alliance legitimacy. That said, the most common business–conservation alliances in South Africa include the sponsoring of conservation ventures by private business elites (Benjaminsen, Kepe and Brathen 2008; Ramutsindela, Spierenburg and Wels 2011) and eco-tourism ventures run by private businesses (Büscher 2010). Additionally, given that most of the conservation areas that are implicated in conservation–land rights tensions in South Africa are managed by the state, it is important to take heed of Corson's (2010) suggestion that business–conservation alliances have compromised the role of the state, whereby private capital interests end up influencing state policy. In other words, local people's fight for land and resource rights on conservation land is not only against the state; it is a fight that involves these private business interests, with all their other alliances. Dzingirai (2003) has argued that in these private–public alliances in conservation or natural resource management, the local poor are unlikely to emerge as winners. Before discussing more reasons why alliances within the conservation sector exacerbate the conservation–land rights tensions in South Africa, below I briefly discuss the dynamics of the land rights alliances that feature in the tensions with conservation.

Land rights alliances

In the conservation–land rights tension, conservation has a far better level of support from the elite and powerful, both politically and financially, than is the case for land rights for the local poor (Benjaminsen, Kepe and Brathen 2008). In South Africa, however, one advantage for the advocacy of local people's land rights is that the loss of land was a symbol of colonial conquest, and therefore resistance against forces of colonialism and apartheid focused on land as a one of the crucial symbols of emancipation (Kepe 2012). This made land a central feature of the ideals of decolonization, redress against apartheid and social justice in general (Hall and Kepe 2017). By extension, to speak of a fight against rural poverty in South Africa is to speak of a fight for land rights for many blacks who live in rural areas, who either lost land during apartheid or who hold insecure land rights on the land they occupy (Marco-Thyse 2006). In other words, struggles for land rights and livelihoods are often intertwined. So, in the case of poor people's land rights on conservation land, what kind of support have they historically received and what is the current state of affairs?

Before the end of apartheid the African National Congress (ANC), which has been the ruling party since 1994, was seen as the champion of land rights for the poor in South Africa. In one of the clauses of the ANC's Freedom Charter, the ANC envisaged a situation where "The land shall be shared among those who work it!" (ANC 1955). Early in the 1990s the ANC formed the Land and Agriculture Policy Centre (LAPC), which engaged in numerous situational analyses and policy formulation excises in preparing for the post-apartheid period (Weideman 2004). The main focus of the LAPC's many studies was rural areas, particularly on thinking about policies and legislation on land redistribution, land claims and land tenure reform. The early 1990s also saw the surge of the South African National Civic Organization (SANCO), an ANC-aligned community-based movement, which took up the fight for land rights in urban and rural areas. SANCO and the local branch of the ANC, for example, combined forces to fight for local land rights in the Mkhambathi area, which involved a conservation area (Kepe 2011).

For most of the 1990s a land NGO, the National Land Committee (NLC), and its affiliates took up advocacy for rural people's land rights in a significant way (Weideman 2004). Even though the NLC began as a sympathizer of the ANC, Mngxitama (2006) has argued that over time the new ANC government, having subscribed to a neoliberal approach to redressing the ills of apartheid, sought to tame NGOs like the NLC, especially when they began questioning this shift from people-focused land reform to World Bank–influenced neoliberal land reform. The weakening of land NGOs, including through having difficulty raising funds to do their work, meant that many land advocacy causes in rural areas lacked the strong external support they once had. Some of this past support by NGOs could be credited for "successful" land claims against sections of Kruger National Park (Wynberg and Kepe 1999; Ramutsindela 2003, 2004), Kalahari Gemsbok National Park (Ellis 2010) and Dwesa-Cwebe Nature Reserve (Ntshona, Kraai, Kepe and Saliwa 2010). However, subsequent work on successful land claims in conservation areas has shown that land rights for the successful claimants remain unclear, as the state still maintains control of management decisions of these areas (Kepe, 2008; Ntshona, Kraai, Kepe and Saliwa 2010; Thondhlana, Cundill and Kepe 2016).

Conservation and land rights: a clash of values?

It can be argued that the strength of any of the alliances or networks on both conservation and land rights that are discussed above is dependent on numerous factors, including the perceived power that different partners hold, political support, finances and public support. In this section I do not wish to focus on these. I wish to focus on the perceived meanings of both land or land rights and biodiversity conservation to those who support each of these disparate goals. Therefore, in the case of biodiversity conservation a question can be asked: what allows it to be so easy to defend and support by the alliance partners? I believe there are several points that are fairly obvious. First, biodiversity conservation anywhere, including in South Africa, easily draws public sympathy and understanding owing to the constant bombardment that we all receive about the damage human beings are doing to the Earth and that, if nothing is done, life as we know it will cease to exist. Second, in the case of South Africa biodiversity conservation has long been the terrain of white people (Kepe 2009; Cock and Fig 2000), who have continued to carry that aura of power, expertise and invincibility. This also explains the current racial differences in support of conservation, where white people are seen as supporters while blacks are still largely perceived as a threat (Hockey, Lombard and Siegfried 1994; Kepe 2014). Third, biodiversity conservation draws the support of many alliance partners because for the most part it has quantifiable aspects to it. Protected areas are already an important statistic in IUCN's target percentage of area of each country that is under protection (IUCN 2017); species lists, including those of endangered plants and animals, are a common tool for convincing outsiders, most of whom are nonscientists (Fairhead and Leach 2003), of the perceived value of a conservation area; and economic evaluation of biodiversity within protected areas makes it possible for capital to insert itself in biodiversity conservation (See Costanza et al. 1998), among others. All of these quantifiable aspects fit what Li (2014, 589) calls "statistical picturing" devices, which are used by experts to make it easy for the markets to see value in land and natural resources, which is often followed by appropriation from local resource users. Fourth, and related to the previous point, is that science in biodiversity conservation is dominant and hegemonic (Fairhead and Leach 2003; Kepe 2014). Hastie (2007) and Gillespie (2012), among others, have even argued that for most of the twentieth century environmental policy making would have been nearly impossible without science. Fifth, the idea of nature for recreation, especially through ventures such as eco-tourism, has helped legitimize the existence of some protected areas. In South Africa, management plans of most public conservation areas include recreational activities as the most important justification why these areas need to be supported (Carruthers 2007; Kepe, 2009). However, again, in the case of South Africa, studies show that nature for recreation in these protected areas is still dominated by whites. For example, Butler and Richardson (2015) have argued that, despite black South Africans making up about 80 percent of the population, only 8.8 percent of them visit national parks for recreation.

I consider these five points above, collectively, as what constitutes meanings and values of conservation in South Africa. This is not to say that all of these are widely rejected by the public. They simply represent one side of the explanation of why conservation and land rights are in such tension in South Africa. This is why it is important to reflect on alternative understandings of the meanings and values relating to land that may be tied up in disputed conservation land. As many scholars have shown, land has multiple meanings that go beyond its use as a natural resource for agriculture, collection of wild resources, shelter and recreation, to mention a few. It has many other important, yet often subtle meanings to different people in any particular locality (Kepe et al. 2008; Ferguson 2013; Li, 2014). Meanings of land that are found in conservation areas are often a form of identity for the people concerned, owing to their historical roots to it; it could have sentimental attachment to it as a result of ancestral graves or other rituals that are attached to the area; and it could serve as a bargaining power to leverage resources or other concessions that strengthen political positions and contribute to livelihoods (Marco-Thyse 2006; Kepe et al. 2008; James 2009; Li 2014). What is challenging for outsiders about these different ways of thinking about land is that they are not seen as quantifiable, and are often viewed as nonscientific, as well as possibly going against conservation goals. Most importantly, unless there is some academic research, or elite advocates for local people, many of these meanings and values are either ignored or are never articulated in forums that matter for policy making. In my opinion, here might lie one of the reasons why land claims in conservation areas are difficult to resolve. In South Africa, owing to the enduring frustrations of many communities fighting for their land rights within protected areas, violence and vandalism is often common. In the Wild Coast of the Eastern Cape Province, at least three prominent nature reserves were, at some point during the post-apartheid dispensation, invaded and vandalized by local people who felt that they needed to take that action to just be heard by those in power. These include Dwesa-Cwebe (Ntshona, Kraai, Kepe and Saliwa 2010), Mkhambathi (Kepe 2009) and Silaka (Thondhlana, Cundill and Kepe 2016). Obviously, whenever there is violence and vandalism, there is often widespread condemnation of those actions by those in power. In the case of these areas mentioned above, temporary solutions were put in place, but the failure to fully understand, let alone embrace, alternative ways of viewing conservation land that has a history of occupation and use by neighboring local communities who are claiming it sets land rights and biodiversity conservation on collision course. At the core then, the problem is with the reluctance to broaden our conceptions of justice that include intuitive justice.

Ambiguous role of the state

The last major explanation that I wish to offer for the continuing tension between biodiversity conservation and land rights in South Africa is the ambiguous role that the state plays in both policy creation and policy implementation. As hinted in this chapter, land claims by black people on land that is currently conservation area make up most of the tension we have discussed here. How is the state playing an ambiguous role in these cases? First, based on the Land Restitution Act (22 of 1994), people who lost land owing to racially motivated policy or practice have a right to lodge a claim. According to the Act, all land claims are against the state, not the individuals or groups currently occupying the land. This made sense, as all land reform is the responsibility of the state and the state is seen as an entity that seeks to undo injustices brought by the previous (apartheid) state (Department of Land Affairs, 1997). However, as Kepe (2012) shows, the state has not been a neutral player in implementing policy on land affecting conservation areas. In particular, based on the Memorandum of Understanding between the Minister of Agriculture and Land Affairs and the Minister of Environmental Affairs and Tourism, signed on 2 May 2007 (Government of South Africa 2007), all successful land claimants must undertake to keep the land a conservation area. This means that, despite the purported choice that is given to successful land claimants on what to do with their returned land, the state leaves them no choice but to accept conservation. This means that no other land uses are allowed and that the protected area is managed by the state, while the new "owners" (land claimants) are told they can benefit from eco-tourism and employment inside the protected area (Ntshona, Kraai, Kepe and Saliwa 2010; Taylor and Atkinson 2012). In the end, local people's land rights become fuzzy, as they only end up with paper land rights and no decision-making powers. This is despite common emphasis on co-management between the state and the successful claimants. These communities are given limited options but to view the state and all its representatives in their localities with deep suspicion.

What is not clear, however, is why, upon seeing study after study highlighting this ambiguity, the state continues to use the same tactics to deal with local people. I argue that, even if politicians see the looming dangers as a result of mollifying local people with "development" and cash, while not acknowledging the meanings and values they attach to the land, the conservation lobby ensures that conservation emerges a winner.

Discussion and conclusion

This chapter has highlighted some possible reasons why biodiversity conservation and land rights in South Africa remain in tension with each other. It has suggested that, first, the ideal of justice that is the hallmark of the post-apartheid dispensation has not been achieved in land reform on conservation areas. One of the reasons for this is that models of justice, and therefore models of redress, tend to solely focus on land as a commodity, thus ignoring the multiple meanings of land and natural resources to local people. Also, as Atuahene (2007) argues, a mere return of land as a material resource does nothing to restore the "social death" or invisibility that people suffered when they lost their land. Thus, in concurring with Atuahene (2007) and Andrews (2006), who feel that land reform should restore the victims' dignity, I believe the debate about how land reform is carried out should be revisited. If the state is sincere about land justice, then it needs to seriously consider the negative impacts that land loss might have had on the people. That understanding could allow for alternative models of land justice that are much broader than just land as a physical resource. This is also consistent with what Holtzhausen (2015) proposes for land reform – *ubuntu*. Ubuntu is a South African concept that includes a strong belief in that individual people are better off because others are better off. The focus, therefore, is on people appreciating their value and gaining confidence in that. Second, this chapter has argued that both biodiversity conservation and land rights have supporters who loosely organize into networks or alliances. For conservation, these alliance partners include scientists, elite private investors, international environmental NGOs, conservation sponsors etc., who operate based on what they see as the meanings and values of conservation. But these meanings attached to biodiversity conservation by the networks or alliances tend to be miles apart from the meanings and values that local people attach to land in conservation areas. Local people, many of whom lay claim to land in conservation areas in this case, tend to have a broader understanding of the meanings and values of land to them, including its importance to their identity, the power that land holds in terms of leveraging resources, and its sentimental value based on history of occupation, among other things. This means that any model of redress that ignores the multiple meanings of land to local people will not do away with the tensions that currently exist in conservation areas in South Africa.

The last main point that I have highlighted is the ambiguous role of the state in dealing with land reform in conservation areas. This begins with a particular tension in the country's Bill of Rights. The Bill of Rights enshrines both conservation (Section 24) and land reform (Section 25). In trying to reconcile the two, the state appears to be favoring conservation, even though there is always the risk of widespread discontent, including violence, when land claim resolution on conservation areas are not consistent with local people's understandings of land justice. It is curious, but understandable, why the state opts to be softer to conservation and less sympathetic to local people's land needs. There might be many reasons for this, but it is clear that conservation has a stronger lobby that is global; it involves financial resources that come from the public and private sectors, and it is backed by powerful international agencies and the international conventions that South Africa has signed over the years. The remaining challenge would be to see how long this can go on before the state can realize that their very own actions or inactions potentially undermine conservation. But, as Dowie (2006) has proposed, poorly conceptualized and implemented conservation has in many instances also wrecked the lives of people who live in the area. Suggestions have long been made about how the quest for biological diversity should be viewed in the context of conservation's competition with other land uses and needs of local people. Thus, as Minin, Macmillan, Goodman, Escott, Slotow and Moilanen (2013) remind us, trade-offs between conservation and land rights and land uses should be seen as central to mitigating the tension between the two.

References

Adger, W. N., Benjaminsen, T. A., Brown, K. and Svarstad, H. "Advancing a Political Ecology of Global Environmental Discourses." *Development and Change*, 32 (2001): 681–715.

ANC (African National Congress). Freedom Charter, adopted at the Congress of the People, Kliptown, 26 June 1955.

Andrews, M. Struggling for a Life in Dignity. In L. Ntsebeza and R. Hall. (eds), *The Land Question in South Africa: The Challenge of Transformation and Reconciliation*. Cape Town: HSRC Press, 2006.

Atuahene, B. "From Reparation to Restoration: Moving Beyond Restoring Property Rights to Restoring Political and Economic Visibility." *SMU Law Review*, 60, no. 4. (2007): 1419–1470.

AWF. Our Mission. AWF: www.awf.org (accessed November 13, 2017), 2017.

Beinart, W. "African History and Environmental History." *African Affairs*, 99 (2000): 269–302.

Benjaminsen, T. A., Kepe, T. and Brathen, S. "Between Global Interests and Local Needs: Conservation and Land Reform in Namaqualand, South Africa." *Africa*, 78, no. 2 (2008): 223–243.

Brockington, D. and Duffy, R. "Capitalism and Conservation: The Production and Reproduction of Biodiversity Conservation." *Antipode*, 42, no. 2 (2010): 469–484.

Büscher, B. "Conservation, Neoliberalism, and Social Science: A Critical Reflection on the SCB 2007 Annual Meeting in South Africa." *Conservation Biology*, 22, no. 2 (2008): 229–231.

Büscher, B. "Derivative Nature: Interrogating the Value of Conservation in 'Boundless Southern Africa.'" *Third World Quarterly*, 31, no. 2 (2010): 259–276.

Butler, G. and Richardson, S. "Barriers to Visiting South Africa's National Parks in the Post-apartheid Era: Black South African Perspectives from Soweto." *Journal of Sustainable Tourism*, 23, no. 1 (2015): 146–166.

Carruthers, J. "'South Africa: A World in One Country': Land Restitution in National Parks and Protected Areas." *Conservation & Society*, 5, no. 3 (2007): 292–306.

Cock, J. and Fig, D. "From Colonial to Community Based Conservation: Environmental Justice and the National Parks of South Africa." *Society in Transition*, 31, no. 1 (2000): 22–35.

Comi, A., Lurati, F. and Zamparini, A. "Green Alliances: How Does Ecophilosophy Shape the Strategies of Environmental Organizations?" *Voluntas*, 26 (2015): 1288–1313.

Corson, C. "Shifting Environmental Governance in a Neoliberal World: US AID for Conservation." *Antipode*, 42, no. 3 (2010): 576–602.

Costanza, R., d'Arge, R., deGroot, R., Farber, S., Grasso, M., Hannon, B., Limburg, K., Naeem, S., O'Neill, R. V., Paruelo, J., Raskin, R. G., Sutton, P. and vandenBelt, M "The Value of the World's Ecosystem Services and Natural Capital" *Ecological Economics*, 25 (1998): 3–15.

Department of Land Affairs. White Paper on South African Land Policy. Pretoria: Department of Land Affairs, 1997.

Dowie, M. "Enemies of Conservation: Enlightened Conservationists Admit that Wrecking the Lives of Millions of Poor, Powerless People Has Been an Enormous Mistake." *Range Magazine*, Summer (2006), 24–27.

Dzingirai, V. "The New Scramble for the African Countryside." *Development and Change*, 34, no. 2 (2003): 243–264.

Ellis, W. "The ‡Khomani San Land Claim against the Kalahari Gemsbok National Park Land." In *Memory, Reconstruction and Justice: Perspectives on Land Claims in South Africa* ed. C. Walker, A. Bohlin, R. Hall and T. Kepe. Athens, OH: Ohio University Press, 2010.

Fairhead, J. and Leach, M. "Practising 'Biodiversity' in Guinea: Nature, Nation and an International Convention." *Oxford Development Studies*, 31 (2003): 427–439.

Ferguson, J. "How to Do Things with Land: A Distributive Perspective on Rural Livelihoods in Southern Africa." *Journal of Agrarian Change*, 13, no. 1 (2013): 166–174.

Gibson, J. L. "Group Identities and Theories of Justice: An Experimental Investigation into the Justice and Injustice of Land Squatting in South Africa." *The Journal of Politics*, 70, no. 3 (2008): 700–716.

Gillespie, A. "Science, Values and People: The Three Factors that Will Define the Next Generation of International Conservation Agreements." *Transnational Environmental Law*, 1, no. 1 (2012): 169–182.

Government of South Africa. Memorandum of Agreement between the Minister of Agriculture and Land Affairs and the Minister of Environmental Affairs and Tourism. Pretoria: Government of South Africa, 2007.

Grove, R. *Green Imperialism: Colonial Expansion, Tropical Island Edens and the Origins of Environmentalism, 1600–1860*. Cambridge: Cambridge University Press, 1995.

Hall, R. and Kepe, T. "Elite Capture and State Neglect: New Evidence on South Africa's Land Reform." *Review of African Political Economy*, 44, no. 151 (2017): 122–130.

Hastie, J. "The Role of Science and Scientists in Environmental Policy." In *The Sage Handbook of Environment and Society* eds J. Pretty, A. S. Ball, T. Benton, J. S. Guivant, D. R. Lee, D. Orr, M. J. Pfeffer and H. Ward. London: Sage, 2007, 519–535.

Hockey, P. A. R., Lombard, A. T. and Siegfried, W. R. "South Africa's Commitment to Preserving Biodiversity: Can We See the Wood for the Trees?" *South African Journal of Science*, 90 (1994): 105–107.

Holtzhausen, H. "*Ubuntu* and the Quest for Land Reform in South Africa." *Verbum et Ecclesia*, 36, no. 2 (2015): 1–8.

IUCN (International Union for the Conservation of Nature). New UNEP Report Unveils World on Track to Meet 2020 Target for Protected Areas on Land and Sea. www.iucn.org/content/new-unep-report-unveils-world-track-meet-2020-target-protected-areas-land-and-sea (accessed November 16, 2017), 2017.

James, D. "Burial Sites, Informal Rights and Lost Kingdoms: Contesting Land Claims in Mpumalanga, South Africa." *Africa*, 79, no. 2 (2009): 228–251.

Kepe, T. "Land Claims and Co-management of Protected Areas in South Africa: Exploring the Challenges." *Environmental Management*, 41, no. 3 (2008): 311–321.

Kepe, T. "Shaped by Race: Why 'Race' Still Matters in the Challenges Facing Biodiversity Conservation in Africa." *Local Environment*, 14, no. 9 (2009): 871–878.

Kepe, T. "Environment and Development." In *Encyclopedia of Human Geography* ed. B. Warf. London: Sage, 2010, 1003–1007.

Kepe, T. "Discontent and Apathy: Post-apartheid Rural Land Reform in the Context of the Mpondo Revolts." In *Rural Resistance in South Africa: The Mpondo Revolts after Fifty Years* eds T. Kepe and L. Ntsebeza. Leiden: Brill; Cape Town: UCT Press, 2011.

Kepe, T. "Land and Justice in South Africa: Exploring the Ambiguous Role of the State in the Land Claims Process." *African and Asian Studies*, 11, no. 4 (2012): 391–409.

Kepe, T. "Globalization, Science and the Making of an Environmental Discourse on the Wild Coast, South Africa." *Environment and Planning A*, 46, no. 9 (2014): 2143–2159.

Kepe, T., Hall, R. and Cousins, B. "Land." In *The New South African Key Words* eds N. Sheppard and S. Robins. Athens, OH: Ohio University Press; Johannesburg: Jacana Media, 2008.

Kepe, T. and Tessaro, D. "Trading-off: Rural Food Security and Land Rights in South Africa." *Land Use Policy*, 36 (2014): 267–274.

Kepe, T., Fukuda, K., Hicks, M., Shortly, A. and Brode, L. *Unlimiting Land Justice: The Importance of Acknowledging Multiplicity and Complexity of Meanings of Land and Justice*. Unpublished paper, University of Toronto, 2017.

Lee, E. "Protected Areas, Country and Value: The Nature-Culture Tyranny of the IUCN's Protected Area Guidelines for Indigenous Australians." *Antipode*, 48, no. 2 (2016): 355–374.

Li, T. M. "What Is Land? Assembling a Resource for Global Investment." *Transactions of the Institute of British Geographers*, 39, no. 4 (2014): 589–602.

Marco-Thyse, S. "Land Rights in South Africa: A Mechanism against Poverty?" *Development*, 49, no. 3 (2006): 133–137.

Minin, E. D., Macmillan, D. C., Goodman, P. S., Escott, B., Slotow, R. and Moilanen, A. "Conservation Business and Conservation Planning in a Biological Diversity Hotspot" *Conservation Biology*, 27, no. 4 (2013): 808–820.

Mngxitama, A. "The Taming of Land Resistance: Lessons from the National Land Committee." *Journal of Asian and African Studies*, 41, no. 1–2 (2006): 39–69.

Ntshona, Z., Kraai, M., Kepe, T. and Saliwa, P. "From Land Rights to Environmental Entitlements: Community Discontent in the 'Successful' Dwesa-Cwebe Land Claim in South Africa." *Development Southern Africa*, 27, no. 3 (2010): 353–361.

Osmani, S. R. "Theory of Justice for an Imperfect World: Exploring Amartya Sen's Idea of Justice." *Journal of Human Development and Capabilities*, 11, no. 4 (2010): 599–607.

Paterson, A. R. "Wandering about South Africa's New Protected Areas Regime." *SA Public Law*, 1 (2007): 1–33.

Ramutsindela, M. "Land Reform in South Africa's National Parks: A Catalyst for the Human–Nature Nexus." *Land Use Policy*, 20, no. 1 (2003): 41–49.

Ramutsindela, M. *Parks and People in Postcolonial Societies: Experiences in Southern Africa*. Dordrecht, Boston and London: Kluwer, 2004.

Ramutsindela, M., Spierenburg, M and Wels, H. Editors. *Sponsoring Nature: Environmental Philanthropy for Conservation*. London: Earthscan, 2011.

Scoones, I. "Sustainability." *Development in Practice*, 17 (2007): 589–596.

Shah, K. U. "Organizational Legitimacy and the Strategic Bridging Ability of Green Alliances." *Business Strategy and the Environment*, 20 (2011): 498–511.

Spencely, A. and Meyer, D. "Tourism and Poverty Reduction: Theory and Practice in Less Economically Developed Countries." *Journal of Sustainable Tourism*, 20, no. 3 (2012): 297–317.

Springett, D. "Critical Perspectives on Sustainable Development." *Sustainable Development*, 21 (2013): 73–82.

Steiner, A., Kimball, L. A. and Scanlon, J. "Global Governance for the Environment and the Role of Multilateral Environmental Agreements in Conservation." *Oryx*, 37, no. 2 (2003): 227–237.

Taylor, S. J. and Atkinson, D. "Delivering Community Benefits Acts as Insurance for the Survival of Small Protected Areas Such as the Abe Bailey Nature Reserve, South Africa." *Koedoe*, 54, 1 (2012): 1–9.

Thondhlana, G., Cundill, G. and Kepe, T. "Co-management, Land Rights and Conflicts around South Africa's Silaka Nature Reserve." *Society and Natural Resources*, 29, no. 4 (2016): 403–417.

Walker, C. "Land Claims, Land Conservation and the Public Interest in Protected Areas." *South African Review of Sociology*, 39, no. 2 (2008): 232–244.

Walker, C. "Finite Land: Challenges Institutionalising Land Restitution in South Africa, 1995–2000." *Journal of Southern African Studies*, 38, 4 (2012): 809–826.

Weideman, M. "Who Shaped South Africa's Land Reform Policy?" *Politikon*, 31, no. 2 (2004): 219–238.

WWF. WWF Mission Statement. www.worldwildlife.org (accessed November 12, 2017), 2017.

Wynberg, R. "A Decade of Biodiversity Conservation and Use in South Africa: Tracking Progress from Rio Earth Summit on Sustainable Development." *South African Journal of Science*, 98 (2002): 233–243.

Wynberg, R. and Kepe, T. *Land Reform and Conservation Areas in South Africa – Towards a Mutually Beneficial Approach*. Pretoria: IUCN, 1999.

3 The promise and limit of environmental justice through land restitution in protected areas in South Africa

Maano Ramutsindela and Medupi Shabangu

Introduction

The Global South is an epicentre for global efforts to conserve biodiversity but it is also characterized by struggles for rights to land and other natural resources. These struggles are prominent in protected areas from which local people were removed and in which their access to resources for livelihood are rendered illegal by the state. This troubled relationship between society and its biophysical environment has been one of the main foci of scholarship and policy interventions for many years (Neumann 2000; Brockington and Igoe 2006; Nash 2014), yet the gap between the needs and aspirations of society in most developing countries and environmental imperatives still exists. The reasons for this are many: they include the hegemonic ideology of nature conservation; the power imbalance between the environmental movement and local people whose livelihood depends on natural resources; the cumulative effects of global environmental conventions and protocols on national policies; and the framing of and universalized approaches to the crisis of biodiversity loss that has given rise to the Nature Needs Half (NNH) movement. The NNH movement argues for the need to protect approximately 50 per cent of the earth's landscapes and seascapes from intensive human economic use in order to prevent further extinction of species (Locke 2014; Wilson 2016).

The question that arises from global concerns with the health of the planet and the need for land reform, especially in the postcolony, is not so much whether there should be a balance between the two but how that balance could be achieved. To be sure, a number of scholars in both the environmental and social sciences have called for such balance (Magome and Murombedzi 2003; Kepe, Wynberg and Ellis 2005; Adenle 2012; Ghimire and Pimbert 2013; Redford *et al.* 2015) but approaches to achieve it are still lacking. In this chapter we draw on the concept of environmental justice and relate it to land restitution in South Africa to contribute to approaches that hold the potential for narrowing the gap between the goals of nature conservation and land restitution.

Our main argument is that the strong divide between conservationists and proponents of land rights can be narrowed down by infusing environmental justice into both land restitution and biodiversity conservation. While conservationists have used various strategies to push back environmental justice agendas in protected areas, there is no guarantee that South Africa's land restitution process in these areas would translate into environmental justice. We should be critical of land restitution as much as we are about nature conservation. Thus, the question of what kind of environmental justice is delivered by land restitution and through conservation is pertinent. We grapple with this question by first recontextualizing environmental justice as a background to our analysis. Thereafter we discuss the tension between land restitution and biodiversity conservation in protected areas before we refer to the case study of Makahane–Maritenga land claim in the Kruger National Park (KNP), South Africa.

Environmental justice recontextualized

In this chapter we deploy environmental justice as a concept that opens up new epistemological and ontological possibilities that should be harnessed to speak to a wide range of contexts, including the conflictual situation of land reform in protected areas. We acknowledge that, over time, understandings of environmental justice have shifted from a preoccupation with the distributional risks faced by the poor and people of colour in the United States, to embrace environmental inequalities around the world (Bassa 1998; Castree *et al.* 2009). This shift is relevant to the discussion of this chapter as it points to the need to re-contextualize environmental justice so as to embrace its multiple meanings. In short, environmental justice derived its particular meaning from the United States, where it was largely associated with the proximity of hazardous waste to areas occupied by the poor and people of colour (Bullard 1990; Goldman 1996; Pulido 1996). As a result of this conceptualization, earlier debates on environmental justice were on exposing and measuring injustices emanating from national environmental policies and actions. Central to those debates were questions around the empirical evidence of distributional inequality, the relationships between exposure to environmental harms and race or class, and the factors behind the proximity of poor people to industrial wastes or the location of polluting industries to areas occupied by the poor (Bowen and Wells 2002; Holified, Porter and Walker 2010).

Though these questions continue to inspire research in many parts of the world (Wayessa and Nygren 2016) environmental justice research has moved on to embrace multiple contexts and scales. For example, the causes of environmental injustice have been analysed through Marxist urban political ecology in which capitalism and class are the main drivers of socio-environmental change (Arboleda 2015; Heynen 2016). Spaces of environmental injustice are also analysed as a product of historical-geographical dynamics of colonialism and oppression (Warlenius and Ramasar 2015). Others have suggested that environmental justice should combine notions of distribution, participation, and recognition as these are often used by activists in their struggles for justice (Walker 2012; Martinez-Alier *et al.* 2014).

Issues of environmental justice have been elevated to the global scale and are at the core of the North-South divide on environmental related resolutions.

Okereke (2007) ascribes this divide to competing views of justice as utilitarianism, liberal egalitarianism, property rights, mutual advantage, communitarianism and meeting basic needs. These views are not stagnant (Najam 2005) but remain central to the geopolitics of the environment. Given these shifts and innovations in the environmental justice literature, how should we understand environmental justice in protected areas? We ask this question not to blunt the radical edges of the environmental justice frame but to come to terms with contradictory outcomes of processes that aim for some form of justice. In terms of the scope of this chapter, progressive scholarship considers land restitution as a just process (Walker *et al.* 2010) but not much attention is given to how these processes could and do perpetuate forms of injustice.

The tension between land restitution and biodiversity conservation

Almost all countries, regions and population groups that have experienced oppression of one type or another are confronted with land-related questions arising from such political systems. Answers to those questions have been many and varied: they range from self-determination to land restitution. Ongoing processes of green grabbing – as 'new ways through which land or resources are appropriated for environmental purposes' (Apostolopoulou and Adams 2015, 16) – exacerbate the problem of land dispossession that was set in motion by colonialism in much of the Global South. They also powerfully bring to the fore the tension between nature conservation and land reform. In countries where land restitution is seen as an appropriate measure for redress, the clash between land restitution and biodiversity protection is unavoidable. This is so because attempts to address the legacy of land dispossession appear to go against the need to halt biodiversity loss by putting more land under nature conservation.

Pursuing land rights through restitution and biodiversity conservation simultaneously is a complex undertaking in many former colonies. In South Africa, attempts to restore land rights in protected areas have faltered because of at least four main reasons. First, the process and objectives of land reform have shifted over time and this complicates but also limits the scope of land restitution in protected areas (Kepe 2012; McCusker, Moseley and Ramutsindela 2016). Second, the entrenched oppositional stances between proponents of land and resource rights and conservationists militate against reconciliatory approaches (Ramutsindela 2002; Magome and Murombedzi 2003; Ramutsindela and Shabangu 2013). Third, the hegemony of the conservation bloc leads to the prioritization of conservation above other land use options (Kepe 2012). The conservation bloc is a world phenomenon, which is integral to the neo-liberalization of nature (Brockington and Duffy 2010). Fourth, in South Africa and elsewhere there is no clarity on what constitutes the glue that binds together land reform and biodiversity conservation. Our premise in this chapter is that land reform and biodiversity conservation should be given equal weight. We argue that pursuing the goals of land restitution and biodiversity protection in tandem is contingent on notions of environment justice and their relevance to both land claimants and specific conservation goals.

The tendency to prioritize biodiversity conservation over land reform has its roots in the Eurocentric hegemonic binary world view of the environment that divides society and nature, and that also presents the cultures of non-Europeans as inherently inimical to nature (Ramutsindela 2004). Such a world view is also underpinned by a great deal of racism wrapped up in the framing of environmental problems, or presented in the form of environmental knowledge and skills, or as global environmental solutions (Lohmann 2000; Shiva 2001; Biermann and Mansfield 2014). To be sure, Indigenous populations and local people[1] have been categorized as one of the main causes of environmental problems. They have been accused of causing the loss of wildlife (Lenggenhager 2016), of lacking environmental ethic and of harvesting natural resources irresponsibly even as the plundering of resources is done by, say, big companies (Shiva 2001; Chiaravalloti 2017). From the perspective of deep ecology, Indigenous groups and local people are seen as violating the rights of non-humans. For deep ecologists those rights need to be restored to achieve what we think is a one-sided view of environmental justice, i.e. restoring the integrity of the environment at the expense of the needs of Indigenous and local people. In South Africa, environmental non-governmental organizations and environmental scientists emphasize the need to preserve and protect the environment, and are concerned with the impact that land reform has on the environment (Puttick, Hoffman and Gambiza 2014). Whereas these organizations and scientists are concerned with the implications of environmental and land use change on land reform and on the impact of land reform on the environment (Meadows 2012; Hoffman 2015), they are silent about how land restitution should be implemented in the country's protected areas.

For their part, proponents of resource rights and victims of land dispossession constitute a camp that seeks to challenge the ideology of nature conservation and the practices that flow from it (Coates 2004; Dowie 2011; Torpey-Saboe 2015). Rights-based civil society groups are conscious of variations among Indigenous populations but nonetheless share a common concern with their marginalization. It is on this basis that rights-based civil society groups and academics have championed the recognition of rights of Indigenous people that entail land restitution where it is permissible. For example, the Brazilian-based Movimento Dos Trabalhadores Rurais Sem Terra (Movement of Rural Landless Workers) (MST) was founded in 1984 'to fight for an agrarian reform that distributed land to those who would work it, and for the development of a just, fraternal society' (Wolford 2003, 500). It championed land rights through land occupations from which it created agrarian reform settlements. The MST supports agroecology in these settlements (Lerrer and de Medeiros 2014).[2] In South Africa, the Landless People's Movement aims to:

> unite all the landless people of South Africa, to end the legacy of colonial and apartheid land dispossession in all its forms and transform South

> Africa's land and asset distribution pattern as rapidly as possible by returning the land and other stolen assets-including [mineral] rights to [their] rightful owners, to struggle for land and for secure land tenure for farm dwellers, to empower, educate and build capacity of the landless to return to the land and use it effectively to meet their multiple social, cultural and economic needs, etc.
>
> (Landless People's Movement 2004)

The point here is that land rights movements are preoccupied with giving ordinary citizens access to land but are less concerned with the implications of land redistribution for nature conservation. The reason for this is clear: it would be illogical for advocates of land rights to consider conservation imperatives given that local people lost land and resource rights due to conservation. In other words, how can pro-local people campaigners be sympathetic to nature conservation that led to land alienation and that continues to marginalize local people?

Concerns with the tension between land reform and biodiversity conservation have led to the development of mitigating strategies such as co-management. In the context of land restitution, co-management acknowledges the need for restitution in national parks and nature/game reserves but the land involved is jointly managed by conservation agencies and land claimants. Co-management arrangements are characterized by unequal power relations that often lead to tension among land claimants and between state agencies and land claimants (Thondhlana, Cundill and Kepe 2016). In some cases, co-management has resulted in short-term financial benefits (Ramutsindela and Shabangu 2013). Our point here is that co-management subdues rather than dissolves the tension between land restitution and biodiversity conservation. We argue that identifying elements that bind land restitution and biodiversity conservation demands a rigorous critique of land restitution within protected areas – where restitution and conservation meet head-on – and a reassessment of claims that 'new conservation' delivers a win–win solution. The win–win solution implies that the success of land claims should not compromise the integrity of protected areas, though such a solution often relies on coercion (Kepe 2012). In other words, land claimants receive some form of justice on condition their land use does not interfere with the goals of biodiversity conservation.

Our concern here is with the conceptualization and implementation of justice as an aspect of land reform policy. During the struggle for liberation in South Africa and at the dawn of democracy in the country in the early 1990s, certain notions of land-related justice were espoused. These ranged from the Freedom Charter's vision of sharing land among those who work it to the current practice of financial compensation to victims of racially motivated land dispossession. Our view is that notions of justice in land restitution have changed over time and that this change manifests in the settlement of land claims in protected areas in South Africa. The apartheid government injected its idea of justice into its land reform policy derived from the Abolition of Racially Based Land Measures Act of 1991, which was passed in the run-up to a political negotiated settlement for a democratic South Africa in 1992/93. The focus at that time was on transferring state land to black people who lost their land owing to racially motivated land planning, including the creation of Bantustans. Such land restoration was overseen by the Advisory Commission on Land Allocation, which was later renamed the Commission on Land Allocation and had the mandate to order organs of the state to transfer and redistribute land. Issues of environmental sustainability were marginal to this process (Wynberg and Sowman 2007).[3] Though the work of the Commission was largely a pre-emptive strategy to design a land reform policy that steered attention away from white-owned farms, it entertained land restoration as a form of justice. At the end of the life of the Commission on 30 September 1993, the idea of justice in land restitution had been broadened to include two pillars, namely land restoration and compensation measures that were backed up by the interim constitution of 1993 – and later by the final constitution of 1996. The central question in this chapter is: which ideas of justice underpin and also manifest in the Makahane–Maritenga land claim?

Makahane–Maritenga land claim

In this section we consider the local people of Makahane–Maritenga not as an isolated clan but rather as one thread in the tapestry of the social, political and environmental history of the KNP in South Africa. Their historical conditions and the consequent experiences with land restitution in democratic South Africa offer a window through which we can grasp the contested nature of land claims in protected areas, and how issues of environmental justice permeate such contestations. The section also highlights that the need to break down the land restitution–biodiversity conservation dichotomy in protected areas is not simply an intellectual exercise but is instead a necessary condition for achieving an environmentally and social just dispensation. We briefly recount the history of the people of Makahane–Maritenga and their land claim to contextualize our argument.

Dispossession: a brief history of injustice

The group known as Makahane–Maritenga, who lodged the land claim discussed below, are descendants of the Makahane clan, who built the Iron Age site of Thulamela in the northern part of the KNP, and those of the Mhinga, who came to live in Thulamela (Ralushai 1998).[4] Thulamela is therefore a multicultural site that brings together the ancestry of the Venda and Shangaan people. It was also shaped by trade between these cultural groups and traders in East Africa between AD 1200 and 1600 (Hall 1987). Their trade was part of the broader history of commercial and cultural networks that African kingdoms developed with other regions of the world as well as waves of migration that led to the development of Thulamela. The cultural foundation of Thulamela is linked to that of Mapungubwe, one of the largest African kingdoms, which developed on the Limpopo valley on the present-day Botswana–South Africa–Zimbabwe borderlands

(Pikirayi 2001). Following the collapse of Mapungubwe, people dispersed to the south of the Limpopo (Thulamela in South Africa) and to the north of Limpopo (Zimbabwe) (Ralushai 1998). These links are corroborated by archaeological findings in the ruins of Great Zimbabwe and Thulamela (Steyn, Miller, Nienaber and Loots 1998). The ruins in Thulamela are commonly known as the Makahane ruins and are one of approximately 254 cultural sites found in the KNP (Nemaheni 2003; Meskell 2005). The former minister of environmental affairs and tourism, Pallo Jordan, officially opened the Thulamela Heritage Site on national heritage day, 24 September 1996. As we show below, this heritage status played no significant role in the settlement of the land claim. Instead, the Makahane–Maritenga land claim was treated just like any other land claim in the KNP.

African settlements in Thulamela were hugely affected by the creation of the KNP, a process that was set in motion in 1898 by the Afrikaner nationalist and hunter Paul Kruger (Carruthers 1995). The creation of the KNP from its nuclei in the Sabi Game Reserve in the south and its expansion towards the north was achieved by removing Africans from their land. The removals were underpinned by a combination of racism and the desire by Afrikaner nationalists to divide the African population along linguistic lines as the basis for launching the development of Bantustans (Ramutsindela 2002).

The government's intention to remove Headman Shikokololo to Mhinga's location was hinted in Minute No. 56/707/120, of 5 August 1920 (Land Claims Commission Research Report 2003). By 27 October 1921 the surveyor-general was working on proposals to alter the boundaries of the Shingwedzi Game Reserve, which forms part of the present-day KNP. The removal of Makahane–Maritenga in two phases between 1926 and 1946 can be ascribed to two factors: the political goal of creating native reserves that were to become 'homelands' and the need to keep the area part of the KNP. During these years, they were removed from Makahane Hill and settled at Makuya, Mutele, Tshakhuma, Maphophe, Matiyani, Ka Josefa and Ha-Lambani (Land Claims Commission Research Report 2003). In the process of removal, their cattle were poisoned and their huts burned down. On this note, the injustice suffered by the people of Makahane–Maritenga was more than the loss of land. It included the loss of their heritage and their assets, as well as their human dignity. Next we discuss how this loss was handled through the restitution process.

Restitution for justice for Makahane–Maritenga

Following the promulgation of the Restitution of Land Rights Act (RLRA) in 1994, which sought to restore land to victims of state-sponsored and racially motived removals, eight land claims – with a total of more than 500,000 ha – were lodged in the KNP between 1994 and 1998. One of these was the Makahane–Maritenga land claim, which was lodged by Samuel Tshinakaho Mamphwe Makahane on 28 September 1996. The land claim consisted of 167 households and was registered as Makahane–Maritenga to reflect the two main cultural groups who lived in Thulamela as we noted above. It covers a total surface area of 89,000 ha in the Punda Maria area to the north of the KNP. The land claim by Makahane–Maritenga went through and satisfied the steps required by the RLRA. The restitution process involves the validation and verification of the land claim, and the publication of the claim[5] through a government gazette for public comment, after which options for restitution are considered to enable the parties involved to reach an agreement on the settlement of the claim.

As part of the restitution process, a joint meeting was held between the Department of Environment and Tourism (DEAT), the Department of Land Affairs (DLA) and the Regional Land Claims Commission: Limpopo, KNP, as well as the people of Makahane–Maritenga to discuss the settlement of the land claim. The community wanted to settle their land claim through land restoration. The leader of the land claimants, Matodzi Makahane, maintained that, 'it's our land – it must be returned to us.... My people are getting very angry' (Matodzi Makahane, interview, 19 October 2007). The same view was expressed by other land claimants in the KNP (participatory observations, 2008–09). Senior officials in the Regional Land Claims Commission (Limpopo) and in the Office of the Chief Land Claims Commissioner supported the demand for land restoration by the people of Makahane–Maritenga (Blessing Mphela [Acting Chief Land Claim commissioner], interviewed by the *Financial Mail*, 23 May 2008). In terms of the theme of this chapter, land claimants and officials in the Land Claims Commission considered land restoration a key component of justice in the restitution process.

South African National Parks (SANParks) and the South African government, however, broadened the notion of justice in land restitution to refer to the national interest of the entire South African nation. These interests refer to the preservation of the KNP as a national heritage and as a cash cow for the national park system. The former chairperson of the Portfolio Committee on Land, Stone Sizani, referred to these interests when commenting that the 'Kruger National Park is our collective heritage as South Africans and therefore having it sliced up and ownership vesting in individual communities will not be in the public interest' (Stone Sizani, pers. comm., 19 September 2011). In the same vein government officials drew on a post-apartheid notion of heritage to argue that it is in the national interest not to give the KNP to any community (Miyelani Nkatingi, interview, 16 March 2011). This narrative of national interest ignores the constitutional provision that land reform is a national interest (Republic of South Africa 1996). These officials hold the view that giving land in the KNP to land claimants is tantamount to privatizing the ownership of state land. In their view, such a process would also compromise the biodiversity protocols and treaties that the South African government has signed with international organizations and institutions. This means that South Africa's international obligations towards biodiversity conservation constrain its domestic pursuit of justice through land restitution.

Translating the heritage of land claimants into that of the nation means that Thulamela cannot be claimed by the clans whose ancestry has produced it. It also renders heritage a weak link in the settlement of the land claim. It could also be argued that the Makahane–Maritenga land claim challenges another heritage, i.e. the establishment of the KNP as an exclusive heritage of white South Africans, particularly Afrikaners. The name of the park reflects this heritage, which has not changed much in a democratic South Africa, where the park remains a symbol of Afrikaner nationalism and territory. It could be argued that the current rhino poaching crisis in the KNP (see Lunstrum and Ybarra, this volume) is not only an environmental crisis but also a serious threat to the park as a symbol of Afrikaner nationalism and heritage. The defence of that heritage is bolstered by a sprinkle of 'the colours of the rainbow nation', i.e. the incorporation of the black elite into the conservation enterprise and the enlisting of local people[6] into the war against poachers in the KNP.

In addition to the KNP as a national heritage, the South African government and SANParks see the Makahane–Maritenga land claim as a threat to the financial viability of the country's national park system. Currently, profit from the KNP is used to subsidize other national parks in the country. SANParks fears that giving land rights within the park to claimants would compromise its monopoly over financial operations in the park, and would also potentially weaken its ability to exercise full control over the management of the KNP.[7] This fear appears to come from SANParks's experiences with the first and most well-known land claim by the people of Makuleke.

The Makuleke land claim has been fully discussed elsewhere (Tapela and Omara-Ojungu 1999; Ramutsindela 2002; Ramutsindela and Shabangu 2013). It suffices here to say the land claim was settled by giving claimants land title to the Pafuri corner located within the northern section of the KNP, currently known as Makuleke region. The settlement of the claim meant that the Makuleke region would be co-managed by the claimants – represented by the legal entity known as Makuleke Communal Property Association[8] – and SANParks. In return for preserving the conservation status of the park, the Makuleke were coerced to use their region in the park for eco-tourism purposes. Subsequent to the settlement of the Makuleke land claim in December 1998, the claimants thought they had the powers to pursue any form of eco-tourism in their newly acquired piece of the KNP and allowed the hunting of wildlife as a quick way of making money. SANParks stopped hunting in the park and, together with government, encouraged the people of Makuleke to enter into partnerships with the private sector to develop non-consumptive tourism. Through partnerships with eco-tourism companies such as Outpost and Wilderness Safaris, they have developed lodges in the park as their primary means of income generation, though the success of these partnerships have been questioned (Shabangu 2014).

It should be noted that the settlement of the Makuleke land claim was hailed by the South African government, environmental non-governmental organizations and the national and international media as an innovative and progressive solution. In the context of environmental justice, the Makuleke model appeared to balance the imperatives of both restitution and biodiversity conservation – it restores land rights without threatening the conservation status of the park. Whereas the Makuleke model recognized the rights of the claimants inside the KNP, the South African government moved away from land restoration as the goal of land restitution in conservation areas in the country. In 2007, the Department of Environmental Affairs and Tourism and the DLA signed a memorandum of understanding in which they agreed to settle land claims in protected areas on state land without giving land title to claimants. On 3 December 2008 the South African Cabinet took a decision not to restore land rights in the KNP. This decision meant that the state would retain land rights even if the land claim in the KNP were to be successful. In doing so, the Cabinet undermined land restoration as the primary goal of land restitution.

Cabinet decision: environmental justice redefined?

In 2009 the Departments of Environmental Affairs and Tourism and Land Affairs informed land claimants in the provinces of Limpopo and Mpumalanga of the Cabinet's decision (Republic of South Africa 2009). That decision effectively nullified the Makuleke model referred to above at the time the people of Makahane–Maritenga were considering it as an option. SANParks dismissed such an option on the basis that it did not take into account the financial viability and ecological integrity of Punda Maria in the northern part of the KNP. It argued that the portion of the KNP under claim is predominantly a wilderness area, is not profitable and is subsidized by other camps in the park. Furthermore, SANParks posits that the community had been misled by unscrupulous private investors who made them believe that they could realize profits from Punda Maria (Wanda Mkhutshulwa, interviewed by *Mail and Guardian*, 19 October 2007).

SANParks used the Makahane–Maritenga land claim as an opportunity to articulate its disapproval of the Makuleke land settlement model. In its view, such a model prevented the national conservation agency from exercising greater and significant control on decision making regarding resource collection, allocation and use of the Makuleke region of the KNP. They viewed the Makuleke land claim as a symbolic land claim that benefited a few people, and that also stood as a political statement by former Land Affairs Minister Derek Hanekom on transformation and land reform.

The notion of justice in Makahane–Maritenga land claim was also complicated by the legal interpretation of feasibility of land restoration. The concept of feasibility is not defined in the Land Restitution Act of 1994. Section 123(1) of the interim constitution provided that restoration of a right in land could only be granted, in the case of state land, if the state certified that restoration of the land was feasible and in the case of private land, if the state certified that the acquisition of the right in land was feasible (Republic of South Africa 1993). This constitutional requirement of a certificate of feasibility was given effect by Section 15, which required that, before a land claim for restoration is referred to the Land Claims Court, the chief land claims commissioner should obtain a certificate of feasibility from the minister of land affairs. Section 15(6) reads:

> In considering whether restoration or acquisition by the state is feasible … the Minister shall, in addition to any other factor, take into account –
>
> (a) whether the zoning of the land in question has since the dispossession been altered and whether the land has been transformed to such an extent that it is not practicable to restore the right in question;
> (b) any relevant urban development plan;
> (c) any other matter which makes the restoration or acquisition of the right in question unfeasible; and
> (d) any physical or inherent defect in the land which may cause it to be hazardous for human habitation.
>
> (Land Claim Court 138/99)

The final constitution did not contain the same level of detail in the provision for restitution as the interim constitution did. In particular, Section 25(7) makes no reference to feasibility but does make the right subject to the limitations contained in an Act of Parliament. The Restitution Act was amended in 1997 to take into account the constitutional changes. These included amendments to the provisions dealing with feasibility. With reference to factors in Section 15(6), Bundlender, Latzky and Roux (1998, 135) concluded that:

> [i]n essence, whenever land has been substantially transformed or developed, the Minister will have good reason to refuse a feasibility certificate. Also in relation to the now-repealed Section 15, expressed the view that [f]easibility addresses the question of whether restoration is practically achievable.

In the case of Makahane–Maritenga, the necessity for a feasibility certificate had fallen away but the current zoning of the KNP had significantly altered the land use patterns and prevents any type of residential or agricultural activities consistent with the period prior to land dispossession. In our view, questions of feasibility deviate from concerns with environmental justice.

A senior official in the Regional Land Claims Commission suggested that the people of Makahane–Maritenga could pursue environmental justice by asking the Land Claims Court to advise them on what it entails and how their land rights could be enforced (Richard Mulaudzi, interview, 4 March 2012). He opined that it was through the Land Claims Court that plans by the government and SANParks to give the Makuleke alternative forms of redress failed. The Regional Land Claims Commission in Mpumalanga thought that another way of pursuing justice in the KNP might be to de-proclaim 2–3 per cent of the 200,000 ha along the park border and give it to successful land claimants. The procedure for doing this could be thrashed out by the Commission in consultation with representatives from the DLA, the DEAT, SANParks and the claimants (*Financial Mail*, 23 May 2008). Officials in Limpopo wanted all land to be restored, with certain restrictions placed in some areas. It is claimed that

SANParks was entertaining the idea of releasing 10 per cent of the land under claim. None of these proposals came to fruition.

Attempts to pursue environmental justice through land restoration were dealt a final blow when President Zuma implemented the Cabinet decision on land claims in the KNP through cash payments. At the celebration and handover ceremony for land claims in the KNP, President Zuma quoted the statements from the former president of the African National Congress, Alfred Bixini Xuma, who said that:

> The fundamental basis of all wealth and power is the ownership and acquisition of freehold title to land. From land, we derive our existence. We derive our wealth in minerals, food, and other essentials. On land we build our homes. Without land we cannot exist. To all men of whatever race or colour land, therefore, is essential for their wealth, prosperity, and health. Without land-rights any race will be doomed to poverty, destitution, ill-health and lack of all life's essentials.
>
> (Xuma, cited in Zuma 2016)

Ironically, this quotation was followed by President Zuma's statement that the government will not give back land to claimants in the KNP in accordance with the Cabinet decision we noted above. Instead, the government offered cash compensation to six land claims in the KNP on 21 May 2016. Three of these claims in the Mpumalanga section of the KNP were the Mhlanganisweni and Sibuyi families, who received R12.8 million for 116 households; Mathebula Ngirivane, with 135 households sharing R15 million; and Mahashi, with R21 million for 191 households. The other three in Limpopo were Madonsi/Nwazekuzeku (R14.9 million for 135 households), Ndindani (R5.7 million for 52 households) and Muyexe (R14.2 million for 128 households). In handing out these payments in what the government described as a compensation and handover celebration, President Jacob Zuma upheld the hegemony of conservation over land rights when he said:

> The settlement model took into account the significance of the Kruger National Park as a home to an unparalleled diversity of wildlife and embraced an effort to save this National Monument for generations to come. It was therefore agreed that the settlement model will be one that takes the very important role of conservation into account.
>
> (Zuma 2016)

While the Makahane–Maritenga land claim committee refused to include financial compensation in the negotiation, the lure of money that was paid out to six land claimants has divided the Makahane–Maritenga land claimants. It is said that some members of Makahane–Maritenga have approached the Regional Land Claims Commission in Limpopo to get information about financial compensation (Manager of Land Claims Research (Limpopo), interview, 28 July 2016). At the time of writing (27 May 2017), their land claim was not yet settled. Indications are, however, that the government has closed the door for land restoration in the KNP. We would be surprised if the Makahane–Maritenga land claim is not settled through cash payments.

Conclusion

In this chapter we set out to contribute to approaches that hold the potential for narrowing the gap between the goals of nature conservation and land reform through the lens of land restitution in the KNP. Environmental justice is crucial for narrowing that gap. The case study of the Makahane–Maritenga and the experiences from land claims in the KNP offer three important lessons on what environmental justice in land restitution in protected areas should entail. The first lesson is that restoration of land rights is a key component of environmental justice as it allows land claimants to regain their material and non-material values of the land that had been lost through forced removals. The restoration of land rights does not automatically translate into a threat to the protection and management of South Africa's national park system. Environmental justice in land restitution cannot be achieved outside the property rights system. Arrangements such as co-management depend on the recognition of land rights.

The second lesson is that shifts in land restitution work against possibilities for striking a balance between the goals of land restitution and that of biodiversity conservation. These shifts reflect lack of policy coherence and also highlight lack of commitment to land reform by the South African government (see Ntsebeza and Hall 2007). The cumulative effects of shifts in restitution policy in protected areas are that they undermine the development and refinement of a credible strategy for settling land claims and also allow SANParks and government to retreat to their conservative approach to land restitution in protected areas. The form that land restitution in South Africa's protected areas should take was never made clear till Cabinet took the decision that, as from 2008, no restoration of land rights would be permissible in the KNP. Since that decision has not been tested in court, there is no guarantee that it paves the way for settling land claims in the country's protected areas.

Third, while environmental justice holds promise for just outcomes in land restitution in protected areas, the notion of justice is however diluted by attempts to separate land claims from national interests. This local–national dichotomy has no constitutional basis, and it instead contributes to the tension among land claimants and between land claimants and the state. The case of Makahane–Maritenga reveals that the source of this tension is also wider in scope. For example, it includes South Africa's obligations to international biodiversity protocols and agreements to which it is a signatory. On this basis we submit that environmental justice as land rights should be infused into conservation agreements at the international level. This would not only resolve the competing views of justice that Okereke (2007) referred to but also opens up possibilities for translating the concept of justice into the settlement of land claims in protected areas.

Land reform in protected areas offers a useful platform on which the multiple meanings of environmental justice could be recovered to enhance the prospects for justice to land claimants. Such recovery is possible when the tension between land claims and protected areas is understood more as a product of competing and shifting notions of justice than as simply a result of contested land use options. The tension has philosophical and practical dimensions that can only be resolved by solutions and strategies that speak to these dimensions in clear terms. In this chapter we have suggested that the possibilities for environmental justice through land restitution in protected areas hinge on three approaches. The first approach entails recontextualizing environmental justice to free it from its North American lineage, while the second one involves subjecting land restitution to rigorous scrutiny. The third approach revolves around agency. The pursuit of environmental justice in protected areas should be understood as a shared mandate between advocates of land rights, conservation agencies and the state. In the absence of this shared mandate, the tension between land restitution and biodiversity conservation will remain a feature of protected areas in South Africa and elsewhere.

Notes

1 Local people are commonly referred to in the literature on conservation and society as local communities. We prefer the term local people here to free the term from its anthropological baggage.
2 The MST supports conventional agriculture, which includes the use of chemical fertilizers (Wolford 2003).
3 There was however reference to sustainable rural development, which had very little or nothing to do with biodiversity conservation but everything to do with supporting agriculture and infrastructure development in rural areas. It was a continuation of betterment planning (see Letsoalo 1982).
4 Makahane people are part of the Nyai group – considered to be the first Venda clan to live in the mountains closer to Limpopo – who built Thulamela (Ralushai 1998).
5 The Makahane–Maritenga land claim was publicized for comments by affected parties in the Government Gazette Notice No. 2391 of 26 September 2003.
6 These local people are now told that the rhinos under threat are theirs, too. This message was muted when the rhinos appeared safe!
7 Lena Lukhele (interview, 18 February 2012) adds that SANParks is not financially and structurally ready to deal with multiple ownership of the KNP administratively. That is to say, SANParks does not want to govern the KNP with various groups of local people represented by different structures as such an arrangement would, in its view, make it hard to exercise its monopoly over the KNP.
8 A communal property association is a legal entity created in terms of the Communal Property Association Act 28 of 1996 for purposes of registering, holding and managing land acquired through land reform.

References

Adenle, Ademola A. 'Failure to Achieve 2010 Biodiversity's Target in Developing Countries: How Can Conservation Help'. *Biodiversity Conservation* 21, no. 10 (2012): 2435–2442.

Apostolopoulou, Evangelia and William Adams. 'Neoliberal Capitalism and Conservation in the Post-crisis Era: The Dialectics of "Green" and "Un-green" Grabbing in Greece and the UK'. *Antipode* 47, no. 1 (2015): 15–35.

Arboleda, Martin. 'The Biopolitical Production of the City: Urban Political Ecology in the Age of Immaterial Labour'. *Environment and Planning D: Society and Space* 33, no. 1 (2015): 35–51.

Bassa, Ronald. 'Evaluating Environmental Justice under the National Environmental Policy Act'. *Environmental Impact Assessment Review* 18, no. 1 (1998): 83–92.

Biermann, Christin and Becky Mansfield. 'Biodiversity, Purity, and Death: Conservation Biology as Biopolitics'. *Environment and Planning D: Society and Space* 32, no. 2 (2014): 257–273.

Bowen, William M. and Michael V. Wells. 'The Politics and Reality of Environmental Justice: A History and Considerations for Public Administrators and Policy Makers'. *Public Administration Review* 62 (2002): 688–698.

Brockington, Daniel and Rosaleen Duffy. 'Capitalism and Conservation: The Production and Reproduction of Biodiversity Conservation'. *Antipode* 42, no. 3 (2010): 469–484.

Brockington, Daniel and James Igoe. 'Eviction for Conservation: A Global Overview'. *Conservation and Society* 4, no. 3 (2006): 424–470.

Bullard, Robert D. *Dumping in Dixie: Race, Class and Environmental Quality*. Boulder, CO: Westview Press, 1990.

Bundlender, Geoff, Johan Latzky and Theunis Roux. *Juta's New Land Law*. Kenwyn: Juta, 1998.

Carruthers, Jane. *The Kruger National Park: A Social and Political History*. Pietermaritzburg: University of Natal Press, 1995.

Castree, Noel, David Demeritt, Diana Liverman and Bruce Rhoads. *A Companion to Environmental Geography*. Chichester: Wiley-Blackwell, 2009.

Chiaravalloti, Rafael M. 'Overfishing or Over Reacting? Management of Fisheries in the Pantanal Wetland, Brazil'. *Conservation and Society* 15, no. 1 (2017): 111–122.

Coates, Ken S. *A Global History of Indigenous Peoples: Struggles and Survival*. New York, NY: Palgrave Macmillan, 2004.

Dowie, Mark. *Conservation Refugees: The Hundred-Year Conflict between Global Conservation and Native Peoples*. Cambridge, MA: MIT Press, 2011.

Ghimire, Krishna B. and Michael P. Pimbert. *Social Change and Conservation*. London: Routledge, 2013.

Goldman, Benjamin. What Is the Future of Environmental Justice? *Antipode* 28 (1996): 122–141.

Hall, Martin. *The Changing Past: Farmers, Kings and Traders in Southern Africa 200–1860*. Cape Town: David Philip, 1987.

Heynen, Nik. 'Urban Political Ecology II: The Abolitionist Century'. *Progress in Human Geography* 40, no. 6 (2016): 839–845.

Hoffman, M. Timm. 'Environmental Change in Twentieth Century South Africa & Its Implications for Land Reform'. In *Land Divided Land Restored: Land Reform in South Africa for the 21st Century*, edited by Ben Cousins and Cherryl Walker, 56–67. Auckland Park: Jacana, 2015.

Holified, Ryan, Michael Porter and Gordon Walker. *Spaces of Environmental Justice*. Chichester: Wiley-Blackwell, 2010.

Kepe, Thembela. 'Land and Justice in South Africa: Exploring the Ambiguous Role of the State in the Land Claims Process'. *African and Asian Studies* 11, no. 4 (2012): 391–409.

Kepe, Thembela, Rachel Wynberg and William Ellis. 'Land Reform and Biodiversity Conservation in South Africa: Complementary or in Conflict?' *The International Journal of Biodiversity Science and Management* 1, no. 1 (2005): 3–16.

Landless People's Movement. Request for a Slot at the Parliamentary Portfolio Committee (Land Hearing). Cape Town, 2004.

Lenggenhager, Luregn. 'Circulating Nature: From North-Eastern Namibia to South Africa and Back, 1960–1990'. In *The Politics of Nature and Science in Southern Africa*, edited by Maano Ramutsindela, Giorgio Miescher and Melanie Boehi, 87–105. Basel: Basler Afrika Bibliographien, 2016.

Lerrer, Débora F. and Leonilde Servolo de Medeiros. 'Food Sovereignty and Struggle for Land: The Experience of the MST in Brazil'. In *Alternative Agrifood Movements: Patterns of Convergence and Divergence*, edited by Douglas H. Constance, Marie-Christine Renard and Marta G. Rivera-Ferre, 111–135. Bingley: Emerald Group, 2014.

Letsoalo, Essy M. 'Survival Strategies in Rural Lebowa: A Study of Geography of Poverty'. MA dissertation, Department of Geography, University of the Witwatersrand, 1982.

Locke, Harvey. 'Nature Needs Half: A Necessary and Hopeful New Agenda for Protected Areas in North America and around the World'. *George Wright Forum* 31 (2014): 59–371.

Lohmann, Larry. *Ethnic Discrimination in 'Global' Conservation*. London: Goldsmiths College University of London, 2000.

Magome, Hector and James Murombedzi. Sharing South African National Parks: Community Land and Conservation in a Democratic South Africa. In *Decolonising Nature: Strategies for Conservation in a Post-colonial Era*, edited by William M. Adams and Martin Mulligan, 135–151. London: Earthscan, 2003.

Martinez-Alier, Joan, Isabelle Anguelovski, Patrick Bond, Daniela Del Bene, Federico Demaria, Julien-Francois Gerber, Lucie Greyl, Willi Haas, Hali Healy, Victoria Marín-Burgos and Godwin Ojo. 'Between Activism and Science: Grassroots Concepts for Sustainability Coined by Environmental Justice Organizations'. *Journal of Political Ecology* 21, no. 1 (2014): 19–60.

McCusker, Brent, William G. Moseley and Maano Ramutsindela. *Land Reform in South Africa: An Uneven Transformation*. Lanham, MD: Rowman & Littlefield, 2016.

Meadows Michael E. 'Contemporary Land Reform Policy and Practice in South Africa and Its Environmental Implications: New Ideas, Old Problems?' *Geography, Environment and Sustainability* 5, no. 4 (2012): 33–45.

Meskell, Lynn. 'Archaeological Ethnography: Conversations around Kruger National Park'. *Archaeologies* 1, no. 1 (2005): 81–100.

Nash, Roderick F. *Wilderness and the American Mind*. New Haven, CT: Yale University Press, 2014.

Najam, Adil. 'Developing Countries and Global Environmental Governance: From Contestation to Participation to Engagement'. *International Environmental Agreements* 5 (2005): 303–321.

Nemaheni, Tshimangadzo I. 'A Cultural Heritage Resource Management Plan for Thulamela Heritage Site'. MA dissertation, Department of Historical and Heritage Studies, University of Pretoria, 2003.

Neumann, Roderick, P. 'Land, Justice, and the Politics of Conservation in Tanzania'. In *People, Plants, and Justice: The Politics of Nature Conservation*, edited by Charles Zerner, 117–133. New York, NY: Columbia University Press, 2000.

Ntsebeza, Lungisile and Ruth Hall. *The Land Question in South Africa: The Challenge of Transformation and Redistribution*. Cape Town: Human Sciences Research Council, 2007.

Okereke, Chukwumerije. *Global Justice and Neoliberal Environmental Governance: Ethics, Sustainable Development and International Co-Operation*. Abingdon: Routledge, 2007.

Pikirayi, Innocent. *The Zimbabwe Culture: Origins and Decline in Southern Zambesia States*. Walnut Creek, CA: Altamira Press, 2001.

Pulido, Laura. 'A Critical Review of the Methodology of Environmental Racism Research'. *Antipode* 28 (1996): 142–159.

Puttick, James R., M. Timm Hoffman and James Gambiza. 'The Impact of Land Use on Woody Plant Cover and Species Composition on the Grahamstown Municipal Commonage: Implications for South Africa's Land Reform Programme'. *African Journal of Range & Forage Science* 31, no. 2 (2014): 123–133.

Ralushai, N. Victor *A Preliminary Report on the Early History of Thulamela Archaeological Site*. Unpublished document: Kruger National Park, 1998.

Ramutsindela, Maano. *Parks and People in Postcolonial Societies: Experiences in Southern Africa*. Dordrecht, Boston, MA, and London: Kluwer (Springer), 2004.

Ramutsindela, Maano. 'The Perfect Way to Ending a Painful Past? Makuleke Land Deal in South Africa'. *Geoforum* 33, no. 1 (2002): 15–24.

Ramutsindela, Maano and Medupi Shabangu. 'Conditioned by Neoliberalism: A Reassessment of Land Claim Resolutions in the Kruger National Park'. *Journal of Contemporary African Studies* 31, no. 3 (2013): 441–456.

Redford, Kent H., Brian J. Huntley, Dilys Roe, Tom Hammond, Mark Zimsky, Tomas E. Lovejoy, Gustavo A. da Fonseca, Carlos M. Rodriguez and Richard M. Cowling. 'Mainstreaming Biodiversity: Conservation for the Twenty-First Century'. *Frontiers in Ecology and Evolution*, 2015. doi:10.3389/fevo.2015.00137.

Republic of South Africa. Interim Constitution of the Republic of South Africa. Pretoria: Government Gazette, 1993.

Republic of South Africa. Constitution of the Republic of South Africa. Pretoria: Government Printer, 1996.

Republic of South Africa. *Media Statement*. Pretoria: Department of Government Communications and Information Systems, 2009.

Shabangu, Medupi. 'The Neo-liberalisation of Nature: Contextualising the Resolution of Land Claims in the Kruger National Park'. MA dissertation, Department of Environmental and Geographical Science, University of Cape Town, 2014.

Shiva, Vandana. *Protect or Plunder? Understanding Intellectual Property Rights*. London: Zed, 2001.

Steyn, Maryna, Sidney Miller, Willem C. Nienaber and Marius Loots 'Late Iron Age Gold Burials from Thulamela (Pafuri Region, Kruger National Park)'. *South African Archaeological Bulletin* 53, no. 168 (1998): 73–85.

Tapela, Barbara N. and Peter H. Omara-Ojungu. 'Towards Bridging the Gap between Wildlife Conservation and Rural Development in Post-apartheid South Africa: The Case of the Makuleke Community and the Kruger National Park'. *South African Geographical Journal* 81, no. 3 (1999): 148–155.

Thondhlana, Gladman, Cundill, G. and Thembela Kepe. 'Co-management, Land Rights, and Conflicts around South Africa's Silaka Nature Reserve'. *Society & Natural Resources* 29, no. 4 (2016): 403–417.

Torpey-Saboe, Nichole, Krister Andersson, Esther Mwangi, Lauren Persha, Carl Salk and Glenn Wright. 'Benefit Sharing among Local Resource Users: The Role of Property Rights'. *World Development* 72 (2015): 408–418.

Walker, Gordon. *Environmental Justice: Concepts, Evidence and Politics*. London: Routledge, 2012.

Walker, Cherryl, Anna Bohlin, Ruth Hall and Thembela Kepe. *Land, Memory, Reconstruction, and Justice: Perspectives on Land Claims in South Africa*. Athens, OH: Ohio University Press, 2010.

Warlenius, Rikard, Gregory Pierce and Vasna Ramasar, 'Reversing the Arrow of Arrears: The Concept of "Ecological Debt" and Its Value for Environmental Justice'. *Global Environmental Change* 30 (2015): 21–30.

Wayessa, Gutu O. and Anja Nygren. 'Whose Decisions, Whose Livelihoods? Resettlement and Environmental Justice in Ethiopia'. *Society & Natural Resources* 29, no. 4 (2016): 387–402.

Wilson, Edward O. *Half-Earth: Our Planet's Fight for Life*. London: Liferight, 2016.

Wolford, Wendy. 'Producing Community: The MST and Land Reform Settlements in Brazil'. *Journal of Agrarian Change* 3, no. 4 (2003): 500–520.

Wynberg, Rachel and Merle Sowman. 'Environmental Sustainability and Land Reform in South Africa: A Neglected Dimension'. *Journal of Environmental Planning and Management* 50, no. 6 (2007): 783–802.

Zuma, Jacob. Remarks by President Jacob Zuma at the Compensation and Handover Celebration for Various Land Claims on the Kruger National Park, Ehlanzeni District Municipality, Mpumalanga, 21 May 2016.

Part II

Militarization, violence, and exclusion

4 Deploying difference

Security threat narratives and state displacement from protected areas

Elizabeth Lunstrum and Megan Ybarra

Introduction

South Africa, and its cherished Kruger National Park, has emerged as the epicenter of commercial rhino poaching. Under public pressure to ramp up its response, the Department of Environmental Affairs presented a media release outlining its "progress in the war against poaching and plans for 2015" (Environmental Affairs 2015). Despite its provocative title, the report reads as a technical list of responses, many amounting to a militarization of conservation practice, reflecting the fact that rhino poaching is understood as at once a threat to both conservation and national security. Yet, also tucked within the release is a reference to the displacement of communities from Mozambique's adjacent Limpopo National Park (LNP) (also see Environmental Affairs 2014). How did eviction from a national park come to be seen as a legitimate *security* strategy, proof of progress in the "war against poaching"?

Moving from Africa to the Americas, Guatemala's Maya Biosphere Reserve (MBR) has become a key site for interventions at the nexus of conservation and drug trafficking (McSweeney et al. 2014). The MBR is part of Guatemala's protected areas system, which was created during the end of the 1960–96 civil war and before a return to democratic processes through the Peace Accords. More than two-thirds of the subtropical lowlands of the Petén region have state protected area status. In cooperation with other state agencies, the Guatemalan security state uses conservation laws to draw on historical practices of evicting poor Indigenous peoples and burning their homes and crops. This is not simply a case of conservation-induced displacement. During the civil war, and now the drug war, the state authorizes displacement on the grounds of security threats rooted in racial ideologies of dangerous subjects.

What unites these cases is that these displacements from both the LNP and MBR are justified increasingly by *security* considerations and not solely conservation concerns. Hence we bring the cases together as a comparative study to highlight this broader trend and expose how it is unfolding. In attending to this, we show how state authorities authorize these security-provoked displacements by deploying interlocking axes of difference. While difference is not inherently dangerous, state agents mobilize it to articulate anxieties of territorial trespass with a racialized enemy. Together, these reframe residents as security threats – whether the insurgent-poacher or subversive-narco – in need of relocation. Such difference, we illustrate, is rooted in prior histories, Cold War histories in both cases and older colonial histories with the LNP. In relation, we show that it is discourses of the nation-state under threat combined with state territorialization practices that ultimately enable eviction. The cases, however, differ in one telling respect. While displacement from the LNP is an instance of conservation-induced displacement (CID), albeit one reworked with security considerations, contemporary eviction from the MBR is justified primarily by security concerns. It is hence an example of the broader category of displacement from conservation areas rather than CID. Nonetheless, the state takes advantage of protected area legislation to enable these evictions. The cases hence offer insight into different articulations of conservation, security, and displacement. Finally, we show that the justifications for eviction make a difference. Namely, more than offering a new rationale for eviction, once security rationales begin to transform conservation space and practice, it becomes more difficult to contest the resulting land tenure regimes, as security itself is presumably at stake. We turn to these arguments after a brief review of methodology and the relevant scholarly literature.[1]

Where conservation meets displacement, security, and difference

Large-scale evictions from national parks began in the late nineteenth century at the same time as the world's national parks came into existence. The timing was not by accident, as such removal was seen as necessary to realizing the essence of national parks as spaces of "wilderness," especially in North America and Africa. As the national park model spread, so too did displacements of residents living within recently designated park borders from Africa to the Americas, with displacements and hence violence often amounting to originary moments in the creation of protected areas. While colonial and post-independence-era displacements from parks have largely been tied to this colonial "wilderness" imaginary, independent nation-states have also evicted residents from parks on the grounds that these projects would enable national development (Neumann 1998; Spence 1999; Wakild 2011). Such evictions both historically and today share qualities well documented in the scholarly literature.

First, they are often organized by state offices and actors. It is states, both colonial and postcolonial, that have had the means and desire to gazette large land tracts and repurpose them into protected areas. Once reclassified as national (or colonial) territory, states can then override tenure rights and, with varying degrees of success, clear lands of human settlements, agriculture, and small-scale resource extraction. Relatedly, protected areas have become consequential sites of territorialization and state formation. More explicitly, protected areas enable states to transform land into state territory or symbolically loaded state property and enable states to consolidate power over these spaces, enabling state formation. They do so by creating various opportunities from revenue generation, national subject–formation (of displaced communities and colonial settlers alike), and the protection of resources deemed valuable and vulnerable to the rescripting of nonhuman nature as "national resources" or "national heritage" (Jazeel 2005; Carruthers 1995; Vandergeest and Peluso 1995; Brockington 2002; Neumann 1998). More recent scholarship on neoliberal conservation has investigated how such displacement is motivated or encouraged by private actors who work through the state to profit from recently emptied landscapes (Gardner 2016; Ojeda 2012). The larger point, however, is that, as states are still the primary actors behind these evictions, protected area designation and the underlying displacements enable states to consolidate power over newly created conservation territory, resources, and populations (even if this is done in consort with private actors).

Second, protected areas eviction (and creation) has long been a racialized form of dispossession. While racism shapes simultaneous processes of inclusion and exclusion, specifying who is included in the nation and who must be banished elsewhere, this plays out in specific ways in protected areas. Here, the state participates in interpellating nondominant populations with cultural, linguistic, class, and national markers of difference as territorial trespassers – as invaders or interlopers. More specifically, the supposedly dangerous figure that stalks the jungle or lurks within the bush takes on the connotations of the racialized, savage interloper: a greedy, slippery, opportunistic, or lazy person who takes without investing in the land (Slater 2002; Hartmann et al. 2005; Neumann 2004a; Mavhunga 2014). While the primary marker of difference deployed here is that of race, this racialized transgressor is also typically constructed as male (Neumann 2004a). Stepping back from these studies, we see the category of the "park invader" as one that is formed through the deployment of politically loaded meanings associated with axes of difference, ones that enable conservation agents to disavow residents' land rights. Here we are building on critical race and postcolonial theories that explain axes of difference not as "objective" markers of difference but as the politically loaded social construction of multiple forms of difference that intersect to create mutually reinforcing systems of discrimination (Hall et al. 1978; Crenshaw 1991; Gilmore 2002). To be clear, difference is not inherently negative, nor does it authorize displacement. Rather, various actors actively articulate racialized difference with understandings of territorial exclusion and trespass. It is the deployment of this reworked, loaded notion of difference, unfolding across unequal power relations, that provokes displacement.

Beyond these similarities, evictions from protected areas are marked by consequential differences. Most salient for our purposes is the fact that not all are justified solely or even centrally on conservation grounds, as Neumann (2004b) powerfully shows. Other rationales include evicting people to "develop" them or interpellate them as national subjects and also to access valuable natural resources (Sandlos 2008; Brockington and Igoe 2006; Dowie 2009; Spence 1999). This moves us to distinguish between *CID*, where eviction is justified on conservation-related grounds, and a broader trend of *displacement from protected areas*, where justifications may spill beyond the bounds of conservation rationales. In fact, even looking back at the multiple state rationales behind conservation makes us complicate the assumption that all evictions from protected areas are motivated strictly or even primarily by conservation concerns.

These trends of state creation and territorialization of protected areas, racialized dispossession from their borders, and the multiple rationales behind these evictions have characterized displacements from protected areas historically and today. Set against this background, we are beginning to see a new rationale for such displacements. Namely, while the 1980s marked a turn away from protected area displacement on the grounds that it violated human rights and led to poorer conservation outcomes, the pendulum has swung back toward acceptance of eviction (Wilson 2016; Wilshusen et al. 2002; Terborgh 1999). Increasingly, these evictions are justified at least in part on security grounds. Built upon a long history of conservation's ties to military personnel, logics, and organizational structure (Ellis 1994; Neumann 2004a), we are seeing a growing trend in treating conservation issues as security issues and responding accordingly (Kelly and Ybarra 2016; Massé and Lunstrum 2016). In extreme cases, this amounts to green militarization (Lunstrum 2014) or the use of military personnel, logics, and technologies in the pursuit of conservation (Lunstrum 2014; Devine 2014; Ojeda 2012; Ybarra 2012; Duffy 2016), along with a broader buildup of military actors in conservation spaces, whether or not their mandate is environmental protection (Ybarra 2016). Firmly rooted in this broader context, military actors and security logics are beginning to play a pivotal role in authorizing the removal of communities from protected areas (Lunstrum 2016; Massé and Lunstrum 2016; Ojeda 2012; Devine 2014).

We build from these trends to show first how the dovetailing of conservation and security leads to evictions from protected areas motivated by security considerations across geographically distant locations, namely southern Africa and Central America. These evictions, moreover, are authorized by mobilizing notions of difference, bringing together notions of territorial trespass and racialized difference rooted in prior histories. We also show how, while some examples of security-provoked displacements from protected areas are instances of CID, in other cases conservation rationales all but disappear and hence are examples of displacement from conservation areas more broadly. But, even in these cases, protected area territorialization, including related legislation, facilitates displacement. Together these cases suggest complex, diverse articulations of conservation, security, and displacement. Our concern is that, regardless of whether eviction is motivated equally by security and conservation concerns (LNP) or much more centrally by security concerns (MBR), the result is that it is more difficult to contest the evictions once security is a motivating factor, a theme we return to in the conclusion.

Before we turn to these issues, we would first like to make a point about terminology. There now exists a rich literature on CID. While some scholars have adopted an expansive understanding of the concept that includes restrictions on access to resources (Witter 2013; Cernea 2005), we follow Agarwal and Redmond's stricter definition, that is, the *physical* removal or eviction of communities from their homes. In both of our empirical cases, moreover, the displacement unfolding is involuntary.[2] Hence we use the terms "displacement," "removal," "dispossession," and "eviction" interchangeably all to mean involuntary physical removal and relocation (also see Agarwal and Redford 2009).

Conservation security–provoked displacement from Mozambique's Limpopo National Park

To understand current rationales behind displacement from Mozambique's LNP, we must jump the border into South Africa's adjacent Kruger National Park. Kruger is now the epicenter of the so-called "rhino wars." Incidents of commercial rhino poaching have grown from 13 in 2007 to 1,054 in 2016, reflecting the escalating value of rhino horn on Asian markets. These numbers are concerning given that South Africa is home to the majority of the world's remaining 25,000 rhinos. As the name "rhino war" suggests, the problem is increasingly framed as an issue of security, beginning with national security (Molewa 2013). This spins on the fact that South African state actors and segments of the public routinely understand rhino poachers as decimating rhinos as national treasures and violating territorial sovereignty, especially given that many come from neighboring Mozambique. As such, their border crossings are repeatedly read as infiltrations undertaken by nefarious foreign nationals bent on destroying the nation's heritage (Lunstrum 2014; 2017). While unfolding within South Africa and the adjacent borderlands, these practices reflect a larger rendering of commercial poaching as an issue of national if not global security. Poaching within and beyond South Africa is orchestrated by global criminal syndicates, often a concern of national security (Molewa 2013). Poaching in East and Central Africa, moreover, is suggested to have ties to alleged terrorist groups like al-Qaeda and the Lord's Resistance Army, despite a general lack of evidence (Duffy 2016). As such, commercial poaching was even understood as a national if not global security threat by the Obama administration (Obama 2014). Framed as a security issue, it hence becomes commonplace to speak not of rhino and biodiversity conservation but "rhino wars" and the larger "war to save biodiversity."

The securitization of commercial poaching – that is, the rendering of poaching as a security threat – has shaped South Africa's response, for example with the deployment of the army within Kruger and along the border with Mozambique (interviews 2015; Lunstrum 2014; Environmental Affairs 2015). Militarization is likewise heading into Mozambique as the country beefs up its own security forces to stop the movement of poachers into Kruger (interviews 2013, 2015, 2016; do Limpopo 2013; Massé and Lunstrum 2016).

Yet a more subtle form of conservation security is underway. Approximately 7,000 people are currently being relocated from Mozambique's LNP, an eviction justified increasingly as an anti-poaching security strategy and promoted heavily by South Africa. To grasp this, it is instructive briefly to look back at the park's history. In the late 1980s, South African officials began to meet with counterparts in Mozambique and Zimbabwe to discuss possibilities for joining the Kruger National Park with adjacent lands in neighboring countries. The result was the creation of the tri-country Great Limpopo Transfrontier Park in 2002. While Zimbabwe had a pre-existing park to contribute, Mozambique did not. So, with strong pressure from South Africa, Mozambique transformed a defunct colonial hunting reserve into the LNP. Before the LNP's designation in the early 2000s, Mozambican officials argued that the reserve should become a multi-use zone that would allow human habitation. South African state and NGO officials, however, insisted that the core of the land be gazetted as a more restrictive national park, requiring the removal of resident communities. Their rationale was that inhabitants would disrupt the feel of "wilderness" that could bring tourism revenues and that they would threaten Kruger's wildlife (Büscher and Schoon 2009). After South African demands won out, Mozambican officials also began to justify the evictions but on the grounds that this was for community safety, as the park was being restocked with dangerous wildlife (interviews 2004–05).

While relocation stalled for a number of years, it began to pick up pace around 2012 after rhino poaching hit the scene (Lunstrum 2016). The arrival of rhino poaching helped rekindle the urgency around relocation, transforming its rationale. Today, while the initial rationales for relocation remain, it is now also deeply motivated by a sense that young men from communities in and near the LNP are hired by criminal syndicates to hunt rhino while others harbor weapons and poachers from the outside (interviews 2013, 2015, 2016). With some communities only a short walking distance to Kruger, an emptied park would create a spatial barrier between Kruger and potential poachers. As a high-ranking LNP official explained:

> [H]aving a village within close proximity of the border, it creates a safe-haven near the border and an operational base from where you could launch [poaching operations].... And if you move that safe-haven to the perimeter of the park, the buffer zone, a poacher would now have to walk 50 km through a protected area before they even got to Kruger. And so doing resettlement is one of the strategies to support the reduction in poaching.
>
> (Interview 2013)

The security rationale for relocation is further reinforced by the argument that an emptied park is easier to police as poachers would no longer be able to hide in plain sight (interviews 2011, 2013).

Relocation from the park is technically the responsibility of the Mozambican government, which supports relocation as a security strategy (interviews 2016; also see Republic of Mozambique 2015, 11). But strongly encouraging these displacements is the South African state, as seen in official state documents celebrating relocation as proof of "progress in the war against poaching" (Environmental

Affairs 2014, 2015). What is equally telling is that a number of LNP officials supporting relocation are actually South Africans whose salaries are paid by the South African Peace Parks Foundation. This in fact includes the official quoted immediately above explicitly justifying relocation as an anti-poaching security strategy.

Deploying understandings of difference, organizing evictions from the LNP

South African demands for relocation on security grounds are supported by a particular mobilization of difference, one that brings together notions of territorial trespass and a racialized Other. To understand how such difference is deployed, it is necessary to turn to how it is rooted in regional history, both the Cold War category of the "insurgent" and the colonial category of the "poacher." These come together in the trope of the poacher-as-insurgent.

Beginning with "the insurgent," in South African state discourse, rhino poaching emerges as far more than an environmental threat. It is increasingly framed as a war and more specifically an insurgency, one directed at South Africa. For instance, David Mabunda, former South Africa National Parks (SANParks) CEO and current Ezemvelo KZN Wildlife CEO, has argued that wildlife protection should be handed over to the army, explaining:

> This is no longer a conservation war – it is a war on [South African] sovereignty so we should look at it in terms of our national security. Poachers from neighbouring countries come heavily armed in the still of the night and kill our rhino. This is counter-insurgency and we should respond accordingly.
>
> (Quoted in Defence Web 2015)

The language of insurgency also frames the language of retired Army General Johan Jooste, who oversees SANParks' national anti-poaching operations (Smith and Humphreys 2015; Lunstrum 2014). It is similarly creeping into the tactics and branding of private anti-poaching companies, such as Counter Insurgency Tracker Training (CITT), which provides "quality man and animal tracking courses" to conservation organizations including SANParks (CITT 2015).

This move to frame poachers as insurgents is evocative not only because it mirrors a powerful global discourse of insurgency given new life within the "War on Terror" (Anderson 2011) and unsubstantiated suggestions that terrorist groups profit from poaching (Duffy 2016), but also because it has historical traction. During the fight against white supremacist rule, anti-apartheid activists coming from within South Africa and neighboring countries like Mozambique were branded as "terrorists" and "insurgents" determined to bring down the apartheid government. Reflecting the broader Cold War context as it was articulated with state racism, insurgents – understood by the ruling party as predominately black political agitators – were seen as infiltrating threats to both white rule and the capitalist economic system (Rich 1984).

The current incarnation of the rhino poacher as "insurgent," a racialized politically threatening and politically motivated trespasser, revives this apartheid Cold War history, giving it discursive punch. In fact, a high-ranking South African anti-poaching official with a background in apartheid counterinsurgency operations drew an explicit connection to the apartheid era, explaining:

> Even in the height of our bad times here in South Africa [i.e., anti-apartheid "insurgency"], there was never a time where you had 2 to 3 insurgencies a day, armed insurgencies, never. Today we have up to 80 a month! A sovereign country allowing armed people, but not only with hunting rifles, often assault rifles as well, to enter illegally and plunder my resources and take them out of the country illegally. That's part of the predicament.
>
> (Interview 2013)

Hence, the predicament is one of mass insurgency, reminiscent of a time when white minority sovereignty itself was felt to be under threat at the hands of black "insurgents." What is ironic is that this new "insurgent-poacher" has no political agenda, hence denying the very essence of what typically constitutes insurgency. Even so, its use is discursively productive.

To fully grasp the racialization of the rhino-poacher-as-insurgent, however, we must grapple with the older colonial construct of "the poacher." The origin of many national parks across sub-Saharan Africa, especially white settler states like South Africa, rested in European settlers creating Edenic landscapes in which to nurture a European sense of belonging, a move itself enabled by Indigenous dispossession (Igoe 2004; Carruthers 1995). In short stride came the criminalization of Indigenous habitation, farming, and hunting. Such racialized dispossession gave life to "the poacher." Necessarily a "black" or "native" African, he is a shifty fellow, albeit one with often impressive bush skills, who threatens the environment, not to mention a European sensibility of Edenic wilderness (Mavhunga 2014; Neumann 2004a). He takes what is not his, what he has invested neither his labor nor money into. This colonial construct haunts the current rhino poacher who is understood as entering where he is not welcome to reap wealth to which he has no claim, in the process threatening wildlife as national treasures and those tasked with its protection. Looking back even further, Indigenous Africans were racialized as Other as a core feature of white settler nation-making long before park boundaries were drawn. It is this prior colonial move of racialized nation-making that made the evictions possible in the first place and hence that is foundational to environmental conservation across much of Africa and beyond (Carruthers 1995; Neumann 1998; Mollett 2010).

In short, the South African trope of the rhino-poacher-as-insurgent emerges from both colonial and Cold War histories. This is a racialized subject position whose race is overdetermined: insurgents during the fight against apartheid and poachers from colonial history onward are both understood as essentially untrustworthy, shifty "black Africans." In a place like Kruger, where protected areas are still largely seen as the provenance of the descendants of European settlers (Kepe 2009; Hughes 2010; Meskell 2012; Büscher 2016) and where men coming to hunt rhinos have largely been "black" Mozambicans, the poacher-as-insurgent is rendered multiply foreign in terms of his nation, labor, and race. So, when a Mozambican enters Kruger to hunt rhinos, he is seen not merely as a poacher but as a dark and menacing insurgent bent on infiltrating South African sovereign territory and greedily decimating its heritage, amounting to an act of war.

This racialized rendering of the rhino poacher is productive: it authorizes displacement. Interestingly, it is not the case that all conservation officials deploy this language, and I have never heard a Mozambican official turn to the language of insurgency. But its routine use in South Africa, a country that has long had substantial influence on the LNP and process of relocation, provides part of the larger context in which displacement comes to make sense. More broadly, it is through these moves that the eviction of communities comes to be understood as an obvious response not only to poaching but ending the *insurgency* and winning the *war*.

Guatemala: security-induced displacement in borderlands, protected areas, and the "drug war"

The crown jewel of Guatemala's protected areas system is the MBR, created in 1990 by expanding a forest reserve and increasing land use restrictions. Today, more than 2.1 million hectares in the Petén department are protected areas on the Mexican border. Most residents did not even know that the MBR had been created until after the laws were passed. Thus, conservation education took the form of telling people about rights they had already lost. As Sundberg (2004, 2003) demonstrates, the 1990s marked a period when marginalized communities maneuvered for land rights after CID took place.

While this conjunctural moment reterritorialized Petén in the name of conservation, its borderland location made it a security concern long before and after this moment. In popular discourses of security and sovereignty, newspaper articles ask questions like "how did Guatemala lose 50,000 square kilometers?" (Gutiérrez Martínez 2017). Guatemalans still decry the loss of Chiapas and Campeche to Mexico. On both sides of the border, non-Indigenous elites raised concerns about Indigenous peoples' loyalty to the postcolonial state. Mexican and Guatemalan central elites made physical and racial difference dangerous when they authorized displacement on that basis (Nolan-Ferrell 2012). Petén's borderland status is why it was later a key site for successive military dictators seeking to (re)make Guatemalan territory as part of an anti-guerilla Cold War campaign during the civil war (1960–96). During the war, the military state first declared Petén an empty frontier that needed to be incorporated into the nation; then the military collaborated with USAID in promoting settlement, where forest-clearing was evidence of ownership required by Guatemalan law to obtain formal land titles; and finally both USAID and the state decried settlement as deforestation (Grandia 2012; Ybarra 2012). State territorial claims repeatedly disavow collective memories and associated land justice claims – for settlement, then for conservation, and today to fight the so-called drug war. Across all three moments, the military territorialized the lowlands under a security framework.

Eventually, military claims to save the Guatemalan nation from the threat of Cold War communism were revealed as thin facades for genocidal massacres. This broader context set the stage for the ways in which Petén's territorialization coalesced on three interrelated threat narratives that framed residents as conservation's constitutive Outsiders, rationalizing CID. First, illegal logging was identified as a "Mexican" problem, where supposed foreigners were stealing valuable Guatemalan natural resources. Second, Petén was supposed to suffer from a "population bomb." When the population seemed to rise precipitously in a short period of time, international conservationists decried "immigration" and even refugees' right to return (Ybarra 2017). Finally, Petenero locals successfully institutionalized their stereotype of Indigenous Q'eqchi's as forest-eating "termites." This narrative served to frame forest-clearing practices as pathological to a supposedly nomadic people, naturalizing their dispossession. Whereas poor farmers were potentially politically dangerous during the Cold War, in the conservation era they became environmentally dangerous. It is of note that park officials call communities "invaders" even if they acknowledge their existence predates the creation of protected areas (interviews 2008). In all three narratives, threats to the environment became read as threats to the postwar state, where protected areas conservation required displacement. Hence, communities were displaced from the protected area on conservation grounds, but these environmental threats were first understood as security threats.

There were dozens of evictions in MBR communities in the 1990s, as well as a series of voluntary resettlement agreements. Today, however, most conservation displacement amounts to a war of attrition. Rather than physical violence, CONAP (Consejo Nacional de Area Protegidas, the national parks agency) has primarily worked with cognizant state agencies to ensure that they do not provide basic services like schools and running water to "invader" communities. Rather than a singular moment, state agencies coordinate to ensure that families cannot send their children to school or bathe in their homes.

By the mid-2000s, in a rising tide of drug trafficking territorial violence, the Guatemalan borderlands became a security threat again. Conservationists were part of a rising tide that brushed off postgenocide calls for demilitarization in favor of increased funding for the drug war (Ybarra, 2017). Scientists coined phrases like "narco-deforestation" (McSweeney et al. 2014), and the *New York Times* warned that the MBR was becoming a "rapidly deforesting mini-narco-state" (Schmidt 2010). This hyperbolic language offers no evidence that drug trafficking organizations (DTOs) have any interest in deforestation, much less a political agenda to take over the state, but threat narratives nonetheless authorize violence on their behalf.

A 2004 drug trafficking–related "state of emergency" deployed the military in Laguna del Tigre National Park. Rather than query the effect of massive troop deployment in tropical forests, US conservationists hailed this as an important victory to save the endangered scarlet macaw (e.g., Gunyup 2005, 62). Hence, conservationists strategically endorsed military buildup, justified by narco-security threats, as a means of ecological protection. The author, however, was unable to find any information that confirmed either that macaw protection was part of the army's mandate in Laguna del Tigre or that massive deployment saved the macaw. In recent years, state laws formalized the military's territorial claims to patrol the Maya Forest. Conservation practitioners suggest that this is necessary because CONAP officials do not carry weapons, so only the military can patrol the forest. At the same time, they acknowledge that soldiers sometimes kill endangered species for food, or even just out of boredom (interviews 2009). As I discuss below, it is during states of emergency that the military evicts communities from protected areas.

While the Inter-American Commission on Human Rights (IACHR 2015) found that the central state declared 10 states of emergency within a decade "as a means of social control" for prolonged and unstated periods of time, it noted that those in northern Guatemala (including the MBR) were in response to valid drug trafficking threats. The problem with the security state's resurgence during states of emergency in protected areas is that securitization strips people of their rights, treating them as presumptive criminals, instead of protecting them. As Oscar Martínez explains,

> International organizations have pumped Guatemala with money intended to protect forested areas and archaeological sites. How does the state show the donors they're tough? By targeting the weakest, and accusing them of being narco-traffickers, which makes the state look even stronger.
>
> (2016, 66)

In other words, state security forces do not evict drug traffickers or ranchers who illegally clear land, build airstrips, and use core protected areas for cattle grazing.

Instead, state security forces target vulnerable communities: those that are poor and Indigenous and often do not speak Spanish, comprising the majority of the 35 "population fronts" that CONAP identifies as "invaded areas" (Rojas 2013). Even when Indigenous communities have historical grounds for their land claims, they are repeatedly evicted (e.g., Corzo Márquez 1999). Images of Indigenous families displaced by the army in national press evoke little popular sympathy because government functionaries describe these operations as having "strategic objectives to find criminal structures, particularly those linked to drug trafficking," claiming that the community was "supporting or collaborating with drug traffickers" (Valdez and Escobar 2011).

In short, it is increasingly not conservation concerns but rather security concerns that are provoking displacement. The fact that the evictions are unfolding within the MBR as a conservation space are, however, significant. Put simply, it is the protected areas laws that make these military operations possible, something state press releases do not mention. Hence, military actions during states of emergency target vulnerable communities for displacement using conservation laws for their eviction, and then claim their numbers as a success for the war on drugs.

The Maya Biosphere Reserve: where the security state makes difference dangerous

In the initial MBR plan, US consultants uncritically observed that "attitudes by most everyone (government officials, industrialists, conservationists) hold that the *milperos* [farmers] are the 'bad guys' – destroyers of the forest" (USAID 1990, 262). The common thread is that the security state had a mandate to displace the bad guys, during Cold War, "drug war," and "war on terror" states of emergency. In the absence of due process, state security forces mobilize racialized threat narratives against Indigenous peoples in protected area policing and eviction. In this section, I explain how "narco" maps onto "Maya" and how this is core to authorizing displacement. Key to this analysis is that conservation goals are largely irrelevant to contemporary security concerns and judgments of the state regarding which communities should be evicted from the Maya Forest.

While international conservationists do not call for large-scale displacement of poor Maya communities, Cold War era sedimentations of the "bad guy" who justifies military action – and increased budgets – necessarily tend to fall on a racialized Other, where the narco-Maya becomes commonsense in the twenty-first century the same way commonsense notions of Mayas were guerrillas in the twentieth century (Nelson 2009). Today, state actors rework civil war narratives of Indigenous peoples as guerrillas with that of narcos. As K'iche' Maya activist Domingo Hernando Ixcoy explains, "They still see indigenous people as a mass.… If they catch people with drugs they become narco-Mayas. You never see headlines about narco-Ladinos! We participate as individuals but we are seen as a collective" (Nelson 2015, 21). While media and state security forces treat ladinos (non-Indigenous people) as individuals who can be judged by their actions, they judge Indigenous people through racialized interpellations first, and only then by their actions. During the Cold War, the counterinsurgency state mobilized the trope of the two-faced Indian to question the loyalty of many rural Mayas, shifting the burden of proof onto citizens that they were not guerrilla collaborators. The trope of difference as disloyalty continues to shape state security logics long after the Cold War's end.

As above, government press releases do not claim that Indigenous peoples in protected areas are drug traffickers – they are read as "supporting or collaborating" these efforts because they are not sophisticated enough to organize crime themselves. To the extent that drug trafficking is understood as a problem of the "two-faced" Maya, this is because he is the same ignorant (read non-Spanish-speaking) figure who was "duped" by guerrillas during the civil war. Today, many Guatemalans question whether DTOs operate with impunity because they travel only through willing communities. If this were the case, any "narco-Maya" who is displaced or killed brought his fate on himself. This framing allows everyday Guatemalans to reassure themselves that they are only vulnerable to drug violence if they are "narcos." Likewise, state officials claim that people they evict, arrest, and/or kill are narcos who deserved it.

Even Guatemalans who reject conservation-motivated displacement see evicting drug trafficking collaborators as urgent for the nation's safety. As Guatemalan homicide rates rose through the 2000s (reaching 40 per 100,000 at its peak), security became people's primary political focus. Following from this, a 2011 state of emergency in Petén evicted communities illegally settled in MBR core areas in the name of the drug war. In her work on Mexico, Wright (2012) explains how the central state's failure to provide security is transformed through narco narratives, where anyone who suffers violence is at fault for associating with so-called narcos. Rather than small-time users or dealers who can be rehabilitated, the rural sites of landing strips in the MBR means that people associated with them are assumed to be traffickers, responsible for driving supply of harmful drugs. Beyond this, the former head of the US Department of Homeland Security, John Kelly, has repeatedly referred to smugglers as "narco-terrorists," citing the Central America route north as a route vulnerable to disease (such as Ebola virus) and ideology (such as ISIS) (Kelly 2014). When the Guatemalan state takes up the US's call to fight back against "narco-terrorists," it does so based on Cold War strategies. In short, what we are seeing is that the state's deployment of a racialized Maya articulates with fears of territorial trespass to make displacement from the MBR seem an obvious security strategy in the face of narco-trafficking.

Deploying understandings of difference, provoking displacement in the LNP and MBR

The land tenure rights of resident communities have long been severed within and in the name of protected areas, with such dispossession routinely justified by mobilizing understandings of difference. What the LNP and MBR draw our attention to is *security* as a growing rationale for displacement from protected areas. In both cases, land tenure rights are overridden at least partially on the grounds communities pose security risks, actual or potential. And in both cases, the security threat hinges upon the Othering of communities slated for displacement rooted in prior histories.

Recognizing this new trend allows us to see both how these displacements fit within historical patterns and to grasp what is new. First, standing behind both evictions is the nation-state. In both cases, it is state practices of territorialization along with the special legal status of protected areas that enable displacement. In the LNP, the resettlement now underway was initially scheduled a decade ago for the reasons outline above. This was long before rhino poaching entered the scene. This earlier context is important. A massive wildlife restocking program – itself a key feature of state protected area territorialization giving rise to the LNP – makes it all but impossible for communities to live in the park (Witter 2013; interviews 2004–05). But if this were not enough to provoke their movement, the state ultimately holds a "trump card" whose power rests in the legal status afforded to national parks. More specifically, both the 1997 Land Law and the national constitution make an exemption for protected areas, giving the state right of eminent domain and therefore the right to evict (Lunstrum 2008). And it is state territorization embodied in protected area and broader legislation that will ensure the eviction takes place. In short, as rhino poaching now provides urgency for relocation, evictions were already underway given state terrorization unfolding as human–wildlife conflict and are ultimately guaranteed by existing protected area legislation.

A similar dynamic is at play in Guatemala's MBR, where the military state called on communities to settle the land in the name of the nation and then decried this settlement as deforestation. Since 1990, police and military forces enforce CONAP's land claim, even against returned war refugees (Corzo Márquez 1999). While communities with registered land titles that predate the Protected Areas Law cannot be evicted, those that did not finish the onerous land titling and registration project can be. Again, even before the cadastral park boundaries were mapped, protected areas trumped individual property claims, often not even allowing remuneration for lost land. By the 2000s, those same communities were read as threats to security in terms of drugs and/or terrorism, which further erodes legitimacy they might have to land claims, claims already weakened by prior protected area legislation.

The state also rests behind these evictions in a way that pushes us beyond historical patterns of forced removal. Namely, conservation displacements are justified increasingly by security discourses – and the underlying constructions of resident communities as the insurgent-poacher and subversive-narco, that is, as racialized Others involved in threat economies. In both cases, the threat is deemed as one directed against a nation-state, whether South Africa or Guatemala, and their too-porous national borders, reflecting that the LNP and MBR are both borderland conservation areas.

Despite their telling similarities, the cases differ in a key respect that sheds light on the growing articulation of security and conservation. With the LNP, the desire to stop rhino poaching emerges from a sense that South African territory is under "foreign attack" but equally a commitment to protect the rhino. As such, displacement from the LNP is an example of CID, that is, displacement in the name of ecological protection. This is the case even given the security twist, which only heightens the seeming need for displacement. With the MBR, however, the state justifies current eviction on the basis of the drug war, even though protected areas laws make evictions possible. So this is a case of *displacement from protected areas more broadly* and not CID given that conservation concerns are not a motivating factor. This distinction allows us to see, once more, how not all displacements from protected areas are motivated by conservation concerns and how different articulations of security and displacement unfold within protected areas. Sometimes security-provoked displacements are equally examples of CIDs, but sometimes not. Regardless of whether eviction is motivated by conservation concerns, protected area territorialization and related legislation help make displacement possible as we saw above. What this shows is that *state protected areas* – including their special legal status and the territorializing acts through which they are created – *are useful to the realization of security agendas*.

Conclusion: implications for biodiversity and land justice agendas

Perhaps the most prescient insight gleaned from the comparison of the cases is that the addition of security as a rationale for displacements *makes a difference*. Simply put, once displacement is motivated on security grounds, it is more difficult to contest. This emerges from the notion that it is the security of the nation-state, if not global security, that is at stake. As such, security-based rationales provide an alibi for displacement from protected areas (Massé and Lunstrum 2016). In this way, placing the issue of community tenure within a national security framework makes it difficult to reconcile biodiversity and land justice agendas precisely because it interferes with the ability of communities to contest displacement once they are framed as security threats. Beyond concerns over the rights and well-being of already-vulnerable rural communities, these evictions fly in the face of conventional wisdom that, for biodiversity agendas to be effective, they must actively respect, engage with, and show the benefits of conservation to resident communities (Child 2004; Wilshusen et al. 2002). It is these very communities, after all, that have the power to protect not abstracted "resources" but these as embedded within the sociocultural environments of daily life.

Even from an instrumental perspective, to remove resident communities is to remove the protections they afford. For instance, some protected areas post-relocation have seen the arrival of commercial poachers or cattle ranchers who find it easy to exploit an emptied landscape (McElwee 2006; Greenough 2003; Grandia 2012). Displacement, in other words, can provoke ecological harm. Once displaced, moreover, members of affected communities may be more likely to turn to ecologically damaging practices like commercial poaching and deforestation either to make a living in the face of poverty (made worse by eviction) or as explicit acts of resistance (Mavhunga 2014). In fact, we are beginning to see preliminary evidence of this in the LNP: relocated to poorer environments outside the park, young men are more amenable to being recruited by poaching syndicates (Lunstrum 2016; Serino 2015; Hübschle 2016). This leads us to the stark conclusion not merely that the best way to ensure *biodiversity agendas* is to protect land tenure (Brashares et al. 2014; Dowie 2009) but that not doing so may reinforce the very *security* challenges that are calling for relocation in the first place. In short, once security imaginaries transform rural stakeholders into insurgent-poachers or narco-Mayas – that is, as security threats – these imaginaries strip these groups of legitimacy to demand land justice. Hence, to defend the land tenure of vulnerable communities it is necessary to critically engage with not only conservation agendas. It is increasingly important to grapple with and in turn disrupt security agendas and the notions of difference upon which these agendas and their resulting displacements come to make sense.

Notes

1 This chapter employs a comparative case study approach, the value of which rests in its ability to investigate similarities and differences across particular phenomena unfolding in geographically distinct spaces. This, in turn, enables understanding of deeper or broader processes. Our selection of the LNP and MBR rests in the fact that, in both locations, we are seeing the rise of evictions from protected areas justified increasingly on security grounds. The Southern African portion of the research is based on 44 interviews in Mozambique and South Africa with park officials, anti-poaching officials, and community representatives in 2013, 2015, and 2016 along with several earlier interviews in 2004–05 and review of government documents, newspaper articles, and websites. The Guatemalan portion of the research is based on over two years of participant observation from 2006–15, a survey on land tenure and conservation, and 31 interviews in Petén.

2 In the early days of the LNP (2001–12), displacement was technically voluntary. In practice, there was no real element of volition given that communities were routinely the victim of growing human–wildlife conflict as the park was restocked with wildlife and as social services were progressively moved outside park boundaries (interviews 2004–05; also see Witter 2013). In the current context of rhino poaching, there is no longer talk of the relocation being voluntary.

References

Agarwal, Arun, and Kent Redford. "Place, Conservation, and Displacement: An Overview." *Conservation and Society* 7 (2009): 1–10.

Anderson, Ben. "Facing the Future Enemy: US Counterinsurgency Doctrine and the Pre-insurgent." *Theory, Culture & Society* 28 (2011): 216–240.

Brashares, Justin S., Briana Abrahms, Kathryn J. Fiorella, et al. "Wildlife Decline and Social Conflict." *Science* 345 (2014): 376–378.

Brockington, Dan. *Fortress Conservation: The Preservation of the Mkomazi Game Reserve, Tanzania*. Bloomington, IN: Indiana University Press, 2002.

Brockington, Daniel, and James Igoe. "Eviction for Conservation: A Global Overview." *Conservation & Society* 4 (2006): 424–470.

Büscher, Bram, and Michael Schoon. "Competition over Conservation: Collective Action and Negotiating Transfrontier Conservation in Southern Africa." *Journal of International Wildlife Law and Policy* 12 (2009): 33–59.

Büscher, Bram. " 'Rhino Poaching Is Out of Control!' Violence, Race and the Politics of Hysteria in Online Conservation." *Environment and Planning A* 48 (2016): 979–998.

Carruthers, Jane. *The Kruger National Park: A Social and Political History*. Pietermaritzburg: University of Kwazulu Natal Press, 1995.

Cernea, M. M. " 'Restriction of Access' Is Displacement: A Broader Concept and Policy." *Forced Migration Review* 23 (2005): 48–49.

Child, Brian. *Parks in Transition: Biodiversity, Rural Development, and the Bottom Line*. London: Earthscan, 2004.

Corzo Márquez, A. R. "Vida, Migración, Tragedia." *Delaware Review of Latin American Studies* 1 (1999): 1. http://udspace.udel.edu/bitstream/handle/19716/19485/Vol.1–1 CorzoMarquez.pdf?sequence=3&isAllowed=y.

Counter Insurgency Tracker Training (CITT). "About CITT." www.cit-training.co.za (accessed February 4, 2018), 2015.

Crenshaw, Kimberle. "Mapping the Margins: Intersectionality, Identity Politics, and Violence against Women of Color." *Stanford Law Review* 43, no. 6 (1991): 1241–1299.

Defence Web. "Rhino Poaching Continues Apace." www.defenceweb.co.za/index.php?option=com_content&view=article&id=37674:rhino-poaching-continues-apace&catid=87:border-security&Itemid=188 (accessed February 4, 2018), January 23, 2015.

Devine, Jennifer. "Counterinsurgency Ecotourism in Guatemala's Maya Biosphere Reserve." *Environment and Planning D-Society & Space* 32 (2014): 984–1001.

Dowie, Mark. *Conservation Refugees: The Hundred-Year Conflict between Global Conservation and Native Peoples*. Cambridge, MA: MIT Press, 2009.

Duffy, Rosaleen. "War, by Conservation." *Geoforum* 69 (2016): 238–248.

Ellis, Stephen. "Of Elephants and Men: Politics and Nature Conservation in South Africa." *Journal of Southern African Studies* 20, no. 1 (1994): 53–69.

Environmental Affairs. "Minister Edna Molewa Highlights Progress in the War against Poaching and Plans for 2015." www.environment.gov.za/mediarelease/molewa_waragainstpoaching2015 (accessed January 22, 2015).

Environmental Affairs. Minister, Question No. 2615 for Written Reply: National Assembly, 2014.

Gardner, Benjamin. *Selling the Serengeti: The Cultural Politics of Safari Tourism*. Athens, OH: The University of Georgia Press, 2016.

Gilmore, Ruth W. "Fatal Couplings of Power and Difference: Notes on Racism and Geography." *Professional Geographer* 54, no. 1 (2002): 15–24.

Grandia, Liza. *Enclosed: Conservation, Cattle, and Commerce among the Q'eqchi' Maya Lowlanders*. Seattle, WA: University of Washington Press, 2012.

Great Limpopo: Wilderness Camps and Trails. "PNL [LNP] anti-poaching successes." www.dolimpopo.com/blog/pnl-anti-poaching-successes (accessed …), 2013.

Greenough, Paul. "Bio-ironies of the Fractured Forest: India's Tiger Reserves." In *Nature in the Global South: Environmental Projects in South and Southeast Asia*, edited by Greenough, P. R., and Tsing, A. L. Durham, NC: Duke University Press, 2003.

Gunyup, Sharon. "State of the Wild 2006: A Global Portrait of Wildlife, Wildlands and Oceans." Washington, DC, and London: Island Press, 2005.

Gutiérrez Martínez, Fancisco R. "De Cómo Guatemala Perdió 50 Mil Kilómetros Cuadrados" [How Guatemala lost 50 thousand square kilometers]. *El Periodico*, February 9, 2017. https://elperiodico.com.gt/opinion/2017/02/09/de-como-guatemala-perdio-50-mil-kilometros-cuadrados (**accessed …**), 2017.

Hall, Stuart, Charles Critcher, Tony Jefferson, John Clarke and Brian Roberts. *Policing the Crisis: Mugging, the State, and Law and Order*. New York, NY: Holmes and Meier, 1978.

Hartmann, Betsy, Banu Subramanian and Charles Zerner. *Making Threats: Biofears and Environmental Anxieties*. Lanham, MD: Rowman & Littlefield, 2005.

Hübschle, Annette M. "The Social Economy of Rhino Poaching: Of Economic Freedom Fighters, Professional Hunters and Marginalized Local People." *Current Sociology* 65, no. 3 (2016): 1–21.

Hughes, David M. *Whiteness in Zimbabwe: Race, Landscape, and the Problem of Belonging*. New York, NY: Palgrave Macmillan, 2010.

Igoe, Jim. *Conservation and Globalization: A Study of the National Parks and Indigenous Communities from East Africa to South Dakota*. Belmont, CA: Thomson/Wadsworth, 2004.

Inter-American Commission on Human Rights (IACHR). *Situation of Human Rights in Guatemala: Diversity, Inequality and Exclusion*. Washington, DC: IACHR, Organization of American States (OAS), 2015.

Jazeel, Tariq. "'Nature', Nationhood and the Poetics of Meaning in Ruhuna (Yala) National Park, Sri Lanka." *Cultural Geographies* 12, no. 2 (2005): 199–227.

Kelly, Alice and Megan Ybarra. "Introduction to Themed Issue: 'Green Security in Protected Areas.'" *Geoforum* 69 (2016): 171–175.

Kelly, J. "SOUTHCOM chief: Central America Drug War a Dire Threat to U.S. National Security". *Military Times*. www.militarytimes.com/article/20140708/NEWS01/307080064/SOUTHCOM-chief-Central-America-drug-war-dire-threat-U-S-national-security (accessed June 4th, 2017), 2014.

Kepe, Thembela. "Shaped by Race: Why 'Race' Still Matters in the Challenges Facing Biodiversity Conservation in Africa." *Local Environment* 14 (2009): 871–878.

Lunstrum Elizabeth. "Mozambique, Neoliberal Land Reform, and the Limpopo National Park." *Geographical Review* 98 (2008): 339–355.

Lunstrum, Elizabeth. "Green Militarization: Anti-Poaching Efforts and the Spatial Contours of Kruger National Park." *Annals of the Association of American Geographers* 104 (2014): 816–832.

Lunstrum, Elizabeth. "Land Grabs, Green Grabs, and the Spatiality of Displacement: Eviction from Mozambique's Limpopo National Park." *Area* 48 (2016): 142–152.

Lunstrum, Elizabeth. Feed Them to the Lions: Conservation Violence Goes Online. *Geoforum* 79 (2017): 134–143.

Martínez, Oscar. *A History of Violence: Living and Dying in Central America*. New York, NY: Verso, 2016.

Massé, Francis and Lunstrum Elizabeth. "Accumulation by Securitization: Commercial Poaching, Neoliberal Conservation, and the Creation of New Wildlife Frontiers." *Geoforum* 69 (2016): 227–237.

Mavhunga, Claperton C. *Transient Workspaces: Technologies of Everyday Innovation in Zimbabwe*. Cambridge, MA: MIT Press, 2014.

McElwee, Pamela. "Displacement and Relocation Redux: Stories from Southeast Asia." *Conservation & Society* 4, no. 3 (2006): 396–403.

McSweeney, Kendra, Erik A. Nielsen, Matthew J. Taylor, David J. Wrathall, Zoe Pearson, Ophelia Wang and Spencer T. Plub. "Drug Policy as Conservation Policy: Narco-Deforestation." *Science* 343 (2014): 489–490.

Meskell, Lynn. *The Nature of Heritage: The New South Africa*. Malden, MA: Wiley-Blackwell, 2012.

Molewa, Edna. Media Statement by the Minister Edna Molewa on Rhino Poaching Intervention and the Position of South Africa to the 16th Conference of Parties CITES, 2013.

Mollett, Sharlene. "Racial Narratives: Miskito and Colono Land Struggles in the Honduran Mosquitia." *Cultural Geographies* 18, no. 1 (2010): 43–62.

Nelson, Diane M. *Reckoning: The Ends of War in Guatemala*. Durham, NC, and London: Duke University Press, 2009.

Nelson, Diane M. *Who Counts?: The Mathematics of Death and Life after Genocide*. Durham, NC: Duke University Press, 2015.

Neumann, Roderick P. "Moral and Discursive Geographies in the War for Biodiversity in Africa." *Political Geography* 23, no. 7 (2004a): 813–837.

Neumann, Roderick P. "Nature-State-Territory: Toward a Critical Theorization of Conservation Enclosures." In *Liberation Ecologies: Environment, Development, Social*

Movements, edited by Peet, R., and M. Watts, 2nd edn. London: Routledge, 179–199, 2004b.

Neumann, Roderick P. *Imposing Wilderness: Struggles over Livelihood and Nature Preservation in Africa*. Berkeley, CA: University of California Press, 1998.

Nolan-Ferrell, Catherine. *Constructing Citizenship: Transnational Workers and Revolution on the Mexico-Guatemala Border, 1880–1950*. Tucson, AZ: University of Arizona Press, 2012.

Ojeda, Diana. "Green Pretexts: Ecotourism, Neoliberal Conservation and Land Grabbing in Tayrona National Natural Park, Colombia." *Journal of Peasant Studies* 39 (2012): 357–375.

Republic of Mozambique. *National Rhino and Ivory Action Plan (NIRAP) 2015–2016*, Mozambique, 2015.

Rich, Paul. "Insurgency, Terrorism and the Apartheid System in South Africa." *Political Studies* 32, no. 1 (1984): 68–85.

Rojas A. "Agoniza la Eterna Primavera." *La Prensa Libre*, 2013.

Sandlos, John. "Not Wanted in the Boundary: The Expulsion of the Keeseekoowenin Ojibway Band from Riding Mountain National Park." *Canadian Historical Review* 89, no. 2 (2008): 189–221.

Schmidt, Blake. "Ranchers and Drug Barons Threaten Rain Forest." *New York Times*, A6, July 17, 2010.

Serino, Kenichi. "The Human Victims in the Fight over Rhino Poaching in Africa." *Al Jazeera*, January 7, 2015.

Slater, Candace. *Entangled Edens*. Berkeley, CA, and Los Angeles: University of California Press, 2002.

Smith, M. L. R. and J. Humphreys. "The Poaching Paradox: Why South Africa's 'Rhino Wars' Shine a Harsh Spotlight on Security and Conservation." In *Environmental Crime and Social Conflict: Contemporary and Emerging Issues*, edited by Brisman, A., N. South and R. White. Farnham: Ashgate, 197–220, 2015.

Spence, Mark. *Dispossessing the Wilderness: Indian Removal and the Making of the National Parks*. New York, NY: Oxford University Press, 1999.

Sundberg Juanita. "Identities in the Making: Conservation, Race and Gender in the Maya Biosphere Reserve, Guatemala." *Gender, Place & Culture* 11, no. 1 (2004): 43–66.

Sundberg, Juanita. "Conservation and Democratization: Constituting Citizenship in the Maya Biosphere Reserve, Guatemala." *Political Geography* 22, no. 7 (2003): 715–740.

Terborgh, John. *Requiem for Nature*. Washington, DC: Island Press, 1999.

The White House, Barack Obama Administration. *National Strategy for Combatting Wildlife Trafficking*. Washington, DC: The United Stated of America. 2014.

USAID. *Guatemala Project Paper: Maya Biosphere Project*. In: 520–0395 P (ed.), Guatemala City: USAID Mission to Guatemala, 1990.

Valdez, S. and R. Escobar. "Desalojan a 300 Campesinos de la Sierra del Lacandón." Guatemala City: *Prensa Libre*, www.prensalibre.com/noticias/Sacan-Lacandon_0_542945718.html (accessed May 27, 2013), 2011.

Vandergeest, Peter, and Nancy Lee Peluso. "Territorialization and State Power in Thailand." *Theory and Society* 24, no. 3 (1995): 385–426.

Wakild, Emily. *Revolutionary Parks: Conservation, Social Justice, and Mexico's National Parks, 1910–1940*. Tucson, AZ: University of Arizona Press, 2011.

Wilshusen, Peter R., Steven R. Brechin, Crystal L. Fortwangler and Patrick C. West. "Reinventing a Square Wheel: Critique of a Resurgent 'Protection Paradigm' in International Biodiversity Conservation." *Society & Natural Resources* 15, no. 1 (2002): 17–40.

Wilson, Edward O. *Half-Earth: Our Planet's Fight for Life*. New York, NY: W. W. Norton, 2016.

Witter Rebecca. "Elephant-Induced Displacement and the Power of Choice: Moral Narratives about Resettlement in Mozambique's Limpopo National Park." *Conservation and Society* 11, no. 4 (2013): 406–419.

Wright, Melissa W. Wars of Interpretations. *Antipode* 44, no. 3 (2012): 564–580.

Ybarra, Megan. "'Blind Passes' and the Production of Green Security through Violence on the Guatemalan Border." *Geoforum* 69 (2016): 194–206.

Ybarra, Megan. "Taming the Jungle, saving the Maya Forest: Sedimented Counterinsurgency Practices in Contemporary Guatemalan Conservation." *Journal of Peasant Studies* 39, no. 2 (2012): 479–502.

Ybarra, Megan. *Green Wars: Conservation and Decolonization in Guatemala's Maya Forest*. Berkeley, CA: University of California Press, 2017.

5 Green violence

Market-driven conservation and the reforeignization of space in Laikipia, Kenya

Brock Bersaglio

Introduction

The Laikipia Plateau is a vast highland area located west of Mt Kenya in Kenya, East Africa. The bulk of the plateau's land mass is located within the present-day boundaries of Laikipia County. Laikipia has been described as a land use mosaic, as it supports numerous livelihoods including commercial and subsistence forms of agricultural and pastoral production, commercial wildlife conservation (i.e. market-driven conservation (MDC)), and commercial horticulture, as well as mixed-use ranching in which livestock production occurs alongside wildlife conservation on private land (Georgiadis 2011). Amid such land uses, 48 large-scale properties comprise about 382,000 hectares – or roughly 40 per cent of Laikipia (Letai 2015; LWF 2012). Twenty-nine of these properties are wildlife conservancies and 17 are mixed-use ranches (LWF 2012). Many of the 48 properties are owned by white settlers and are used for MDC, with organizations such as the African Wildlife Foundation (AWF), Fauna and Flora International, and the Nature Conservancy having also acquired property in Laikipia for conservation purposes. The rest of the county is largely held and used by Indigenous groups or the government: small-scale properties of less than 2,000 acres comprise about 334,700 hectares (roughly 34 per cent) of Laikipia (LWF 2012). These small-scale properties belong to diverse groups of smallholders disposed to agricultural production, such as Kikuyus, Merus, and many others. Three group ranches held by collectives of Maasais, for conservation and pastoralism, account for an additional 71,200 hectares (roughly 7 per cent) of Laikipia. The rest of the county is under some form of government ownership or is classified as urban (LWF 2012).

Although there are diverse land uses in Laikipia, much of the landscape remains under the occupation or control of white settlers and is being used for some type of MDC. Like all rural groups, white settlers in sub-Saharan Africa make up a heterogeneous class comprised of its own forms of social differentiation and stratification (Hughes 2010; McIntosh 2016). Relationships between white settlers and Indigenous groups on the continent lack uniformity in day-to-day life, although they generally display the racialized power dynamics that made settler capitalism possible in the first place. The term "white settler" is used loosely in this chapter to refer to whites who occupy or control large-scale landholdings in Laikipia (greater than 10,000 hectares) – regardless of whether such individuals hold British, Kenyan, or other passports. This is because, collectively, this demographic continues to function as a settler class in rural society. However, the statistical rendering of land use and tenure in Laikipia above is not an indictment against white settlers en masse. Such a rendering instead serves as a pivot point for tracing the shifting trajectories of social life in what was a formal "white reserve" – a designated area for whites to own freehold property in a space geographically segregated from communal "native reserves", which served as labour reserves for white-owned farms and ranches (Morgan 1963).

Tracing these shifting trajectories in Laikipia reveals insights that are pertinent to ideas about "green violence", a concept that is increasingly being deployed in analyses of violence perpetrated in the name of conservation (Büscher and Ramutsindela 2016; Anneke and Masubelele 2016; Marijnen and Verweijen 2016). This approach to analysis emphasizes the temporal dimensions of green violence and serves to nuance its effect in rural society. As will be discussed later in this chapter, property ownership in Laikipia continues to effect differences in social status, wealth, and well-being according to historical boundaries of cultural and racial segregation (Blomley 2003). Moreover, it is argued in this chapter that the ability to obtain and maintain control over property in Laikipia rests on landholders' aptitude for embracing the violent ideas and aspirations of MDC. For example, global support for militarized conservation has enabled settler-landowners in Laikipia to reinforce their property rights with, and to pursue capital accumulation through, green violence – mainly under the guise of "anti-poaching" and "wildlife protection" activities carried out by paramilitary forces deployed on their land. Green violence, in this format, does not simply threaten would-be encroachers or poachers with bodily harm; it reinforces a status quo in property relationships that perpetuates racialized forms of structural violence rooted in settler capitalism. When pursued in tandem with other practices associated with MDC, green violence in Laikipia brings the effects of a deferred colonial past to bear on present-day rural society (Campbell 2016) – this has been a gradual, often hidden, process with no less destructive consequences for social relationships tied to land and resources.

After briefly describing the concept of green violence in greater detail, the next section proceeds to analyse the "greening" of settler ranches in Laikipia during the post-independence era. Following formal independence from Britain in 1964, white settlers subsequently perceived informal and unorganized efforts to redistribute white-owned land, legislation that banned sport hunting, and under-performing beef markets as threats to the survival of their class and privilege. It is in this context that MDC was rolled out over the county's landscape, partly as a livelihood diversification strategy for white settlers that began to identify as a subaltern group fighting to belong and survive in the absence of a paternalistic colonial state that once privileged their well-being over that of other races (McIntosh 2016). After describing how the green economy took root in

Laikipia, subsequent sections analyse the use of (para)military instruments, personnel, and tactics in private conservation areas alongside the de facto provision of social services by conservation organizations in the human settlements that surround these same areas. This leads to a summative section that recaps some of the ways that green violence has facilitated the reforeignization of space in Laikipia – a process understood in this chapter as the ongoing reinvention of settler capitalism and reproduction of colonial property relationships through MDC. Recently, this process has coincided with the intensification of material violence between settler-landowners and migrant pastoralists in the region (Mbaria 2017).

These conclusions are based on an analysis of qualitative data collected during ten months of fieldwork in Laikipia between October 2014 and June 2015, as well as during follow-up trips to the region in May 2016 and April 2017. Relevant data was procured through participant observation of wildlife conservation and tourism initiatives in Laikipia (including over two months on safari), as well as through key informant interviews (160 in total) and close readings of primary and secondary sources of information on the history of conservation policy and practice in the region. The analysis in this chapter is primarily based on data collected on three of the largest and most influential private conservancies in the greater Laikipia area. Listed in order of size, these are: Ol Pejeta Conservancy (37,231 hectares in Laikipia County), Lewa Wildlife Conservancy (18,211 hectares in Isiolo/Meru County), and Borana Conservancy (14,164 hectares in Laikipia County). Lewa and Borana recently removed the fence that divided these two neighbouring properties, effectively doubling the size of each conservancy's total land area. This chapter's conclusions are most relevant to these private conservation areas, but they do provide some indirect insights into relationships between mixed-use ranches or pastoralist group ranches and wider society. It is also worth noting that Lewa Wildlife Conservancy is not officially located within the present-day boundaries of Laikipia County; however, it directly borders the county and remains a significant force in the political ecology of the plateau.

Green violence: the violent nature of conservation

Green violence refers to "the deployment of violent instruments and tactics towards the protection of nature and [towards] various ideas and aspirations related to nature conservation" (Büscher and Ramutsindela 2016, 2). Such violence is widespread in sub-Saharan Africa, where "the use of military and paramilitary personnel, training, technologies, and partnerships" has long been associated with colonial and postcolonial efforts to protect wildlife resources (Lunstrum 2014, 816). Much of the existing research on green violence has focused on the direct, material violence commonly associated with militarized conservation in sub-Saharan Africa, such as forced evictions to create space for conservation areas or shoot-on-sight orders that target suspected poachers (Neumann 2004; Duffy 2014; Lunstrum 2016). Only more recently have critical researchers shifted their attention towards discursive and social forms of green violence, such as conversations in online chatrooms that target racialized violence at poachers or the use of conservation initiatives to obtain/maintain class privilege (Büscher and Ramutsindela 2016). Such work has begun to emphasize the relationship between conservation and indirect, structural forms of violence.

Building on the broadening notion of green violence, this chapter highlights the *slow* attributes of green violence in sub-Saharan Africa. Whereas violence is often understood as an event with immediate observable impacts, slow violence "occurs gradually and out of sight, [it is] a violence of delayed destruction that is dispersed across time and space, an attritional violence that is not typically viewed as violence at all" (Nixon 2011, 2). From this perspective, green violence is not only material, social, and/or discursive; it is "incremental and accretive, its calamitous repercussions playing out across a range of temporal scales" (Nixon 2011, 2). This conception of green violence necessitates in-depth and nuanced investigations into discrete genealogies of conservation-cum-violence in sub-Saharan Africa, which could help generate greater historical attunement in the literature than currently exists (Bersaglio 2017). Towards this end, consideration is given to the violence embodied in Laikipia's private enclosures, and how such violence has shaped conservation policy and practice – and vice versa – in a countryside formerly reserved for white settlement only in Kenya.

Making wildlife pay: the greening of white ranches in Laikipia

Exclusive nature: the contemporary landscape of market-driven conservation

Laikipia's total land area of 869,600 hectares contains one of eastern Africa's larger areas of contiguous wildlife-compatible land uses – an interconnected patchwork of properties that comprise about 365,000 hectares altogether (LWF 2012). No single national park in Kenya is larger, except for Tsavo East and West combined. Conservationists also believe Laikipia to be one of the most important wildlife areas in the region, as wildlife either lives on or regularly migrates through a vast network of private properties in the county (LWF 2012). Protecting wildlife outside national parks and reserves is a priority for conservationists, as 75 per cent of Kenya's wildlife reside outside the formal boundaries of such protected areas (LWF 2012).

The most recent aerial census in Laikipia suggests a total wildlife population of about 64,225 animals, including animals of equal or greater size to Thomson's gazelles (LWF 2012). This number is nearly 17,000 more animals than reside in Amboseli, Nairobi, and Tsavo East and West National Parks combined (Kinnaird and O'Brien 2012; LWF 2012). Laikipia's wildlife is also incredibly diverse: "To date 95 species of mammals, 540 species of birds, 87 species of amphibians and reptiles, almost a 1,000 species of invertebrates and over 700 species of plants have been recorded" in the county (LWF 2012, 10). Moreover, the county is prized as a haven for large populations of endangered mega-fauna. Laikipia contains half of Kenya's black rhinos – a species listed as critically endangered on the IUCN Red List – and 7,000 elephants, which is the country's second largest population. Laikipia also boasts a stable lion population of about 250 individuals (15 per cent of Kenya's total population), as well as some 200 Cape hunting dogs (the world's sixth largest population) and a significant number of cheetahs. Some less well known endangered mammals can also be found in Laikipia. This includes two-thirds of the world's reticulated giraffe (*Giraffa camelopardalis reticulata*), 80 per cent of all Grevy's zebras (*Equus grevyi*) on the planet, and the Laikipia hartebeest (a hybrid of *Alcelaphus buselaphus cokei* and *lelwel*) (LWF 2012).

In addition to the conservation of endangered wildlife outside national protected areas, conservationists also believe Laikipia to be significant for the wide range of value-added activities afforded to MDC in private conservation areas – activities such as bush meals and game walks, camel and horse caravans, late-night game drives, and exclusive wilderness lodging, among other additional-cost activities associated with wildlife safaris (LWF 2012). Laikipia's tourism industry is marketed as a highly exclusive destination, as a place where tourists can get a *real* wilderness experience, compared to destinations that are overcrowded with people, such as Maasai Mara National Reserve in southern Kenya. Tourism investors and operators in Laikipia operate on the logic that wealthy clientele are willing to pay a premium for intimate wilderness settings, up-close encounters with endangered/rare wildlife, and the freedom to engage in activities that are not permitted in national protected areas. As a result, Laikipia's 1,230 beds in 43 tourism facilities amount to only one-fifth of the beds in Maasai Mara, which is less than half the size of Laikipia's total wildlife area. Although Laikipia attracts nowhere near the amount of tourists that the Mara does, the wildlife sector is the second most profitable industry in the county next to horticulture (beating out livestock production and agriculture) (LWF 2013).

In brief, the term market-driven conservation refers to conservation programmes designed to catalyse new opportunities for economic growth and development while ensuring that targeted human populations conduct themselves in ways that are believed to protect – rather than degrade – the environment (Igoe and Brockington 2007; Fletcher 2010; Roth and Dressler 2012). In rural parts of sub-Saharan Africa, MDC programmes often involve strategies and technologies that attach economic value to wildlife resources with the goal of incentivizing subsistence producers to behave in ways that protect those resources as a source of financial capital (Roth and Dressler 2012). As such, MDC is considered a hallmark of neoliberal governmental reform – but one that has had contradictory, and sometimes devastating, effects for subsistence rural producers in sub-Saharan Africa (Igoe and Brockington 2007; Fletcher 2010; Roth and Dressler 2012). To fully understand the green violence that has taken form in Laikipia, it is also necessary to consider the origins of MDC in the county.

Racialized dispossession and the origins of market-driven conservation

The history of MDC in Laikipia traces back to the alienation of land in British East Africa by the Colonial Office from 1902 onwards, and to the subsequent implementation of a racialized property regime in what later became the colony of Kenya. Following years of work by the colonial administration to bar and evict Maasais from the Laikipia Plateau, to create a white reserve in the central highlands (later called the "white highlands"), by 1913 the British had moved thousands of Maasais and their livestock off the plateau to a native reserve in the south (Hughes 2006; Matheka 2008). The evictions were also carried out to appease Laikipia's nascent settler community, which perceived Maasai livestock as being in competition with and a threat to white-owned cattle. The contentious process of evicting Maasais and their livestock from Laikipia and moving them to a southern reserve contributed to numerous human and livestock deaths among Maasais (Hughes 2006; Matheka 2008). Ultimately, at least 10,000 Maasai, 175,000 cattle, and over one million goats and sheep were recorded leaving the Laikipia area (Hughes 2006). Following the 1933 report of the Kenya Land Commission, the exclusion of Indigenous ethnic groups from land ownership in the white highlands was formalized – the total amount of land available to white settlers at that time was 2,679,343 hectares (Morgan 1963; Matheka 2008).

The hunting attitudes and habits of Laikipia's settler community contributed to a steady decline in Kenya's wildlife population, both on and off the plateau (Steinhart 2006). Virtually "all the Europeans who came to Kenya in their capacities as explorers, missionaries, administrators, soldiers or settlers also hunted regularly and sometimes prodigiously" (Steinhart 1989, 251). Throughout the colonial era, white settlers were free to hunt (i.e. shoot wildlife for sport), crop (i.e. harvest wildlife for meat/trophies), and cull (i.e. reduce the breeding population of) wildlife on their land – in some cases without the need of permits. Some animals now considered endangered, such as lions, were classified as vermin and could be killed legally by white settlers at their leisure (Steinhart 2006). White settlers in Laikipia were also able to profit from commercial hunting by hosting hunting safaris and selling their services as guides to clients from Europe and North America (Herne 1999; Steinhart 2006).

White settlers in Laikipia have largely reconciled themselves to the fact that their ancestors "shot most of the animals on their land or drove them out" (Huxley 1991, 229). Indeed, "the vast majority of local whites regarded all game as either vermin or target practice … even the sight of elephants was a treasured moment by the 1930s" (Duder and Youé 1994, 266). Recent interviews with white settlers further corroborate such statements, with some appearing bemused by their ancestors' passion for hunting. One white Kenyan said that black rhinos used to be so numerous they were considered pests: "like fucking rabbits", he exclaimed. Another laughed while flipping through his father's photo albums, explaining that he did not "know what to do with all the photos of dad with dead rhinos". The devastation to wildlife caused by white settlers, professional hunters, and tourists led to a nationwide ban on hunting in 1977 (Steinhart 2006).

As early as the 1960s, however, white settlers in Laikipia began to value wildlife on their land for aesthetic and ecological reasons (Denney 1972). Furthermore, as beef markets slumped in the 1980s, some white settlers also began to see economic value in the wildlife that had begun to repopulate their properties amid the hunting ban (Kock 1995; Georgiadis 2011). These white settlers pursued opportunities to profit from growing wildlife numbers on their land in ways that they understood to be "sustainable", in contrast to the "unsustainable" practices of their ancestors, reinvesting income from new wildlife production/tourism ventures on their land back into conservation initiatives. Such notions of sustainability reflect emergent discourses of sustainable development and the green economy at the time, which understood MDC as an effective way to make wild animals "pay" for their own conservation (Elliott and Mwangi 1997). High-profile transnational conservation organizations like the AWF allied with white ranchers and settler associations to experiment with different forms of MDC in Laikipia's privatized landscape, which functioned as a "conservation laboratory" for the green economy.

By the early 2000s, the AWF – and other national and international entities (Bersaglio 2017) – concluded that safari tourism was the most viable, although not the most equitable, way to make wild animals pay for their own conservation given continued support for the hunting ban in Kenya's parliament (Elliott and Mwangi 1997; 1998). A discussion paper produced by the AWF, called *Making Wildlife "Pay" in Laikipia, Kenya,* was influential in promoting this conclusion. In the paper, AWF argues that non-consumptive forms of wildlife tourism (e.g. photographic safaris) provide the best economic justification for wildlife as a land use in Laikipia, alleging returns four times higher than that of livestock production alone. This position assumes, of course, that most Laikipians would be excluded from entering or benefiting from the county's privatized wildlife sector. At the time of the AWF's study, entering the safari market required a "land area of at least 10,000 hectares, good access [for tourists], excellent wildlife viewing opportunities, the right partners, access to capital and a defensible market niche, *factors which exclude most Laikipia landholders from becoming significant players*" (Elliott and Mwangi 1997, 1, emphasis added). Thus, between 1977 and 1997 cattle ranches in Laikipia, once thoroughly and sometimes ferociously hunted by white settlers were transformed, into model spaces for the green economy – spaces built on the cultural, economic, and legal bedrock of a racialized private property regime.

Market-driven conservation and the militarization of private conservancies

In the early 1980s, a recently deceased British conservationist called Anna Merz approached a long-time settler family in Laikipia about creating a rhino sanctuary on their ranch in the northern foothills of Mt Kenya. This family was the Craigs, who had used their land as a cattle ranch since the 1920s but agreed to set aside 2,000 of their original 16,000 hectares for the sanctuary, called Ngare Sergoi (Martin 2013). Merz invested US$1.5 million into Ngare Sergoi, building a fence around the sanctuary, acquiring and translocating rhinos, hiring armed guards, buying a surveillance plane, and developing a network of spies and informants to counter rhino poaching efforts in the region. Merz also helped develop a network of international donors, including the American Association of Zookeepers, to raise additional millions of dollars for both Ngare Sergoi and rhino conservation more generally. In the mid-1990s, the Craigs transformed the rest of their cattle ranch into what is now Lewa Wildlife Conservancy – over 18,000 hectares recognized as a UNESCO World Heritage Site along with the neighbouring Ngare Ndare Forest Reserve on its southern border.

The story of Lewa Wildlife Conservancy is now widely known, and the conservancy has become a world-famous safari destination and conservation organization with significant influence in the region (Bersaglio 2017). Some of Lewa's patrons include the likes of Britain's royal family. In 2016, Ian Craig was awarded the Order of the British Empire for his services to conservation in the region (NRT 2016). Although the conservancy is distinct in terms of its influence, prestige, and wealth, the trajectory that Lewa followed during its transformation from a settler ranch into a rhino sanctuary – and later into a large-scale private wildlife conservancy outfitted with paramilitary personnel and military technology – is similar to that followed by other white ranches in Laikipia. In fact, the Craigs were not the first settler family in the county to get into the business of rhino conservation. The owners of what is now Solio Game Reserve, in southern Laikipia, were breeding rhinos to stock sanctuaries and reserves as early as 1970. Both Ol Jogi Ranch and Sweetwaters Game Reserve established rhino sanctuaries in the 1980s as well. Ol Jogi consists of 23,500 hectares at the foot of the Lolldaiga Hills north of Nanyuki, which is the main urban hub in Laikipia County. Sweetwaters, a sanctuary that is now part of the 37,000-plus hectares of Ol Pejeta Conservancy, has since become the largest black rhino sanctuary in eastern Africa. Each of these conservancies was transformed from a settler ranch into a wildlife conservancy in the 1980s, during the rejuvenation of the wildlife economy. In total, Laikipia is home to approximately 280 black rhinos and 251 white rhinos, which represents 48 and 75 per cent of Kenya's total population, respectively (KWS 2012; LWF 2012). Currently, the majority of Laikipia's rhinos reside in Borana, Lewa, Ol Pejeta, and Solio.

Boasting rhino sanctuary status attracts significant support (moral, financial, political, etc.) to conservancies from national conservation entities, private donors, and transnational conservation organizations, as well as from tourists captivated by the possibility of encountering the Big Five in a single location. It is estimated that gross annual returns for private conservancies in Laikipia range from US$23–$176 per acre (LWF 2013). The minimum annual revenue for these conservancies is US$3.1 million per year, corresponding to only US$127,000 in taxes (LWF 2013). This translates into US$1.5 spent on supplies locally each year, with US$541,000 going towards local wages (LWF 2013). One of the reasons that gross annual returns per acre are so variable in private conservancies is the amount of resources required to conserve rhinos on private land. The cost associated with creating and maintaining suitable, secure rhino habitats is a significant barrier to entering the rhino business. In a 2014 interview, John Weller (general manager at Ol Jogi Conservancy) reported that it costs Ol Jogi about US$5 per acre per year to protect its rhinos. This may not seem like a significant amount, but it adds up to US$3 million per year for the conservancy. Moreover, it is far from guaranteed that rhinos translocated to private sanctuaries will survive long-term.

Laikipia's high density of rhinos has faced a disproportionate amount of Kenya's successful poaching activities in recent years – an outcome in contradiction with KWS's (2012) call for additional and more discrete, fenced, and heavily armed rhino sanctuaries. Between 2008 and 2011, 71 per cent of all rhinos killed as a result of poaching incidents in Kenya were in private conservation areas in Laikipia (KWS 2012). Il Ng'wesi, the only group ranch with a rhino sanctuary in Laikipia, lost its sole black rhino to a poaching incident in 2013. In 2014, nine rhinos were killed illegally on Ol Jogi alone. Coupled with the fact that the world's last three northern white rhinos (*Ceratotherium simum cottoni*) now reside on Ol Pejeta, "rhino panic" is prolific in the discourses of conservation in Laikipia. Narratives about declining rhino populations, the immanent extinction of northern white rhinos, and threats of over-population and poaching are heard frequently on safari. Moreover, such narratives are used by private rhino sanctuaries to attract money from donors around the world – ranging from the Duke of Cambridge to "10-year old Hillary from Ontario, Canada" (Ol Pejeta Conservancy's Facebook Page).

Amid the rhino panic in Laikipia, a major fundraising focus has become financing the recruitment, training, and arming of wildlife rangers. "Wildlife rangers" are teams of paramilitary personnel, often recruited with basic military or police training that use military technology to defend and surveil private conservation areas. Wildlife rangers patrol conservancy land, carry out anti-poaching reconnaissance, and engage in direct combat with poachers when deemed necessary. Rangers are also meant to deter threats by giving the impression that conservancies are defended by well-organized, heavily armed fighter units. Teams of wildlife rangers are often comprised of Kenya Police Reservists (KPR) equipped with military clothing and government-issued rifles. However, conservancies such as Borana, Lewa, and Ol Pejeta, among others, also deploy special units that focus exclusively on protecting rhinos. Ol Pejeta's Rhino Protection Unit and Borana's Armed Anti-Poaching Unit are two examples of such units. Wildlife rangers also tend to be trained in tactics unfamiliar to most KPR, such as conducting military operations or handling attack and sniffer dogs. Borana recently recruited a former British Special Forces instructor to train snipers for its anti-poaching unit. Other technologies of war feature prominently in Laikipia's wildlife sector, including sophisticated electrical fences, communication technologies, and, more recently, unmanned aerial vehicles (i.e. "drones").

Moreover, it appears that increasingly more fundraising activities for general operations in conservancies evoke rhino panic and lionize wildlife rangers represented as being regularly engaged in bush combat or reconnaissance (Bersaglio 2017).

In short, "war" has become a compelling metaphor and common model for conserving wildlife in private conservation areas in Laikipia (Neumann 2004). An interview conducted by the *Telegraph* with the owner of Borana (named Dyer) further illustrates this observation when Dyer is asked about the conservancy's reliance on paramilitary forces to defend its property and the wildlife on it (Madden and Madden 2014):

INTERVIEWER: "... is this the future of rhino conservation?"

DYER: "Yes. This is the frontline. This is relentless. Its 24 hours a day, 365 days a year, and it's going to be like this until this crisis ends. We don't have any choice."

Dyer, along with many of his contemporaries, perceives his conservancy as the frontline of a war that requires the same dedication, ingenuity, and resources as any other war. As this chapter suggests, however, the war referenced by Dyer is not simply being fought over biodiversity conservation goals, objectives, and practices. While this war is justified by the moral and ecological pretext of conservation, at its roots lies a protracted struggle over land, property, and resources that can be traced back to original colonial dispossession. With no clear or obvious "enemy" to defend or fight against, however, conservancies and conservation organizations have jointly pursued soft tactics that aim to win hearts and minds for conservation.

Market-driven conservation via education: "changing a community's mindset"

Virtually all wildlife conservancies in Laikipia have a webpage devoted to "communities" on their websites, where visitors can find information about the outreach programmes the organizations carry out in human settlements neighbouring private conservation areas. For example, Borana's website boasts of the funding it provides to a mobile health clinic, which provides immunizations, voluntary counselling and testing for HIV, and health education in remote communities. "Roads, classrooms, food, peace – this is what Lewa represents in the minds of local people", reads Lewa's "community programmes" webpage. Ol Pejeta's community-focused webpages assure potential tourists and donors that the conservancy uses "regular socio-economic surveys" to "provide the support necessary to address real needs and to make a real difference to the lives of the people who live nearby". Each of these conservancies is engaged in various community development activities, which include education programmes, health care initiatives, and infrastructure projects, such as schools, clinic, boreholes, renewable energy, roadways, and fencing aimed to minimize human–wildlife conflict.

Borana, Lewa, and Ol Pejeta attract at least US$2.5 million per year from conservation organizations investing in community development, resource management, and social services in Laikipia (LWF 2013). Although conservancies are transparent about how they attract funding and where their funding comes from, the actual allocation and distribution of funds is less easy to decipher. Despite this uncertainty, fundraising for the provision of social services in human settlements surrounding private conservation areas has, like the militarization of these same properties, become a priority for conservation organizations. Annual expenditures reported by conservancies and conservation organizations indicate an increasing trend in the amount of conservation funds being spent on education specifically. In some respects, educational fundraising and outreach programmes reflect the biopolitics of conservation – measures designed to improve and sustain both human life and wildlife vis-à-vis MDC (Fletcher 2010). In the context of Laikipia, however, such programmes also draw a shade over the militarization of private land and, more generally, the subtle reproduction of a colonial property regime.

Most of the education programmes funded or operated by conservancies involve partnerships with civil society organizations, such as the Laikipia Wildlife Forum (LWF) and the Northern Rangelands Trust (NRT), a wide range of international organizations and donors (e.g. USAID), and government entities such as Kenya's Ministry of Education, Science, and Technology. The education programme facilitated by the LWF is worth examining closely, as the organization is most explicit about the desired effects of education in rural society.

The LWF's education initiatives occur under the organization's Environmental Education Programme (EEP). As stated, the LWF is explicit about EEP's goal:

> The long-term sustainability of conservation efforts in Laikipia is inextricably linked to the environmental awareness. Awareness is a pre-requisite for the development of attitudes and practices, and so we focus much of our attention on schoolchildren of primary school age.... We hope that by encouraging involvement through environmental education, the next generation of responsible, committed Laikipians will work for the *sustained* conservation of the Laikipia ecosystem.
>
> (LWF 2016b, emphasis added)

In short, the LWF invests in education to create rural citizens that conduct themselves in ways that sustain the ideas and aspirations of MDC in Laikipia. This is evidenced in part by the biographies of Indigenous safari guides that grew up in Laikipia and now work in private conservation areas: all such guides interviewed explained that they got into the safari industry because they attended schools built and supported by conservation organizations and even received bursaries for their secondary and post-secondary education.

One of EEP's core programme areas is supplementing the national curriculum in rural schools with conservation-focused lectures and field trips tailored around conservation efforts in Laikipia. Through EEP, over 1,000 public teachers have been trained using workshops and field trips that provide detailed instruction on how to deliver educational content about conservation in line with the LWF's objectives. Additionally, some 13,000 students across Laikipia have been taken on field trips to conservancies through LWF's educational bus programme, which the organization says covers over 1,000,000 hectares. The bus programme offers experiential learning opportunities in conservancies to students that would otherwise not be able to afford to pass through conservancy gates legally – at least not as tourists. The LWF is also using film to spark an interest in wildlife conservation and management among school-goers, teaching them to value wildlife and other resources in ways that align with MDC (LWF 2016b).

These ideas and aspirations are shared by the conservancies and organizations that the LWF partners with. For example, Borana's community webpage quotes Nelson Mandela's observation that "education is the most powerful weapon which you can use to change the world" and states that education is "an essential part of our conservation mission". Borana's education mission aims to "enhance the conservation efforts for both wildlife and the environment through activities at the five schools" surrounding the conservancy. Like Borana, Lewa too boasts about the role it plays in "shaping conservation's future" (2015, 9) through education and Ol Pejeta states that "the benefits of wildlife conservation must be tangible to even the youngest members of local communities" (OPC 2016) if conservation is going to be sustainable in the long term.

In addition to providing conservation education in neighbouring human settlements, the conservancies raise money for bursaries, curriculum and infrastructure development, energy and water systems, school supplies, and teacher salaries and training. Combined, Lewa and Ol Pejeta provide educational assistance to some 57 schools and 15,500 students in human settlements surrounding each conservancy. Lastly, Lewa facilitates a child/youth sponsorship programme through which tourists and donors can support the education of a young person from a nearby community. According to Lewa, over 75 per cent of the 500 students that have received bursaries later graduated from college or university. "These students are also ambassadors of the Conservancy in their communities, representatives of Lewa's efforts in holistic development" (LWC 2016a). However, when scrutinized in relation to the simultaneous militarization of private conservation areas in Laikipia – and when situated deeper in relation to the historically racialized distribution/control of land and resources in the county – the liberal promise of education as a means to self-determination has subtle, but no less dire, consequences for the autonomy and life chances of individuals from Indigenous communities that rely on subsistence forms of production for their survival and well-being.

Green violence and the reforeignization of space

> The Craigs were smart. They put rhino on their land. That got the whole international community behind them.

It has been argued that "the struggle over hunting and the control of wildlife in Kenya always took second place to struggles over land" (Steinhart 2006, 206). Before concluding, this section recaps a few of the reasons why the struggle for control of wildlife in Laikipia can be understood as a protracted struggle over land with "calamities that are slow and long lasting" (Nixon 2011, 6). Ultimately, this discussion reveals that the ability to obtain and maintain control over property in the county is founded on a historically unequal and prejudicial set of arrangements and institutions. Within these arrangements and institutions, property ownership has become partly contingent on both the ability, and chance, to accumulate entire landscapes for wildlife habitat and on the aptitude or disposition to embrace the ideas and aspiration of MDC. These insights derive from a broad conception of green violence that looks beyond material and spatial manifestations of green violence to consider the immaterial and temporal nature of conservation-cum-violence, as well as the effects of such violence in rural society.

This chapter describes how the wild animals that white settlers once considered "target practice" or "vermin" became a source of staying power for those fighting to defend their property rights, secure their economic interests, and maintain their influence in post-independence Kenya. The notion of "staying power" – used here to describe one's ability to maintain both a literal position on the earth and a figurative position in society – is reflected in the quote at the beginning of this section. During an interview, a white Kenyan of no relation to the Craigs' explained how smart the long-time settler family was for establishing a rhino sanctuary on their land, arguing "that got the whole international community behind them". This statement reflects local awareness for the fact that MDC provided landed white settlers in Laikipia with access to influential supporters, wealthy donors, and foreign capital to fortify the benefits of settler colonialism. This translates into political capital that white settlers use to shape local decisions about land use planning and resource management and, to demand government support for their aspirations, ideas, and presence in the landscape (Enns and Bersaglio, forthcoming).

By allying with transnational conservation actors and entities to slowly transform their cattle ranches into for-profit wildlife conservancies, white settlers were granted access to a portfolio of means and resources that have enabled them to reinforce their rights claims by deploying wildlife rangers on their land and to maintain their influence in wider society by acting as a de facto provider of employment, healthy ecosystems, and social services. First, white settlers have used "military and para-military personnel, training, technologies, and partnerships" to defend their properties (Lunstrum 2014, 816). Although justified amid the rhino poaching panic as an appropriate response to the threat of encroachers and poachers, wildlife rangers are more subtly defending and surveilling green mutations of colonial enclosures. Second, the efforts taken by conservation organizations to "conservationize" education in human settlements surrounding conservancies has equally subtle effects in rural society. In being taught to sustain the conservation of Laikipia's ecosystem in the classroom while also being conditioned to the normalcy of privately secured conservation areas during field trips, children and youth are at risk of being taught to forget the colonial present – namely, the racialized distribution and control of land through MDC. In this context, the LWF's (2016) use of the word "sustain" above highlights the slow nature of green violence in Laikipia, as structural forms of violence rooted in colonial dispossession lurch onwards in time and space under green pretext that are often seemingly benign in the eyes of those within the settler class.

The genealogy of MDC in Laikipia describes both the general conditions and more specific strategies, technologies, and programmes that have enabled the reproduction of what Zoomers (2010) calls a "foreignization of space". Market-driven conservation in Laikipia contributes to a reforeignization of space through the reinvention and reproduction of settler capitalism; the green economy justifies foreign interests, capital, and (white) people to become ever more deeply rooted in the landscape. In this context, MDC functions as both an accumulation strategy for white settlers and as a source of staying power for those equipped to reinvest capital accrued from wildlife back into technologies and programmes that fortify their geographical and societal position. The accretive intensification of foreign control over entire landscapes in the name of conservation has, consequentially, delayed the structural violence of colonial dispossession. Amid the militarization of private conservation areas, privatization of social service provision, and commercialization of land in rural society more broadly, the space for alternative land uses and livelihoods in Laikipia is ever-shrinking. In these shrinking spaces, the slow forms of green violence that are shaded from the sightline of privileged onlookers are all too obvious from the viewpoint of subsistence producers who experience their calamities on a day-to-day basis.

Concluding discussion

Early in 2017, incidences of pastoralists migrating with their livestock to Laikipia from nearby drought-stricken counties and "invading" private conservation areas to access pasture and water began to increase in frequency and intensity. Some of these herders razed tourist lodges, harassed tourists, and killed wildlife they encountered in the process. On 6 March 2017, the body of Tristan Voorspuy, a white Kenyan, was found dead on Sosian Game Ranch. Voorspuy was allegedly shot and killed, along with his horse, by invading herders when he approached them with a gun on horseback. On 22 April 2017, Kuki Gallman, the Italian author of *I Dreamed of Africa*, was shot and injured while patrolling her property – the largest private landholding in Laikipia, called Ol Ari Nyiro – with wildlife rangers. In response to escalating tensions, the British High Commission demanded that the Government of Kenya take immediate action to restore the rule of law in the county (Lang'at and Ringa 2017). This demand was met by scaled-up military interventions that aimed to root out and disarm herders squatting illegally on private wildlife ranches and conservancies, demonstrating the current government's commitment to protecting Laikipia's reputation as a world-class tourism destination (Agutu 2017).

Amid increasing deaths, invasions, and punitive military operations, the world has begun to debate the root causes of such violence in Laikipia. "Are Kenya ranch invasions driven by drought or politics?" asks one BBC article (Leithead 2017), reflecting two of the more common explanations of what drives land invasions cited in the media. More frequent droughts in the context of increasingly degraded rangelands and depleted water sources (i.e. "climate change") are often blamed as a driver of land invasions in Laikipia; and the 2016–17 drought did hit pastoralist communities in the region very hard. Politics have also been blamed for inciting land invasions in Laikipia. Speculation is high that those who shot and killed Voorspuy are connected to local politicians and bullets used to kill a ranch worker elsewhere in Laikipia have been traced to a government-owned ordinance factory in Eldoret (Ndirangu 2017; Start Reporter 2017). The logic in such explanations is that, in the run up to national elections in August 2017, local politicians are attempting to win votes from destitute constituents by promising to give them control over settler-owned land if elected. These beliefs and discourses are also commonly heard on the ground in Laikipia: "Hopefully they [the land invasions] will finish once the rains come", stated a safari guide who identifies as Meru. Additionally, a white rancher explained "if we can just get through the election, hopefully things will calm down".

Less-publicized by the national and international media, however, are explanations that point to structural inequalities centred on land as a driver of land invasions and related violent conflicts (for evidence of growing exceptions, see Burke 2017; Mbaria 2017). This stands in stark contrast to the fact that such explanations are routinely articulated by Maasais and other pastoralist groups in the region. Without negating the fact that drought and politics factor into land invasions, this chapter reveals how the violent ecology of MDC has shaped, and has been shaped by, much deeper and wider struggles over land and resources in Laikipia. Land invasions, in this context, can be understood as a material consequence of green violence – a violence that has subtly brought the effects of a deferred colonial past to bear on peoples' everyday lives now under the moral and ecological pretexts of conservation (Campbell 2016). The case of Laikipia serves to disclose the fact that green violence "needs to be seen – and deeply considered – as a contest not only over space, or bodies, or labor, or resources, but also over *time*" (Nixon 2011, 8, italics added). Failing to probe the temporal dimensions of green violence leaves hidden the colonial roots and racialized histories firmly embedded in discursive justifications for and spectacular displays of violence against local Africans on behalf of a rhino population that aids in the security of settler property rights.

References

Agutu, Nancy. "States Declares Seven Laikipia Areas 'Dangerous, Disturbed' ". *The Star*, March 15, 2017, www.the-star.co.ke/news/2017/03/15/states-declares-seven-laikipia-areas-dangerous-disturbed_c1525640 (accessed 1 June 2017), 2017.

Anneke, Wendy, and Mmoto Masubelele. "A Review of the Impact of Militarisation: The Case of Rhino Poaching in Kruger National Park, South Africa". *Conservation and Society* 14, no. 3 (2016): 195–204.

Bersaglio, Brock. "Green Grabbing and the Contested Nature of Belonging in Laikipia, Kenya: A Genealogy". Doctoral dissertation, University of Toronto, 2017.

Blomley, Nicholas. "Law, Property, and the Geography of Violence: the Frontier, the Survey, and the Grid". *Annals of the Association of American Geographers* 93, no. 1 (2003): 121–141.

Borana Wildlife Conservancy (BWC). "Education". www.borana.co.ke/conservation/education.html#.VvfwPhIrJE4 (accessed 27 March 2016), 2016.

Burke, Jason. "Inequality, Drought and the Deadly Fight for Precious Grazing Land in Kenya". *Guardian*, 3 May 2017. www.theguardian.com/world/2017/may/03/inequality-drought-and-the-deadly-fight-for-precious-grazing-land-in-kenya (accessed 1 June 2017), 2017.

Büscher, Bram, and Maano Ramutsindela. "Green Violence: Rhino Poaching and the War to Save Southern Africa's Peace Parks". *African Affairs* 115, no. 418 (2016): 1–22.

Campbell, Jeremy. *Conjuring Property: Speculation and Environmental Futures in the Brazilian Amazon*. Seattle, WA: University of Washington, 2016.

Denney, Richard. "Relationships of Wildlife to Livestock on Some Developed Ranches on the Laikipia Plateau, Kenya". *Journal of Range Management* 25, no. 6 (1972): 415–425.

Duder, C. J. D., and C. P. Youé. "Paice's Place: Race and Politics in the Nanyuki District, Kenya, in the 1920s". *African Affairs* 93 (1994): 253–278.

Duffy, Rosaleen. "Waging War to Save Biodiversity: the Rise of Militarized Conservation". *International Affairs* 90, no. 4 (2014): 819–834.

Elliott, Joanna, and Muthoni Mwangi. "Making Wildlife 'Pay' in Laikipia, Kenya". In *Laikipia Wildlife Economics Study Discussion Paper CEC-DP-1*. Nairobi: African Wildlife Foundation, 1997.

Elliott, Joanna, and Muthoni Mwangi. "Developing Wildlife Tourism in Laikipia, Kenya – Who Benefits?" In *Laikipia Wildlife Economics Study Discussion Paper CEC-DP-3*. Nairobi: African Wildlife Foundation, 1998.

Enns, Charis, and Brock Bersaglio. "Negotiating Pipeline Projects and Reterritorialising Land through Rural Resistance in Northern Kenya" (forthcoming).

Fletcher, Robert. "Neoliberal Environmentality: Towards a Poststructuralist Political Ecology of the Conservation Debate". *Conservation and Society* 8, no. 3 (2010): 171–181.

Georgiadis, Nicholas. "Introduction: Conserving Wildlife in Kenya's Ewaso landscape". In *Conserving Wildlife in African Landscapes: Kenya's Ewaso Ecosystem*, edited by Nicholas Georgiadis, 1–10. Washington, DC: Smithsonian Institute Scholarly Press, 2011.

Herne, Brian. *White Hunters: The Golden Age of African Safaris*. New York, NY: Henry Holt, 1999.

Hughes, David. *Whiteness in Zimbabwe: Race, Landscape, and the Problem of Belonging*. New York, NY: Palgrave Macmillan, 2010.

Hughes, Lotte. *Moving the Maasai: A Colonial Misadventure*. Basingstoke: Palgrave Macmillan, 2006.

Huxley, Elspeth. *Nine Faces of Kenya*. New York, NY: Viking, 1991.

Igoe, Jim, and Dan Brockington. "Neoliberal Conservation: A Brief Introduction". *Conservation and Society* 5, no. 4 (2007): 432–449.

Kenya Wildlife Service (KWS), *Conservation and Management Strategy for the Black Rhino in Kenya: 2012–2016*. Nairobi: KWS, 2012.

Kock, Richard. "Wildlife Utilization: Use It or Lose It – a Kenyan Perspective". *Biodiversity and Conservation* 4 (1995): 241–256.

Kinnaird, Margaret, and Timothy O'Brien. "Effects of Private-Land Use, Livestock Management, and Human Tolerance on Diversity, Distribution, and Abundance of Large African Mammals". *Conservation Biology* 26, no. 6 (2012): 1026–1039.

Laikipia Wildlife Forum (LWF). *Wildlife Conservation Strategy for Laikipia County: 2012–2030*. Nanyuki: LWF, 2012.

Laikipia Wildlife Forum (LWF). *The Contribution of the Rural Economy of Laikipia as the Basis of a Model Community*. Nanyuki: LWF, 2013.

Laikipia Wildlife Forum (LWF). "Who We Are". www.laikipia.org/about-us/ (accessed 27 March 2016), 2016a.

Laikipia Wildlife Forum (LWF). "Environmental Education". www.laikipia.org/portfolio-item/environmental-education (accessed 27 March 2016), 2016b.

Lang'at, Patrick, and Mathias Ringa. "Britain Reacts to Laikipia Rancher Killing". *Daily Nation*, 6 March 2017. www.nation.co.ke/news/Britain-reacts-to-Laikipia-rancher-killing/1056-3839034-kwk98z (accessed 1 June 2017), 2017.

Leithead, Alastair. "Are Kenya Ranch Invasions Driven by Drought or Politics?". *BBC*, 4 February 2017. www.bbc.co.uk/news/world-africa-38866389 (accessed 1 June 2017), 2017.

Letai, John. "Land Deals and Pastoralist Livelihoods in Laikipia County, Kenya". In *Africa's Land Rush: Rural Livelihoods and Agrarian Change*, edited by Ruth Hall, Ian Scoones and Dzodzi Tsikata, 83–98. Suffolk: James Currey, 2015.

Lewa Wildlife Conservancy (LWC). *Annual Report 2014*. Isiolo: LWC, 2015.

Lewa Wildlife Conservancy (LWC). "Our Communities: Education Programmes: Scholarships". www.lewa.org/our-communities/education-bursariesscholarships (accessed 27 March 2016), 2016a.

Lewa Wildlife Conservancy (LWC). *Annual Report 2015*. Isiolo: LWC, 2016b.

Lunstrum, Elizabeth. "Green Militarization: Anti-poaching Efforts and the Spatial Contours of Kruger National Park". *Annals of the Association of American Geographers* 104, no. 4 (2014): 816–832.

Lunstrum, Elizabeth. "Green Grabs, Land Grabs and the Spatiality of Displacement: Eviction from Mozambique's Limpopo National Park". *Area* 48, no. 2 (2016): 142–152.

Madden, Richard, and Sarah Madden. "Black Rhino Poaching: On the Front Line Fight against Poachers". *Telegraph*, 12 November 2014. www.telegraph.co.uk/travel/activityandadventure/11221205/Black-rhino-poaching-on-the-front-line-fight-against-the-poachers.html (accessed 1 June 2017), 2014.

Marijnen, Esther, and Judith Verweijen. "Selling Green Militarization: The Discursive (Re)production of Militarized Conservation in the Virunga National Park, Democratic Republic of Congo". *Geoforum* 75 (2016): 274–285.

Martin, Douglas. "Anna Merz, Rhino Guardian and Champion, Dies at 81". *New York Times*, 21 April 2013. www.nytimes.com/2013/04/22/world/africa/anna-merz-protector-of-black-rhinos-dies-at-81.html?_r=1. (accessed 1 June 2017), 2013.

Matheka, Reuben. "Decolonisation and Wildlife Conservation in Kenya, 1958–68". *Journal of Imperial and Commonwealth History*, 36, no. 4 (2008): 615–639.

Mbaria, G. "The Laikipia Crisis and the Disenfranchisement of Kenyans in the North". *The Elephant*, 18 May 2017. www.theelephant.info/the-hustle/2017/05/18/the-laikipia-crisis-and-the-disenfranchisement-of-kenyans-in-the-north (accessed 1 June 2017), 2017.

McIntosh, Janet. *Unsettled: Denial and Belonging among White Kenyans*. Berkeley, CA: University of California, 2016.

Morgan, W. T. W. "The 'White Highlands' of Kenya". *The Geographical Journal* 129, no. 2 (1963): 140–155.

Ndirangu, Mwangi. "Herder Charged with Murder of Tristan Voorspuy at Sosian". *Daily Nation*, 4 April 2017. http://allafrica.com/stories/201704050049.html. (accessed 1 June 2017), 2017.

Neumann, Roderick. "Moral and Discursive Geographies in the War for Biodiversity in Africa". *Political Geography* 23 (2004): 813–837.

Nixon, Rob. *Slow Violence and the Environmentalism of the Poor*. Cambridge, MA: Harvard University Press, 2011.

Northern Rangelands Trust (NRT). "NRT Director of Conservation Ian Craig Awarded Order of the British Empire". NRT. www.nrt-kenya.org/news-list/2016/ian-craig-obe (accessed 1 June 2017), 2016.

Ol Pejeta Conservancy (OPC). *2020 Map*. Nanyuki: OPC, 2015.

Ol Pejeta Conservancy (OPC). "Education". OPC. www.olpejetaconservancy.org/community/infrastructure-projects/education/ (accessed 27 March 2016), 2016.

Ol Pejeta Conservancy (OPC). Facebook Page. OPC. www.facebook.com/OlPejetaConservancy (accessed 1 June 2017).

Roth, Robin, and Wolfram Dressler. "Market-Oriented Conservation Governance: The Particularities of Place". *Geoforum* 43 (2012): 363–366.

Star Reporter. "Bullets Used by Pokots in Laikipia Raids Are from State's Eldoret Artillery – Source". *The Star*, April 22, 2017. www.the-star.co.ke/news/2017/04/22/bullets-used-by-pokots-in-laikipia-raids-are-from-states-eldoret_c1547934 (accessed 1 June 2017).

Steinhart, E. I. "Hunters, Poachers and Gamekeepers: Towards a Social History of Hunting in Colonial Kenya". *The Journal of African History* 30, no. 2 (1989): 247–264.

Steinhart, E. I. *Black Poachers, White Hunters: A Social History of Hunting in Colonial Kenya*. Athens, OH: Ohio University Press, 2006.

Zoomers, Annelies. "Globalisation and the Foreignisation of Space: Seven Processes Driving the Current Global Land Grab". *The Journal of Peasant Studies* 37, no. 2 (2010): 429–447.

6 Elusive space

Peasants and resource politics in the Colombian Caribbean

Diana Ojeda and María Camila González

1 Introduction

Colombia ranks among the world's most inequitable countries. In the country's rural areas, unequal distribution of land is rampant and severe (BBC 2016; Sherman 2015). A recent study from Oxfam revealed that properties measuring 500 ha or more (only 0.4 percent of registered properties) comprise nearly 70 percent of the country's productive land, while small land holdings of 2 ha or less (representing 84 percent of properties) correspond to only 4 percent of productive lands. The country's six-decade war and the endurance of power structures that continue to marginalize peasants explain in part this discrepancy (Osorio 2016; Gutiérrez and García 2016), and land grabbing has grown exponentially during the last decade (Betancur 2016). According to official numbers, in Colombia, more than seven million people have been forcibly displaced from their land (RUV 2016), and nearly 10 million ha, nearly a fourth of the national cultivated lands, have been grabbed by paramilitary groups (AMH 2009, 21–23). Millions of rural inhabitants have been victims of violence perpetrated by armed actors – paramilitary, guerrilla, state and private security forces (GMH 2016).

Since 2011, Colombia has undergone a process of transitional justice, in which land has played a central role. While 87,750 ha have been restituted to claimants – peasant, Indigenous and Afro-descendant populations (URT 2016) – the nationwide program presents huge limitations and has shown little progress in terms of communities' actual return to their land (CSM 2015). Limited land access and use is perhaps the most important cause for war in Colombia and was the first negotiation point in the recently signed peace accords between FARC (Armed Revolutionary Forces of Colombia) guerrillas and the government.[1] State-led peacebuilding efforts are undermined because peasant leaders, among them land claimants and environmental defenders, are routinely assassinated. Even after the signing of the accords, the murders of peasant leaders are mounting and so is the impunity of the crimes committed against them (Semana 2016). Since 2012, not a single conviction has been achieved for any of the 124 peasant murders reported (CNN 2016).

The paradox of post-conflict amid war is key to understanding the country's contemporary conjuncture. In the struggle for what peace would look like in rural areas, the state has avidly combined militarization strategies with development interventions. As extractivism is central to the national agenda, different regions face the violence of an ongoing, massive counter-agrarian reform legitimated in the name of development. The dramatic entrenchment of private capital's resource control has been necessary to guarantee the viability of mining, the oil industry and large agribusinesses.

In this chapter, we explore the drastic transformations of peasants' spaces during the last two decades in a context of paramilitary state-sanctioned violence, multi-scaled land grabbing, the war on drugs and sustainable development projects including eco-tourism, agrofuels and timber plantations.[2] In particular, we focus on how peasants in the Colombian Caribbean articulate a resource politics while navigating a very limited political terrain. We draw from seven years of ethnographic and collaborative research carried out independently by each author in different sites of the Colombian Caribbean, in the north of the country. In particular, our case focuses on Tayrona National Natural Park, in the department of Magdalena, and on Montes de María. Tayrona is one of Colombia's most important protected areas, located in the foothills of the Sierra Nevada de Santa Marta. Montes de María is a region composed of 15 municipalities within the departments of Bolívar and Sucre, historically produced as an "agricultural pantry."[3]

We do not understand peasants' political strategies as a set of empty narratives they have adopted to their convenience. They are important means and expressions of ideological struggles, and key elements in the conformation of peasants' subjectivities and ways of acting in (and making) the world (Yié 2015, 41). Taken in a wider sense, we understand these political strategies as the repertoire of action and enunciation available to peasants for them to make their lives possible and meaningful, and to voice their demands. In that sense, peasants' political space is not limited to formal or official spaces of dialogue with the state and other public institutions, but entails a comprehensive understanding of the political that includes the myriad, always-relational and -situated, manifestations of power. This political space is thus the manifestation of intertwined sociospatial processes that give shape to the everyday practices through which *peasant space* is constantly constituted.

Peasants clearly conform a heterogeneous and dynamic group under which many different subjects, experiences and expectations get lumped together. Standard definitions from disciplines such as economics and sociology of "rural laborers" or "small rural producers" do not fully account for the complex historical and geographical processes implied in the production of peasants as social, economic, cultural, political and environmental subjects (Tocancipá 2005). We refer to peasants – men, women and children – as rural inhabitants whose livelihoods are highly dependent on local resources. Most of them are landless and have struggled all their life for the chance to grow their food. Some of them also represent themselves as Indigenous or black/Afro-Colombian.

In the next section, we outline how peasants have been constructed as a category in Colombia's recent history. Drawing from interviews with state officials and discourse analysis of official state documents, we explain how different processes – state multiculturalism among them – have curtailed the possibility of peasants to access both biodiversity conservation and land rights frameworks of representation, interlocution and visibility. In the third section, we examine how rural development discourses, infused with sustainability and conservation imperatives, have shaped the elusive space of peasants. We draw from unstructured interviews, participant observation and life histories with different rural communities (formally organized or not), aiming to understand how they have negotiated the logics of state-led interventions. On the one hand, we examine peasants' elusive space in relation to the pressures of agribusiness – sometimes as workers, but mostly trying to become *small rural entrepreneurs* by participating in partnering models with big companies or by indebting themselves into schemes of financialization of access to land, seeds, fertilizers and pesticides. On the other, we show how such political space is conditioned to the possibility of proving themselves as *green subjects* – either as nature guardians, as "environmental interpreters" for eco-tourism or as agroecological producers. In the fourth section, we explore peasants' territorialities, looking for more politically enabling ways of understanding peasant space and of accounting for their myriad strategies to counter the processes that have enclosed, chased, criminalized and killed them during the last two decades in Colombia. Lastly, in the conclusions, we return to the main contributions and future directions of our work.

2 Placing peasants within national configurations of difference and citizenship

In April 2016, one of us had the chance to attend an informative meeting with state officials from the Unidad de Restitución de Tierras (Land Restitution Unit) in Bogota. The focus of the meeting was to inform about the two possible routes for claiming lands for restitution that victims of the internal armed conflict between 1985 and 2005 could access owing to forced abandonment or dispossession of their lands: the collective route and the individual route. Noticeably, the collective route is limited to nationally imagined collective subjects or "ethnic" subjects – Indigenous and Afro-descendant communities more generally – while the "individual" route is referred to as "the peasant route," as peasants are not considered ethnic subjects in official multicultural discourse in Colombia (Gutiérrez and García 2016; Hoffman 2016). The ethnic/peasant divide corresponds as well to an unsurmountable distinction between territory and *predio* (plot, piece of land) (Herrera 2016). Territories to be restituted to ethnic communities are assumed to have a collective use or destination, and the damages associated to the armed conflict include threats to the group's survival, cultural loss, diminished organizing capacity, environmental damages and "*campesinización*" (peasantization) (see Table 6.1).

From the URT's responses, the sharp distinctions between the two subjects of land restitution became clear. When one of the authors inquired about the differences between territory and *predio*, one of the officials working for the ethnic

Table 6.1 Individual vs. collective restitution

Individual restitution – peasant route	*Collective restitution – ethnic route*
Predio: plot, piece of land.	Territory.
Individual use.	Collective use.
Loss of a *predio*.	Territorial damage. Loss of cultural identity, organizing capacity or collective character of territory.
Testimony and interviews with affected individuals.	Field study and characterization usually based on social cartography and focal groups.
Cannot be done without the previous zoning of the affected area.	The restitution process is advanced in any place of the country with or without the previous zoning of the affected area.
Restitution occurs with or without explicit intentions of return.	A return order is issued by the competent state agency.

Source: Authors, based on information gathered from URT's documents and officers.

area of the URT replied: "Territory implies an ancestral and spiritual relation with land. What needs to be restituted in that case is not the plot, but the whole set of rights the community lost." One of us asked if this was not the case for peasant communities:

> No. What a peasant has with his plot can't be compared to the relationship ethnic communities establish with their territory.... Peasants only look for the overexploitation of land, they don't have a close relation to nature, they don't have a spiritual consideration of their surroundings. Furthermore, they don't use resources collectively.
>
> (Bogota, April 2016)

The narrow definition of the two routes, and the fact that they do not overlap, illustrates well national configurations of difference. That transitional justice in the country is based on unsurmountable and naturalized distinctions speaks of the *elusiveness* of peasant space. Beyond what could be interpreted as the short sight of a state official, his narrative is representative of official discourse. In many other occasions, we have heard from state officials in different agencies in charge of biodiversity conservation, illegal crops elimination, climate change adaptation, tourism development and social integration, among others, similar statements that render peasants as nonethnic, individualistic, environmentally damaging and (potentially) subversive subjects.

Moreover, in a context of increased extractivism, the right to *consulta previa* – established by the International Labor Organization Convention 169 as the right that ethnic communities must be consulted on matters affecting their culture and heritage – has been an important mechanism for Indigenous and Afro-descendant populations in Colombia, a mechanism to which peasants (and communities whose ethnicities are put into question by state mechanisms) are not entitled. The ethnic turn has resulted in new mobilization strategies that have taken particular forms in their intersection with violence and attempts to build a post-conflict society (Aparicio and Jaramillo 2014). As Hoffman notes,

> [u]ntil the end of the 20th century, the struggle in the countryside was aimed at agrarian reforms and led the indigenous peoples to "peasantize themselves", that is, to act as members of a social class, while silencing their ethnic dimension. Today, many peasant communities tend to indigenize themselves in order to access land and services primarily provided to indigenous and Afrodescendant peoples.
>
> (2016, 22)

For the case of the Colombian Caribbean, Johana Herrera (2016) studies how Afro-Colombians have constituted *consejos comunitarios* (community councils), focusing on the transition of the "struggle for land" to the claims for "rights over territory" and how it closely relates to the multicultural discourse.

It should be clear that this is not to say that Indigenous and Afro-descendant groups have it easy. As many authors have pointed out, the narrow definition of what an ethnic subject is or should be is ridden with contradictions and reinforces old forms of racism and colonialism (Agudelo 2005; Restrepo 2007). That return is compulsory in the collective route, for example, speaks of the firm assumptions under which ethnic subjects are categorized on the base of an ancestral, spiritual and more respectful relation to nature in problematic forms of "green multiculturalism" (Cárdenas 2012). What we contend is that, while the constitution of 1991 and the multicultural turn in Colombia have opened important and much needed spaces for difference to be recognized and for the rights of historically subordinated collectives to be acknowledged, they have closed others. Among the rooms of maneuver that were foreclosed are those historically mobilized by peasants, namely, the political languages of class equality, social justice, land tenure and labor rights.

Historically, there have been important forms of organization and mobilization of peasants in the country and in the region (CNRR 2010; Zamosc 1986). Perhaps the most important peasant movement nowadays is the Cumbre Agraria, Campesina, Étnica y Popular – CACEP (Agrarian, Peasant, Ethnic and Popular Summit) in its efforts for constituting peasants as a subject of law (Montenegro 2016). The nationwide peasants' movement responds to dispossession and devastation related to war, neoliberal policies and agroindustrial projects. Nevertheless, myriad forms of peasants' associativity have been criminalized during the last decades. As mentioned above, Colombia presents high records of threatened, forcedly disappeared and assassinated peasant leaders, and in some rural areas, particularly in the Colombian Caribbean, paramilitary forces have eliminated and explicitly prohibited peasants' cooperatives and local councils.

Similarly, Zonas de Reserva Campesina – ZRC (Peasant Reserve Areas), created by Law 160 of 1994 for the promotion of the peasant economy and the protection of populations affected by the armed conflict, have been adamantly opposed by different state instances in the national, regional and local levels.[4] Only six of them have been created after their regulation in 1997. Thought of as dangerous spaces of peasants' autonomy, a former minister of agriculture, Juan Camilo Restrepo, referred to them as a "constellation of independent *republiquetas* [mock republics]" supposedly under the command of armed groups acting at the margin of the law (*El Espectador* 2013).

Attempting to access a viable political language and mend peasants' exclusion from the constitution, last year Senator Alberto Castilla, known as Colombia's first peasant senator, presented a legislative act project to the National Congress, "[b]y means of which the peasantry is recognized as a subject of rights, the right to land and peasant territoriality is recognized, and provisions are adopted for popular consultation." The project intended to modify the 1991 constitution's Articles 64, 65 and 66, pertaining to "rural workers" in order to recognize instead "peasants" as subjects of special protection and to recognize their social construction of their territory. According to the project, "[t]he focus of the Constitution was to understand peasants as subjects in terms of their productive vocation and as a productive sector, rather than as a social group with their own identity and practices" (Congreso de la República 2016). The project was rejected on December 12, 2016, by the Senate, despite the relevance and potential of recognizing peasants – and their economy and culture – as subjects of special protection. This was a failed attempt to make the Colombian state recognize peasants' right to land and territory, as well as their role in defending agrarian production, water and forests, among other commons including native seeds (Senado 2016, online).

This example confirms Hoffman's appreciations that "[p]easants who do not recognize themselves as Indigenous or Afrodescendants enjoy very few political and legal tools to defend themselves against the attacks of their resources, whether material or immaterial" (2016, 19). This is particularly true for the case of the Colombian Caribbean, where ethnicization has become a potential political language in the context of violence and dispossession. Consequently, the creation of *consejos comunitarios* and the request for collective land titles have grown exponentially in the last few years (Herrera 2016).

Manuel is a leader in Montes de María who has actively participated in the formulation of an Intercultural Zone for Territorial Protection along with other leaders from the Organización de Poblaciones Desplazadas de Montes de María – OPDs (Organization of Displaced Populations of Montes de María). OPDs is an umbrella association that gathers together different rural organizations in the departments of Bolívar and Sucre. He expresses the frustration shared by many rural inhabitants in the region: "We are fighting amongst ourselves – peasants against afros, indigenous peoples against peasants, afros and indigenous … and meanwhile the multinationals going forward" (Bogota, May 2013). Or, as Yolima, another leader from OPDs, highlights in relation to increasing tensions within communities, "The war didn't come to pick. It swept us evenly.… And now all this distrust among us" (María la Baja, February 2014).

The examples presented in this section point to the necessity to understand the exclusionary effects of national configurations of difference and citizenship.

El campo (the countryside) and *los/las campesinos/as* (peasants) are fields of constant dispute in Colombia, and even more so in relation to the country's violent history. While national imaginaries harbor dreams of peacebuilding, they remain anchored to an official narrative of peasants' backwardness and (potential) threat. And, while peasants are largely presented as invaders, unproductive and environmental predators, it was not always so.

Official narratives in the nineteenth century confided in peasants to opening the agricultural frontier by civilizing *el monte* (wild lands). During the twentieth century, state-led colonization processes targeted peasants to "populate" different regions of the country. The national colonization project of "filling up" the nation and conquering marginal territories was saturated with moral connotations that glorified the brave men who took on the endeavor of domesticating nature and conquering it with discipline and strength (Bolívar 2006); and produced them as good Christians, Colombian citizens and agrarian producers (Acevedo and Yié 2016). This characterization changed as peasants started to become the ideal target of development interventions and their moral worth was put into question. The image of the poor *colono* (settler) became more popular in the Cold War setting, and later, in the 1970s and 1980s, with the marijuana and coca bonanzas in different regions of the country peasants became associated with illicit crops. Official narratives started to see them as invaders (González 2014; Ruiz 2003) and *guerrilleros* (Espinosa 2010; Ramírez 2001; Vásquez 2006). This shift is deeply felt by peasants in different sites of the Colombian Caribbean, as one peasant leader expressed: "The state has used us historically, as they [the elites] want. They used us to open up the way for capital to advance. Now they want us out. Who understands them?" (Teódulo, Bogota, May 2013).

3 Development, conservation and dispossession

> And I want you, the peasants of Colombia, to hear me in the fields – in the mountains, in the plains, in the jungles, on the shores of our land. We are going to defend the Colombian peasant, we are going to make him an entrepreneur, to support him with technology and credit, to make every peasant a prosperous Juan Valdez.
>
> (Santos 2010)

In his inauguration speech, the current president, Juan Manuel Santos, made clear an official version of peasants as development targets. Adducing to a default backwardness, his vision entailed the conversion of every peasant to Juan Valdez, that is, to the stereotype of a small coffee grower, a self-made man whose product sells in international markets. In the state's version, the desirable peasant is an entrepreneur, a profitable neoliberal subject fully immersed in the logics of the market. The means for such transition are, paradoxically, two powerful mechanisms of dispossession: the further financialization of rural relations and the increase in peasants' indebtment. Moreover, the speech seems to oversee the precarious situation of small coffee growers in the country, and even more so in the region Juan Valdez represents (Patiño 2014).

National Development Plans for Santos's first (2010–14) and second terms (2014–18) insisted on the need to "develop peasants' productive capacities." The state's quest to incorporate peasants to capitalist logics insisted on their inadequacy for making a profitable, and thus acceptable, use of land and other resources; on becoming successful *small rural entrepreneurs*. This has been a powerful narrative in the justification and legitimization of peasants' dispossession in different parts of the country. Peasants' place (or the lack of it) within the extractivist national political strategy is clearly stated in the National Development Plan for 2010–14: "Mechanisms will be developed to facilitate private investment in agroindustrial projects, complemented by business schemes that incorporate the land and labor of small producers and sustainable projects, without necessarily implying the transfer of ownership" (DNP 2010).

These state narratives and practices exemplify well the logics of development and their material consequences over peasant space. They are not just the somewhat expected malfunctioning of a national centralized government but traverse generalized versions of who are (or should be) the peasants and what is (or should be) their political space, delineating its elusiveness. In official discourse, peasants' economy is presented as inviable and peasants are considered incapable of productive land use.

3.1 Alianzas productivas

Since the nineteenth century, the establishment of monocrops of tobacco, sugarcane and rice, as well as cattle ranching, in Montes de María needed a constant supply of labor force. As a result, a group of peasants tied to big haciendas was constituted. In the late 1960s, after decades of peasants' mobilizations and land occupations, state-led attempts at agrarian reform took place. This confluence opened the possibility for some peasants to become small proprietors and resulted in the creation by decree of the Asociación Nacional de Usuarios Campesinos – ANUC (National Association of Peasant Users), one of the most important peasants' organizations nationwide (Verdad Abierta 2010). The following decades were marked by tensions with large landowners and by the presence of guerrilla groups. Later, at the turn of the century, Montes de María's rural populations survived some of the bloodiest episodes of paramilitary violence in the country. During the decade between 1997 and 2007, in Montes de María alone, paramilitary groups forcedly displaced more than 200,000 peasants and over 80,000 ha were grabbed by means of combined strategies of physical violence and the delineation of land titles for large landowners and entrepreneurial elites (De los Ríos et al. 2012, 32). Expropriated lands were quickly incorporated into the market and destined for plantations of oil palm and timber.

In contrast, the militarization of Montes de María by state, paramilitary and private forces has been portrayed as a successful experience of territorial consolidation and sustainable development. One of its most celebrated strategies is *alianzas productivas* (productive alliances), implemented in 2002 by the then minister of agriculture, Carlos Murgas, a key large landowner with oil palm plantations in different regions of the Colombian Caribbean. Under this figure, local peasants are linked as "producers" and the business conglomerates as "strategic partners." Peasants are required to plant at least 10 ha of oil palm or to work tending the crops. In spite of the supposed opportunities for income generation and employment (MinAgricultura 2013), the price of the fruit is set by the big company, usually below the production costs. Moreover, land tenure agreements have an average duration of 25 years, ensuring the control of land by companies. As Manuel from OPDs points out:

> *Alianzas productivas* has been really a mechanism to allow oil palm to take over our region. Becoming a *productor agrario* (agrarian producer) is really a way to say that we put the land, we put the labor … and we get kicked out from our piece of land.
>
> (Bogota, May 2013)

Furthermore, the abovementioned criminalization of peasants as potential insurgents – *guerrilleros* – or their allies has effectively contributed to the naturalization of their ongoing dispossession by processes of privatization and enclosure, as well as by the proletarization of peasants and their incorporation to development projects (Ojeda et al. 2015; Ojeda 2016). Thus, most peasants (like most Indigenous and Afro-descendant populations) in the region survive on renting small pieces of land that have become even harder to access with the rapid expansion of monocrops. Some of them work for the plantations, despite the precarious labor conditions. Moreover, the fact that large-scale plantations need a very limited number of workers and just on a seasonal basis seems to confirm Tania Li's insights on how peasants become "surplus people," as "their land is needed, but their labour is not" (2011, 286).

3.2 Familias Guardabosques

In Tayrona and the Sierra Nevada de Santa Marta, security and development strategies meant the propagation of military actions in guerrilla-controlled zones. With resources from Plan Colombia, and working in tandem with paramilitary groups, state projects of illicit crops eradication set the basis for tourism development in the name of environmental conservation in the area (González 2014; Ojeda 2012). Taryona is perhaps the most emblematic protected area of Colombia, one ridden with conflicts associated to conflicting land use and ownership. Its complex histories and geographies have been marked by marijuana and coca bonanzas, tourism development and paramilitary violence, in all which regional elites have been closely involved.

Familias Guardabosques (Forest Ranger Families) was a program of illicit crop eradication implemented during Uribe's government under the banner of alternative development. As part of the project, a group of peasant families could access portions of land in the immediacies of Tayrona's protected area, where they had to build luxurious tourist lodges. The program sought

> to benefit communities located in strategic ecosystems or conservation areas … with the presence of illicit crops, or risk of being affected by them, so that they are committed as Rangers Families, preventing the expansion of [illegal crops] and contributing to their reduction and eradication.
>
> (DNP 2006)

As a result, 20 families were incorporated to an eco-tourism project with the promise of being able to work within park limits. One such case is Juan. Juan is from Ciénaga Magdalena and came to the region more than 30 years ago, having been trained as an "environmental interpreter" (ecotour guide) within the program.

Juan was one of the many peasants who, for several decades, have had small plots planted with avocados, coffee and bananas within the park. But, in December 2011, curiously following a strong national debate that halted the project to build a seven-star hotel of the exclusive Six Senses chain within the protected area, Juan, along with six other households, was evicted by the National Park Administrative Unit and the National Police. Juan was treated as an invader and illegal occupant. He was outraged:

> If the state thought of the real ranger, this would not happen.… When I got there [to the park] when it was a paddock. And, who knows, if it wasn't for me, maybe in the *marimbera* [marijuana] bonanza they would have taken part of the park.… I got there and planted those trees, I was there and avoided any harm. I was a natural ranger.

And he added: "I was the one who helped the [coca] eradication … today, they are taking away our land" (Tayrona, January 2012). State promises of implementing viable alternatives to drug-traffic, including formal access to land, were quickly broken and the project was deemed a peasants-induced failure.

Peasants in Tayrona and Sierra Nevada de Santa Marta, where there is a strong Indigenous presence, are referred to as *colonos* (settlers, newly arrived), even though they had lived in the area for over six decades.[5] *Colonos* is associated with a series of negative connotations such as an invader, illegal or environmental predator, among others, unlike big landowners and tourist entrepreneurs within the protected area. Drug war policies have also imposed an official narrative of the "need to intervene" in these populations, which has translated in development and conservation projects such as Familias Guardabosques. Such projects have demarcated a very restricted space for peasants, focusing on a profitable use of soil and defining the narrow place that peasants should occupy either as labor force in large-scale projects or as *green subjects*. At the same time, in a region where conservation demands converge with tourism development, paramilitary power and drug trafficking, peasants like Juan mobilize, appropriate and reinterpret environmental identities as a way of staying in place (González 2014).

In this context, land grabbing and green grabbing are inseparable. Portions of land to be protected and portions of land to be developed, even if apparently different in intention and form, lay out a similar terrain of violent exclusion for local rural populations (Brockington and Duffy 2010; Büscher and Arsel 2012; Mollett 2016). Furthermore, as we have shown, the logics of sustainable development and biodiversity conservation have greatly contributed to construct peasants as unproductive and environmentally destructive subjects.

With such restricted room for maneuver, peasants' political strategies have transformed. Peasants across the Colombian Caribbean, among other regions, insist on their importance for development, peacebuilding and conservation (Abad 2016). Their implied disposability translates into anxieties to show the viability and relevance of peasants' forms of production, to prove their practices are profitable (OTEC 2013). Criminalization and fear have diluted the language of *lucha campesina* (peasant struggle) with more palatable narratives of victimhood, food security and biodiversity conservation. Within the context of post-conflict, Law 1448 of 2011 admitted the existence of the internal armed conflict (denied in official discourse before) and established the right of victims to receive state attention, be assisted and be repaired integrally. As members of peasant organizations in Montes de María often assert, a victims' organization is more viable than a peasants' organization.[6] At the same time, peasants have implemented the tropes of global peasant movements, such as Via Campesina, which reinstate their role as agroecological producers and seed guardians. In the next section, we further analyze peasants' territorialities seeking to better understand the material concretions of the political space they struggle for every day.

4 Peasant space

Peasants in Colombia constantly fight to carve out the spaces that sustain life. The women and men who have collaborated with us throughout the years navigate the frameworks of conservation and development and traverse the interconnected geographies of the Colombian Caribbean, negotiating ways to survive in close relation to the land. As we have shown, violent processes of sociospatial exclusion, inequality and dispossession have dramatically constrained peasants' territorialities. At the same time, national configurations of difference and citizenship have reduced peasants' room for maneuver, eroding their political practices and reducing their relationship to land to private property (the plot), which they rarely have, or to economic production (Gutiérrez and García 2016). In this section, we explore peasant space as it is constantly forged amid Colombia's landscape of ongoing violence and profound inequality.

Our notion of political space relates to Hoffman's definition of peasants' political and geographical imagination as a way of challenging the norms imposed by hegemonic actors (2016, 19). Our reflection seeks to point out how peasants' territorialities have been curtailed violently, but also how they attest a continuous struggle against land grabbing – in its rampant, legalized, gradual or green versions. At the same time, we want to point out that the elusive space that peasants constantly build is ridden with contradictions and refuses the fetish implied in the generalized idea that peasants inevitably seek to stay put (León 2015). Peasants move across sites, rural and urban, and devise and adjust their livelihood strategies according to the possibilities they encounter. They negotiate with development projects, opening up spaces to grow yucca, avocados, yams, rice, corn and plantains. From *jornaleros* (day laborers) to tourist guides, from domestic workers to informal vendors, from *cocaleros* (coca growers) to *cacaoteros* (cacao growers), peasants' livelihood strategies attest that peasant space is far from guaranteed or fixed.

Peasants life trajectories and daily itineraries trace out complex interconnected ecologies that result in very dynamic geographies. For example, mule riders incessantly travel the routes that connect distant places in the Colombian Caribbean region. They walk continuously, transporting huge sacks of produce from one place to another, without roads, tracing an itinerant geography. Their travels are a form to survive direct forms of violent, but also the everyday dispossession that has shaped peasant space in the region. They set up a peasant life that cannot be reduced to the plot or the farm but transcends wider spaces – private, communal and state lands – on which a network of knowledge, memories, experiences and valuations rests, interweaving diverse lived ecologies (fieldnotes, 2014).

Peasant space is a vibrant space of life and resistance. Domestic agrarian spaces such as gardens in which every inch of soil is full of herbs, flowers and garlic are a strong reminder that not even the bloodiest forms of intimidation and violence can erase women's spaces of kinship, healing and care. Contested waterscapes that sustain peasants' lived ecologies exemplify too their capacity of negotiation and resistance. In María la Baja, right by the state-built irrigation district, peasants struggle for water access. The dams, canals and gates that constitute the imposing infrastructure have been at the service of large plantations for over two decades, when the district was given in concession to a private association mainly constituted by big landowners. Peasants in this area of Montes de María must walk for many hours a day to collect water for their farming, animals and human consumption. Some of them go to the processing plant that channels potable water to urban areas far down with jugs and ask the workers in charge to please fill them up occasionally. Others fill the streets in protest and even close the floodgates at dawn so that water will reach their plots. They do so in the face of threats and persecution as they refuse to leave their lives behind yet again (fieldnotes, 2016).

In many occasions, we have also seen how thirsty palm workers in María la Baja come out of the plantations nearly fainting, and children from nearby houses besieged by the monocrop run to offer them water (the same water they struggle for daily). In other occasions, we have walked a broken valley on a stretch of road in the Sierra Nevada de Santa Marta, where, almost an hour ahead of the road, there is a cut-in-half bottle of soda, tied with a rope to a log in a ravine. The improvised jug collects water from the ravine, so that passersby can drink from it. Peasants' creative ways of being in the environment often reflect common spaces of care and solidarity. These spaces emerge from their close relations with family members and neighbors, plants, trees, birds, pigs and passing wild animals such as monkeys, deer and armadillos.

In the Colombian Caribbean, within the areas we have worked in, we have found how hegemonic views of peasants and their spaces conceal different forms of land use and tenure, and different practices of nature production. The evident inequitable distribution of resource access and control has led to creative ways of survival. In areas such as Montes de María and Zona Bananera, peasants resort to neighbors, relatives and acquaintances for renting, leasing or caring for small portions of land. Other types of sociospatial agreements include seasonal work in *baldíos* (state lands) such as floodplains of common use in the shores of marshes, wetlands and dams called *playones*.

At the same time, such spaces are shaped by destruction and domination, sustained by peasant narratives of lost practices. Arnorys, a leader from OPDs, puts it this way:

> I remember well how it was like before. The monkey was everywhere. And that jumble of birds. Not anymore [sadly]. There was coconut, cassava and corn … we drank water from the canals.… Everything is gone.… All that disappeared. Land no longer has strength.

And she added: "And it is that now the thing is cruel, if one does not buy, does not eat. Now everything must be paid" (María la Baja, February 2014). The sociospatial rearrangements that dispossession brings upon speak of its multidimensional nature. Green deserts, barbed wire, poisoned waters, devastated soils, smoke from the palm oil processing plant, thirst and hunger, fields with underlying mass graves, the scars of sexual violence and itineraries constrained by fear all also make up a part of peasant space. Ultimately, peasant space is the proof of how spaces of life are carved out from spaces of death, of the destruction they are hinged upon.

Peasant movements such as the CACEP and OPDs defend different territorial forms, including the ZRC, agroecological territories and intercultural territories, all which entail collective forms of property (Montenegro 2016, 191). Nevertheless, these territorial forms do not stand entirely outside or against the state. The languages through which they are legitimated – ancestrality, victimhood, agroecology etc. – fit within an agrarian subject that is either accepted or promoted by the state. "Each territorial figure translates, at the same time that induces, particular relations with space and the power relations inscribed on it" (Hoffman 2016, 28). As such, while peasant space is a space of resistance, it cannot be understood outside to the grids of power laid out by capital, coloniality, elitism, racism or sexism. Indeed, multiple politics shape peasant–state relations (Camargo and Ojeda 2017).

Our ethnographic experience illuminates how peasant space is reproduced through interconnected and lived ecologies, simultaneously material and symbolic, that cannot be reduced to "the plot." They include water basins, wild lands, forests, marshes, gardens and fields, as well as the daily itineraries to collect water and the networks to commercialize produce. As such, peasants' life trajectories and rooted histories involve a constant production of space and a continuous reinvention of politics, which confirm the elusiveness of peasant space in the region and in the country. We insist that what underlies peasant space does not correspond to a given set of characteristics, or to homogenous classifications, but to sociospatial practices that are contradictory and complementary.

We suggest that the notion of peasant space focuses on the material and symbolic ecologies that lay the substratum of life for different rural populations. It is based on everyday practices that include the organization of daily life, combined livelihood strategies, nature production and the definition of dynamic sociospatial arrangements. Providing spaces for bird visitation or for insect-hosting plants on the plots, or maintaining patios destined for subsistence, for example, are constitutive of peasant space and its impossibility to comfortably fit within institutional and market logics.

5 Conclusions

In this chapter, we have explored how peasant space has been dramatically curtailed during the last two decades in Colombia. As we have shown, this space is configured through everyday strategies that stand at odds with an increasingly restricted room for maneuver. We characterize peasants' political space – at the same time material and symbolic – as *elusive*, seeking to tease out their different ways of building and claiming space vis-à-vis the dispossessing narratives and practices set in motion in the Colombian Caribbean. The rampant, yet sustained and gradual, forms of land and water grabbing are a constant attack to peasant space in their lived and imagined materializations. Furthermore, in the not-so-hidden script of the state, peasants are a hindrance to rural development and biodiversity conservation efforts, a version that has proven useful for violent actions of land and labor capture carried out by private and armed actors, illegal and not. In this way, peasant space often "slips through their fingers," often leaving peasants "up in the air" between the broken promises of land rights and biodiversity conservation, which are often portrayed as ways of protecting rural populations. On the contrary, as we have shown, peasants barely manage to navigate the demands of official conservation and entrepreneurization, losing the autonomy over their means and ways of life.

In highlighting peasants' resource politics in the Colombian Caribbean, we seek to contest a violent and highly exclusionary political order under which peasants are not considered full subjects; are criminalized, evicted, chased and exterminated; and their lives are deemed collateral damage of the higher ends of development and biodiversity conservation. We assume the theoretical challenge of thinking peasant space precisely to expand it. As our argument demonstrates, there is urgent need for a wider understanding of peasants' political strategies and their spatial concretions.

Acknowledgments

We want to thank the peasants – women, men and children – who have generously shared their knowledge, stories and experiences with us across the Colombian Caribbean throughout the last seven years. We are grateful for the editors' comments and, in particular, for Sharlene Mollett's insights and suggestions. We want to thank Julio Arias, Alejandro Camargo and María Elvira García for their useful comments, and Fernando Murcia for his research assistance. Fieldwork for this research has been possible thanks to funding of Pontificia Universidad Javeriana, Universidad del Rosario, Instituto Alexander von Humboldt, Ministerio de Cultura, the Inter-American Foundation and the Society of Woman Geographers.

Notes

1 The implementation of this agreement should contribute to reversing the effects of the internal armed conflict and changing the conditions that have facilitated the persistence of violence in the territory. And that in the opinion of the FARC-EP, such transformations must contribute to solving the historical causes of the conflict, such as the unresolved issue of land ownership, particularly its concentration, the exclusion of peasants and the lag of rural communities.

(OACP 2016, 2)

2 These two decades roughly include the presidential terms of Álvaro Uribe (2002–06, 2006–10) and Juan Manuel Santos (2010–14, 2014–18). While different in approach – Uribe's term is identified with the military defeat of FARC guerrillas, while Santos's term is identified with the peace accords with it – both governments have close similarities in their social, political and economic projects, even more so in relation to the country's agrarian structure.

3 Other sites include Zona Bananera (Magdalena), a place configured by the establishment of banana plantations from the United Fruit Company in the early twentieth century, and Montería (Córdoba), a city in one of the most important cattle ranching regions of Colombia and recognized as the birthing place of the paramilitary project.

4 ZRCs consist of a form of territorial organization of peasants' lands or lands that have already been parceled out, in which each family was given or awarded a Family Agricultural Unit, or state lands that can be awarded to small farmers to organize and develop sustainable development plans.… The ZRCs do not involve collective ownership, unlike lands with collective titles that are recognized to Afro-descendant communities. ZRCs are not recognized as having territorial autonomy, although they do require a community organization to assume their representation. Neither do they have the character of territories that are considered imprescriptible, unattachable or inalienable, as collective lands.

(Sergio Latorre, cited in *El Heraldo* 2016)

5 In the late 1940s, several peasant families from Andean regions of the country arrived in the Sierra Nevada de Santa Marta and Tayrona area fleeing political violence.

6 The categorization of victims is contradictory and problematic. See Lemaitre et al. (2014) on the transition from state categorizations of "displaced populations" to "victims" and its depoliticizing effects.

References

Abad, María Mercedes. 2016. Communication Strategy for Political Incidence in Chocó, Magdalena and Bolívar. Unpublished report. *Cuando tengamos la tierra, crecerá la semilla: restitución de tierras y construcción de paz con comunidades étnicas y campesinas*. Bogota: UE, CINEP/PPP, Pontificia Universidad Javeriana.

Acevedo, María José and Yié, Maite. 2016. Nos debemos a la tierra. El Campesino y la creación de una voz para el campo, 1958–1962. *Anuario Colombiano de Historia Social y de la Cultura* 43(1): 165–201.

Agudelo, Carlos. 2005. *Retos del multiculturalismo en Colombia: política y poblaciones negras*. Medellín: La Carreta.

AMH – Área de Memoria Histórica, Línea de Investigación Tierra y Conflicto. 2009. *El Despojo de Tierras y Territorios. Aproximación Conceptual*. Bogota: Área de Memoria Histórica, Comisión Nacional de Reparación y Reconciliación, IEPRI.

Aparicio, Juan Ricardo and Jaramillo, Pablo. 2014. Etnicidad y victimización. Genealogías de la violencia y la indigeneidad en el norte de Colombia. *Antípoda* 22: 171–177.

BBC. 2016. Cuáles son los países más desiguales de América Latina. *BBC Mundo*, March 9.

Betancur, Laura. 2016. Colombia, el país más desigual de A. Latina en el reparto de la tierra. *El Tiempo*, November 29. http://app.eltiempo.com/estilo-de-vida/ciencia/concentracion-de-la-tierra-en-america-latina-oxfam/16762145.

Bolívar, Ingrid. 2006. *Discursos emocionales y experiencias de la política. Las FARC y las Auc en los procesos de negociación del conflicto (1998–2005)*. Bogota: Uniandes.

Brockington, Dan and Duffy, Rosaleen. 2010. Capitalism and Conservation: the Production and Reproduction of Biodiversity Conservation. *Antipode* 42(3): 469–484.

Büscher, Bram and Arsel, Murat. 2012. Neoliberal Conservation and Uneven Geographical Development. Exploring the Changing Nature of Capitalist Modernity in Nature–Society Interactions. *Journal of Economic and Social Geography* 103(2): 129–195.

Camargo, Alejandro and Ojeda, Diana. 2017. Ambivalent Desires: State Formation and Dispossession in the Face of Climate Crisis. *Political Geography* 60: 57–65.

Cárdenas, Roosbelinda. 2012. Green Multiculturalism: Articulations of Ethnic and Environmental Politics in a Colombian "Black Community." *Journal of Peasant Studies* 39(2): 309–333.

CNN. 2016. Asesinato de líderes sociales pone en riesgo construcción de la paz en Colombia. *CNN*, November 23.

CNRR – Comisión Nacional de Reparación y Reconciliación. 2010. *La tierra en disputa. Memorias del despojo y resistencias campesinas en la Costa Caribe: 1960–2010*. Bogota: Ediciones Aguilar.

CSM – Comisión de Seguimiento y Monitoreo al cumplimiento de la Ley 1448 de 2011. 2015. *Segundo informe al Congreso de la República 2014–2015*. Bogota: República de Colombia.

Comisión Nacional de Reparación y Reconciliación (CNRR). 2010. *La tierra en disputa. Memorias del despojo y resistencias campesinas en la Costa Caribe: 1960–2010*. Bogota: Aguilar.

Congreso de la República. 2016. Proyecto Acto Legislativo No. 006 de 2016. "Por medio del cual se reconoce al campesinado como sujeto de derechos, se reconoce el derecho a la tierra y a la territorialidad campesina y se adoptan disposiciones sobre la consulta popular." Bogota: República de Colombia. http://congresodelospueblos.org/images/PDF_Congreso/campesinos.pdf.

De los Ríos, Edwin, Becerra, Carmen Andrea and Oyaga, Fabián Enrique. 2012. *Montes de María. Entre la consolidación del territorio y el acaparamiento de tierras*. Bogota: ILSA.

DNP – Departamento Nacional de Planeación. 2006. *Plan Nacional de Desarrollo 2006–2010, Estado comunitario, desarrollo para todos*. www.dnp.gov.co/Plan-Nacional-de-Desarrollo/PND%202006-2010/Paginas/PND-2006-2010.aspx.

DNP – Departamento Nacional de Planeación. 2010. *Plan Nacional de Desarrollo 2010–2014, Prosperidad para todos*. www.dnp.gov.co/Plan-Nacional-de-Desarrollo/PND-2010-2014/Paginas/Plan-Nacional-De-2010-2014.aspx.

El Espectador. 2013. Zonas de reserva campesina encienden el debate. *El Espectador*, March 13. www.elespectador.com/noticias/politica/zonas-de-reserva-campesina-encienden-el-debate-articulo-410197.

El Heraldo. 2016. Dos modelos de desarrollo rural en tensión. *El Heraldo*, August 30. www.elheraldo.co/politica/dos-modelos-de-desarrollo-rural-en-tension-281645.

Espinosa, Nicolás. 2010. *Política de vida y muerte. Etnografía de la violencia diaria en la Sierra de la Macarena*. Bogota: Instituto Colombiano de Antropología e Historia.

GMH – Grupo de Memoria Histórica. 2016. *BASTA YA! Colombia: Memories of War and Dignity*. Bogota: CNMH. www.centrodememoriahistorica.gov.co/descargas/informes2016/basta-ya-ingles/BASTA-YA-ingles.pdf.

González, María Camila. 2014. *El que tiene tierra, que la atienda*. Undergraduate thesis, Department of Anthropology, Universidad del Rosario, Bogota.

Gutiérrez, Francisco and García, Paola. 2016. Acceso a la tierra y derechos de propiedad campesinos. *Revista Colombiana de Antropología* 52(1): 91–116.

Herrera, Johana. 2016. *Sujetos a mapas: Etnización y luchas por la tierra en el Caribe colombiano*. Bogota: Pontificia Universidad Javeriana.

Hoffman, Odile. 2016. Divergencias construidas, convergencias por construir: identidad territorio y gobierno en la ruralidad colombiana. *Revista Colombiana de Antropología* 52(1): 17–39.

Lemaitre, Julieta, López, Eva Sol, Mosquera, Juan Pablo, Bergtora, Kristin and Vargas, Juliana. 2014. De desplazados a víctimas. Los cambios legales y la participación de la Mesa de Víctimas de Mocoa, Putumayo. *PRIO Report*, 8. Bogota: Universidad de los Andes.

León, Andrés. 2015. *Rebellion under the Palm Trees: Memory, Agrarian Reform and Labor in the Aguán, Honduras*. CUNY Academic Works. http://academicworks.cuny.edu/gc_etds/1019.

Li, Tania. 2011. Centering Labor in the Land Grab Debate. *The Journal of Peasant Studies* 38, no. 2: 281–298.

MinAgricultura – Ministerio de Agricultura y Desarrollo Rural. 2013. *Proyecto apoyo a alianzas productivas*. Bogota: República de Colombia.

Mollett, Sharlene. 2016. The Power to Plunder: Rethinking Land Grabbing in Latin America. *Antipode* 48(2): 412–432.

Montenegro, Camilo. 2016. Ampliaciones y quiebres del reconocimiento político del campesinado colombiano: un análisis a la luz de la Cumbre Agraria, Campesina, Étnica y Popular (Cacep). *Revista Colombiana de Antropología* 52(1): 169–195.

OACP – Oficina del Alto Comisionado para la Paz. 2016. *Texto completo del Acuerdo Final para la Terminación del Conflicto y la Construcción de una Paz Estable y Duradera*. Bogota: República de Colombia. www.altocomisionadoparalapaz.gov.co/procesos-y-conversaciones/Paginas/Texto-completo-del-Acuerdo-Final-para-la-Terminacion-del-conflicto.aspx.

Ojeda, Diana. 2012. Green Pretexts: Ecotourism, Neoliberal Conservation and Land Grabbing in Tayrona National Natural Park, Colombia. *Journal of Peasant Studies* 39(2): 357–375.

Ojeda, Diana. 2016. Los paisajes del despojo: propuestas para un análisis desde las reconfiguraciones socioespaciales. *Revista Colombiana de Antropología* 52(2): 18–43.

Ojeda, Diana, Petzl, Jennifer, Quiroga, Catalina, Rodríguez, Ana Catalina and Rojas, Juan Guillermo. 2015. Paisajes del despojo cotidiano: Acaparamiento de tierra y agua en Montes de María, Colombia. *Revista de Estudios Sociales* 54: 107–119.

Osorio, Flor Edilma. 2016. Campos en movimiento. Algunas reflexiones sobre acciones colectivas de pobladores rurales en Colombia. *Revista Colombiana de Antropología* 52(1): 41–61.

Patiño, Juan Camilo. 2014. *El Paisaje Cultural Cafetero: Patrimonialización, turismo y representaciones de los campesinos en un escenario de crisis*. Master's thesis, Pontificia Universidad Javeriana, Bogota.

Ramírez, María Clemencia. 2001. *Entre el estado y la guerrilla: identidad y ciudadanía en el movimiento de los campesinos cocaleros del Putumayo*. Bogota: Instituto Colombiano de Antropología e Historia, Colciencias.

Restrepo, Eduardo. 2007. El "giro al multiculturalismo" desde un encuadre afro-indígena. *Journal of Latin American and Caribbean Anthropology* 12(2): 475–486.

Ruiz, Daniel. 2003. Campesinos entre la selva, invasores de reservas. *Tabula Rasa* 1: 183–210.

RUV. 2016. Registro Único de Víctimas. Unidad para las Víctimas, República de Colombia. Bogota, December 1. http://rni.unidadvictimas.gov.co/RUV.

Santos, Juan Manuel. 2010. Discurso de posesión del presidente Juan Manuel Santos Calderón. Bogota: República de Colombia. http://wsp.presidencia.gov.co/Prensa/2010/Agosto/Paginas/20100807_15.aspx.

Semana. 2016. Los 13 líderes asesinados después de la firma del acuerdo de paz. *Semana*, December 9. www.semana.com/nacion/articulo/los-13-lideres-asesinados-despues-de-la-firma-del-acuerdo-de-paz/493528.

Senado. 2016. Plenaria del Senado niega reconocimiento del campesinado colombiano, al hundir reforma constitucional que buscaba reconocer sus derechos. *Senado de la República de Colombia*, December 13. www.senado.gov.co/sala-de-prensa/senadores-noticias/item/26262-plenaria-del-senado-niega-reconocimiento-del-campesinado-colombiano-al-hundir-reforma-constitucional-que-buscaba-reconocer-sus-derechos-senador-alberto-castilla.

Sherman, Erik. 2015. America Is the Richest, and Most Uneven, Country. *Fortune*, September 30. http://fortune.com/2015/09/30/america-wealth-inequality/.

Tocancipá, Jairo. 2005. El retorno de lo campesino: una revisión sobre los esencialismos y heterogeneidades en la antropología. *Revista Colombiana de Antropología* 41: 7–41.

Vásquez, María Angélica. 2006. De repúblicas independientes a zonas de despeje: Identidades y estado en los márgenes. In Bolívar, Ingrid (ed.) *Identidades culturales y formación del estado en Colombia: Colonización, naturaleza y cultura*, 119–202. Bogota: Universidad de los Andes.

Verdad Abierta. 2010. El precio que pagó la Anuc por querer la tierra que trabajaban. *Verdad Abierta*, September 1. www.verdadabierta.com/component/content/article/2677.

Yié, Maite. 2015. *Del patrón-Estado, al Estado-patrón. La agencia campesina en las narrativas de la reforma agraria en Nariño*. Bogota: Universidad Nacional de Colombia.

Zamosc, León. 1986. *The Agrarian Question and the Peasant Movement in Colombia*. New York, NY: Cambridge University Press.

7 "When land becomes gold"

Changing political ecology of the commons in a rural–urban frontier

Shubhra Gururani

Introduction

This chapter explores the changing political ecology of the commons that are situated between rural and urban regimes of land and property in India. In a volume on land rights and biodiversity conservation, I focus on urbanizing peripheries because amid extensive urban transformation the social and material relations of land, ecology, property, community, and place are undergoing significant reconfiguration. It is estimated that by 2050 there will be more people living globally in urban areas than in rural ones and close to 90 per cent of the increase will be concentrated in Asia and Africa, continents that are predominantly agrarian today.[1] In this unprecedented socio-spatial change, as vast stretches of agrarian hinterlands are being incorporated into the urban landscape, agricultural fields are turning into housing enclaves, lakes are drying up, and forests are relentlessly being cut down to make room for the city yet to come.[2] The frantic pace of urban expansion amidst regimes of flexible planning[3] and fragmented governmental oversight has resulted in, as many have noted, serious ecological destruction and raised alarm about the ecological stability of such urbanizing terrains.[4] In response to widespread environmental loss, members of civil society as well as state authorities have come forward in different arenas to redress environmental loss and undertake ecological restoration and conservation projects.

In such a scenario, the chapter explores the contours of urban conservation projects as they take shape in urban India and describes the case of biodiversity conservation in the Aravali Hills in the new city of Gurgaon, located on the southwestern edge of New Delhi. Conservation, as Tania Li (2008) has argued, is inherently contradictory as it brings forth competing understandings and relations of nature/land. I would argue that conservation is particularly fraught in urbanizing peripheries that are caught up in rapid conversion of land and are typically characterized by multilayered, heterogeneous, and unclear regimes of property rights, sharp divisions of class, conflicting claims and stakes, and unequal access to basic social services and infrastructure. Increasingly, the middle classes have come forward as key stewards of the urban environment and mobilized their social and political networks, drawn on transnational discourses of environmentalism, cultivated a sense of belonging in nature, filed public-interest litigation, and contested ecological damage.[5] The middle classes constitute, as Sundaresan (2011) argues, a new environmental community that plays an important part in the evolving configurations of urban environmentalisms. In this political-economic moment, as efforts are made to restore local ecologies and contest the long reach of capitalist urbanization, the critical question is not whether to protect local ecologies in places where the boundaries of the village and the city jostle with each other, where cattle herders, tractors, villages, and villagers stand as persistent reminders of an agrarian other, where there are tensions between the villagers and the middle classes and between the villagers and the migrants; the question is *how* to save ecologies and how to reconcile competing interests and visions of land/nature, how to make middle-class environmentalism more inclusive, and how to collectively carve out a just and sustainable urban future. The challenge of urban environmentalism then, as Maringanti (2011) notes, is how to develop an ecological praxis that "assembles actors who can construct new communities based on principles of collaboration and sharing that are at once aware of the inherited inequities and how the old inequities are incorporated into new dispensation of unequal power", and to do so in a socially just and inclusive manner (69). There are no easy prototypes available for such an environmentalism and yet, as we devise strategies to halt reckless environmental destruction and craft new urban commons and communities, it is vital that we do not treat land/nature/ecology as an abstract entity that can be saved from the society in which it is embedded, but instead view ecologies as a composite that are assembled through social relations of power and knowledge. There are only social ecologies that are historically produced and hence, in order to save ecologies, it is urgent that we also strive for equitable and inclusive social relations, acknowledge multiple senses of belonging, sustain diverse forms of livelihoods, and aspire for ecologies that are both biologically and socially diverse and fair.

In the face of serious ecological threats, the goal of the chapter is neither to celebrate a romanticized notion of the commons, simply defending the agro-pastoralists who continue to live in many villages near the park, nor is it to undermine or challenge the efforts of environmental advocates who have come forward to create the park. The making of an urban public biodiversity park in the middle of a land frenzy is a remarkable feat, a bold instance of biodiversity conservation that does not involve coercive displacement at the hands of large corporate or state actors. In many ways, it is an exemplary community-based mobilization and intervention that has worked to check ecologically destructive urbanization and development. Rather, in the context where environmentalism has increasingly become "middle-class" (Mawdsley 2004), "ambient" (Hall, Hirsch, and Li 2011), or "bourgeois" (Baviskar 2003), and a governmental regime (Goldman 2001), the chapter, in thinking with urban environmentalists, shares the predicament of conservation and, in the hope of developing critical ecological praxis, explores how and why projects of conservation on the ground that are well-intentioned and are aimed at restoring local ecologies and serving the larger good generate unintended consequences and get caught up in the *double edge of exclusions*.

I draw from Hall, Hirsch, and Li's (2011) framework of "powers of exclusion". In their book of the same name, *Powers of Exclusion*, they evaluate the changes in rural land relations in Southeast Asia and describe diverse and multi-scalar forms of exclusion (2011). They start with an important observation that "all land use and access requires exclusion of some kind" (4). But exclusion for them "is not a random process, nor does it occur on a level playing field. It is structured by power relations" (4). In adopting a broad understanding of exclusion, they go beyond defining exclusion as the absence or presence of property rights, and instead they show how exclusion takes place through processes of regulation, force, the market, and legitimation (4). All four mechanisms are not always in play but in different contexts they interact with each other and result in exclusions from land. In the case of conservation, they point out that exclusion is increasingly ambient and it has a *double edge*, that is, it does not take place through force, yet it produces exclusions. According to them, exclusion's double edge refers to "the various kinds of exclusivity that different actors want generally bring with them not just the desired positive effects but also a series of other effects that are much less welcome" (8). This double edge "creates both security and insecurity" for different members who are involved in conservation and it subtly, or not, shapes the charged politics of land and conservation (7). The case of the park presented here, as I describe below, also discursively entails exclusion's double edge. Even though the case of the park is a relatively small example, it nonetheless offers an opportunity to explore how projects of urban greening unfold on the ground, how everyday practices and discourses of land, environmentalism, urban propriety, class, and caste relations intersect with each other, and how the politics of difference and "ambient exclusions" contour the social geography of a place that straddles the rural–urban divide (Hall, Hirsch, and Li 2011).

Situating Gurgaon

Until the early 1990s, Gurgaon was a cluster of agro-pastoral settlements and was synonymous with agriculture, farmhouses, and later the Maruti car factory. It was a faraway place, the rural "other" through which the urban and urbane megapolis of New Delhi attempted to define and delineate itself. But, starting in the mid-1980s, Gurgaon's social and material landscape began to change. India embraced economic liberalization and adopted urbanization as one of its key strategies to bolster economic growth and attract corporate investment. In 1985, the Ministry of Housing and Urban Affairs passed the National Capital Region Planning Board Act and the territory of the national capital was extended from 42.7 square kilometres to 1,484 square kilometres to create a National Capital Region, incorporating Gurgaon in its fold. The Act's main goal was to make room for corporate head offices, business processing zones, factories, and housing enclaves for New Delhi's growing numbers. To this end, large parcels of agro-pastoral land were acquired and many land related laws were modified to allow private investors, corporate financiers, and developers to enter urban land markets and creatively turn land into an asset. The complex process of assetization of agrarian land in the urban peripheries all over India resulted in an unprecedented land frenzy and real estate speculation that Michael Goldman (2011) in the case of Bangalore has described as *speculative urbanism*.

While the peripheries of all megacities underwent rapid de-agrarianization in the 1980s and 1990s, Gurgaon became one of the fastest growing cities in India. Its population has increased by 73 per cent since 1991 to over two million residents. The built-up area has increased almost eight times since 1981, while the area under agriculture has decreased from 80 per cent to 26 per cent of the total area.[6] Gurgaon now has dozens of shopping malls, golf courses, and countless housing enclaves that dot its landscape. Owing to its proximity to the international airport, it has also become a desired destination of several multinational companies including Google, HSBC, Nokia, Intel, and many more.

As land was hastily pulled out of agriculture and forests were cut down in this land rush, very little effort was made by developers and urban authorities to follow environmental policies of creating green belts or natural conservation zones (NCZ). Even though in draft plans and master plans there are provisions for creating green areas/belts, and green patches and strips are duly demarcated in the plans, on the ground it is a different story. Mr DR,[7] a retired planner from the Town and Country Planning Office (TCPO), said:

> The green belt is an intention, that is, what we aim to create as planners but on the ground, it unfolds along different intentions. If someone decides to build a highway through it, they will just apply for a CLU (change of land use), talk to the relevant authorities, and it will be done. In that sense, they are not binding, even though they should be, there always are ways to work around them.
>
> (Mr DR, personal communication, February 2017)

Hardly any effort has been made in Gurgaon to protect local ecological sites like sacred groves, water sources, or forests. In the last 10 years, tree cover has receded to less than 2 per cent of the total area; it is reported that, in 2016 alone, more than 8,000 trees were felled for construction purposes with the Forest Department's permission.[8] According to Vivek Kamboj from Hariyali, an environmental NGO, in 2016 an additional "6,600 trees were axed in the name of development of various residential and commercial projects in old and new sectors of the city".[9] In fact, the environmentalists fear that recent policy interventions will result in the state of Haryana losing 70 per cent of its green cover in the next decade. Not only have forests receded, but most of Gurgaon's 300 small ponds, drains, and lakes have dried up, or filled with construction debris and garbage, or sold to private developers for construction purposes. Most recently, the Ghata Lake near Ghata village, which was one of the largest bodies of water in Gurgaon, covering almost 370 acres of land, has been reduced to just about two acres. Ironically, while the natural lakes have been filled up, the TCPO is building a large artificial lake to deal with the huge overflow of rainwater from a drain that comes from Ghata village. The deplorable state of Gurgaon's environment and infrastructure is widely known and headlines like "Gurugram, country's most polluted city again",[10] "Gurgaon is an example of how not to urbanise India",[11] and "Gurgaon is dying a slow death due to urbanization"[12] have become routine.

In response to deteriorating environmental conditions, in 2009–10, when Gurgaon's first Municipal Corporation (MCG) was formed, a consortium of civil society members, represented by the group I Am Gurgaon, mobilized against further construction and ecological destruction and approached the MCG to create a biodiversity park. At that moment, close to 40 villages were municipalized and brought under the MCG's fold. Even as the villages were administratively amalgamated, no clear plan was developed to deal with the village commons and even at the time of writing, in 2017, years after the Municipal Corporation was formed, it is still unclear as to what is planned for some of the former village commons. In this conjuncture of administrative realignment, there was a legitimate concern among the city's middle-class residents that Haryana Urban Development Authority may encroach upon or acquire villages' commons for yet another residential or commercial project, and the members of I Am Gurgaon took matters into their own hands. Fortuitously, the first commissioner of Gurgaon's Municipal Corporation, Mr R. S. Khullar, was environmentally inclined and when I Am Gurgaon approached him in 2010, he eagerly supported the idea of creating a park in the former village commons of Nathupur. The 576 acres of land, on the main road and facing the metro station, was designated by the MCG as the Aravali Biodiversity Park.

Several environmentalists, naturalists, schoolchildren, and civil society members joined hands and initiated the painstaking task of making the idea of a biodiversity ark a possibility. Like the rest of Gurgaon, the land set aside for the park is part of the red rocky 600 kilometres mountainous range of the Aravali Hills, which extend from the southern tip of New Delhi through Haryana to Rajasthan. It is undulating and full of scrub and bushes; long periods of stone quarrying and mining have left this patch of land barren, with almost no soil cover. The park's advocates and their supporters devoted their time and money to convert the arid terrain into a park and to create space for cultural events, nature walks, jogging, and birding.[13] Vijay Dhasmana, a well-known naturalist, was brought on board as a consultant and he, along with others, set about to identify and collect native species of trees to plant in the park and eliminate the invasive species vilayati kikar (*Prosopis juliflora*).[14] I Am Gurgaon launched the "Million Tree Drive" in 2011 and close to 50,000 tree saplings were carefully chosen to ensure that they were ecologically suitable for an arid ecology. In just a few years, the former commons has been transformed into a biodiversity park and is now a much-appreciated open and green venue where residents come regularly for walks, jogging, birding, and other community events. One park supporter referred to the park as the "lung of the city" and said that

> the Park is the best place in Gurgaon, we need more of these. It is not only a charger for the environment, but for all us. It has built a community of nature lovers who put in their time and effort to create this paradise. If it were not for the park, the whole place would have been built up, another shopping mall would have come up or the villagers would have encroached it.
>
> (TK, personal communication, February 2012)

In a place where land is being acquired in all possible ways and converted into real estate, the park's guardians have so far ensured that private developers and land mafia do not appropriate the land, although it is not entirely clear what will happen to it in the future.

The urban land question

The Park is undoubtedly an incredible achievement and presents a powerful example of community efforts. But, like all projects of land conversion and conservation, Park-making is also double edged and must be situated in contested histories of land and livelihood, and take note of the sedimented practices and social relations of land use. In Gurgaon, even though the years of urban transformation have largely dismantled social relations of land, community, and commons, the villages have not disappeared. The agrarian-pastoral history and everyday practices of land and livelihood are a critical part of Gurgaon's social, political, and economic fabric and cannot be easily overlooked or wished away. In fact, the entrenched relations of caste, kin, village, class, gender, and place inform the ongoing conflicts and contentions over land acquisition, conversion, compensation, and exclusion and have to be engaged with in order to make Gurgaon sustainable.

Peluso and Lund (2011) have argued that the question of land control is of one of the key issues in the twenty-first century, "even though the nature of its importance, how it is struggled over, and the effects of these struggles are largely products of their times and geographic locations" (668). In light of extensive acquisition, conversion, and commercialization of land all over the world, there is a rich and growing body of literature on "land grab" that has focused on biofuels, plantations, or Special Economic Zones, analysed the complex and multiscalar processes of large-scale land acquisition, and examined how different actors like multinational corporations, international organizations, wealthy individuals, and foreign governments, often with the backing of national governments, acquire land.[15] A related set of literature has focused on land grab for creating national parks or biodiversity conservation, bio-carbon sequestration, and the protection of ecosystem services. Fairhead, Leach, and Scoones (2012) call the "appropriation of land and resources for environmental ends" *green grabbing*. According to them, "the transfer of ownership, use rights and control over resources that were once publicly or privately owned—or not even the subject of ownership—from the poor (or everyone including the poor) into the hands of the powerful" constitutes the terms of appropriation or green grabbing

(239). They acknowledge the tensions that lie in conservation projects and argue that, even though the contemporary green grabs tend not to necessarily alienate the residents from their land, they nonetheless work to reconfigure the rules and terms of access, use, and management of resources.

Both of these sets of literature focus mostly on rural land and until recently there was relatively little on the question of land in the urban context. Indeed, parallels can be drawn between land acquisition and conversion in urban and rural areas as they are propelled by similar political-economic forces and sometimes involve the same set of actors. The politics of urban land conversion in India, though, diverges from large-scale acquisition for plantations, biofuels or conservation corridors. Urban land transformation in most cases, unlike "land grabs" or "green grabs", is guided by commercial, residential, and infrastructural demands, involves private developers, state authorities, public–private partnerships, and politicians at different levels, and tends to be geared towards land consolidation. The administrative instruments of master planning, particularly "change of land use" (CLU), are creatively deployed to facilitate land conversion. In the urban peripheries, land is usually converted through the consent of landowners, who are almost always upper castes, sometimes with their participation and sometimes through the instruments of the market, but in most instances the complex process of changing land use is gradual, piecemeal, and smaller in scale than in rural areas and necessitates attention to the more intimate, slow, and subtle processes of exclusion and displacement.

In the case of Gurgaon, starting in the 1990s, land became a scandal and converting agricultural land for non-agrarian purposes a masterful art that involved local- and national-level politicians, private land developers, government officials, local leaders, engineers, planners, contractors, and big and small landholders. Until the 1980s, private developers were not involved in urban development but this changed in the 1980s when the Haryana government became the first state to open its doors to private developers, who, with the backing of the state government, purchased land directly from the farmers and converted it into residential or commercial zones. During this period, land changed hands in all possible ways and involved leaders and politicians at all levels of politics. Journalist Shalini Singh writes that the story of land conversion in Gurgaon is "a story of political alchemy in which farmland turns into gold for all those fortunate enough to acquire acreage and the permission required to undertake commercial development on it".[16] A range of creative local arrangements, including the calculated deployment of master plans, draft plans, CLU, and designating and redesignating of "controlled areas" were used to convert land into gold.[17] In this land rush, it is important to note that, first, even though the general impression among middle-class residents is that all villagers in Gurgaon have made impressive gains from selling their land, it is in fact only the members of the dominant castes – the Jats and the Yadav, and among them those who had relatively larger land titles and were able to negotiate a good price for their land – have done well.[18] The majority of Gujars and villagers from the lower castes who are officially designated as "other backward castes" (OBC), and the *Dalits*, previously known as untouchables or *Harijans*, were smallholders or landless did not avail anything from the property boom. Second, amidst urbanization of agrarian, it is the transformation and the conversion of the commons that has left a lasting impact for these smallholders and lies at the heart of most land conflicts and struggles in urban peripheries and is central to understanding the unfolding social geography of urbanizing frontiers.[19]

The contested commons

The commons is a capacious category that encompasses a wide range of meanings and social relations. Historically and theoretically, the concept of the commons is entangled with that of enclosure, discipline, policing, autonomy, authority, and social reproduction. In the main, the commons can be described as a cooperatively shared terrain of land/water/air that is historically embedded in specific social and ecological contexts and carefully negotiated and collaboratively regulated. Importantly, since commons are communally managed, they are intimately enmeshed with community relations and, like the communities themselves, are also marked by highly charged social-spatial relations of power and authority. They do not connote some traditional or romanticized ideal of homogenous or static space of belonging that harks back to an era of imagined ecological harmony. Instead, both the spaces of community and the commons are dynamic and contested socio-ecological entities that are continually remade through everyday practices of livelihood, labour, and leisure.[20]

In India, the history of the commons and with it of grazing land and lands that came to be designated as "wasteland" is complex and variable. There is not enough space to comprehensively discuss the rich literature on the commons and delineate its precolonial, colonial, and contemporary transfigurations and the wide regional variations that have shaped contemporary practices in the commons,[21] but, suffice to say, during the colonial period the generation of revenue from pastoral land or wasteland informed the long history of contestations over rights and governance of the commons. In post-independence India, the goals of enhancing agricultural productivity and implementing land reform contoured the social and legal geography of the commons. In the contemporary context, it is the extensive conversion of agricultural land and real estate speculation that has once again placed the commons at the forefront of political and legal contestations.

Minoti Chakravarty-Kaul's book *Common Lands and Customary Law* (1996) offers a comprehensive historical analysis of the role of the British in shaping the property rights regimes in colonial Punjab, of which Haryana was part until 1966, and shows how regimes of common lands in New Delhi and its surrounding areas were slowly changed. She notes that there was a great deal of variation, both ecological and social, between different regions of the province, which gave rise to vastly different arrangements through which the villagers regulated and accessed grazing lands and the commons. Despite these variations, two main types of agricultural systems prevailed. Typically, in irrigated parts of the province, there was sedentary agriculture in which private and arable land was held in scattered strips, while the pastoral land or the "waste" was held in common (24–40). In villages that combined arable farming and pastoral activities, which is the case for most villages in Gurgaon,

> there were extensive common lands or *banjar kadim*, held collectively by the *Malikan-deh* or village proprietary body.... The *Malikan deh* had a bundle of rights to these categories of land. Of which the principle ones were: the right to hold and to partition, the right to manage, and the right to use.
>
> (24)

The commons, referred to as the *shamalat deh*, incorporated a diversity of social and material meanings like grazing land (*chargah*), short fallow (*banjar jadid*), long fallow (*banjar kadim*), and uncultivable (*gair mumkin*), all which involved a range of negotiations and agreements between different castes. Both agriculturalists and pastoralists relied on these rights but in many instances pastoralists only had usufruct grazing rights or seasonal rights in hills, forests, and riverine areas, while the *Malikan Deh* had the right to the land and its regulation. But, since it is a dry, mountainous ecological terrain, the Aravalis also fostered relations of mutual dependence between the agriculturalists and pastoralists, where the graziers left their cattle in the field to fertilize and in turn received grain, seeds, or jaggery. That is, over decades of co-existence, even though *Malikan Deh* governed the commons, the commons served as a critical glue that maintained a vibrant system of mutuality, sharing, support, and sustenance of both the village and its ecology.

The British reworked the property rights regimes throughout the nineteenth century. In various land settlements, the colonizers undid the existing relations of land and property and introduced a new grammar of land ownership and governance. In 1871, the Punjab Land Revenue Act was passed, mainly to bring more area under cultivation and augment revenue but it also initiated a series of changes that slowly but surely formalized the collective rights of the village proprietary body, the *Malikan Deh*, in the common lands. It was amended in 1887 and over the decades led to what Chakravarty-Kaul identifies as "the partition and privatization of the remaining commons, thereby altering the patterns of land rights" (87). The fixing and formalizing of legal boundaries around the commons and formalizing of rights of the landowning castes like the Jats and Yadavs have continued since[22] and the changes have left a long legacy that has not only shaped the volatile and highly disputed politics of land acquisition in the present but also systematically marginalized landless castes, tenants, and labourers.

The *Malikan Deh* have subsequently consolidated their class position, especially through the implementation of the Intensive Agricultural Development Program (IADP), a.k.a. the Green Revolution, in the 1960s and 1970s. The

Green Revolution, as is widely noted, was not only ecologically ruinous but also resulted in greater inequalities between small and big farmers. Moreover, it changed the configuration of caste politics in Haryana; the landowning caste of Jats emerged as the new political elites and they have gradually come to play a significant role in the evolving land market and speculation (Jodhka n.d.). In Gurgaon, the dominant castes are Yadavs and Jats, and they have consolidated their political standing over time and through village council bodies like the *Panchayat*, or super Panchayats called *Khap* Panchayats, have also come to control the commons. In some instances, the dominant castes have converted common lands for agricultural purposes; they have even sold or auctioned the commons and divided up the money among themselves, and in yet other cases a handful of villagers have entered into surreptitious deals with developers. What is relevant for our discussion here is that the political ecology of the commons is entangled in a multilayered web of tenurial and usufruct arrangements that undergirds the volatile politics of land conversion and acquisition. Most of these arrangements are historically negotiated between different caste groups, sometimes they are seasonal, and in other instances they are worked out through complex regimes of labour and exchange. For example, in one village there may be multiple relations of property that are at play and they contour the charged social-spatial relations of the commons as well as the village. In the context of extended urbanization, the competing claims on the commons have posed a serious challenge as they have confounded the logic of private property and thwarted easy assetization. Today, the majority of legal disputes in urban peripheries take place over the commons, its encroachment, and compensation, and it would not be a stretch to say that the struggle and conflict over the commons is the defining feature of twenty-first-century land conflicts and conversion in the Global South.

The land on which the park sits, even though it is generally described as barren (*banjar*) or empty, was neither empty nor a wasteland. Until 2010, it belonged to the Nathupur village and was governed by the village council, which was constituted of the *Malikan Deh* from mostly the Yadav caste, but also some Gujar families who had come to own land since independence. In addition to big and small landowners, there are 13 other OBCs as well as Dalits who accessed the area prior to its transformation into a park. Different castes and landholders had a range of agreements, some of them seasonal, about grazing, pasturage, fodder, stones and rocks, cultivation, and so on. There are no archives of these rules of use and access. The former village chief, in response to my question about the commons, said:

> this is a very old story, from the time of our forefathers, I don't remember all the details but I know one thing, some people had rights [*haq*] in it, some have captured it [*kabza*], and while others have stolen [*chori*] from the *shamalat*. Earlier no one cared that much but now land has become gold and there is a lot of tension [around it].
>
> (MS, Gujjar, personal communication, April 2015)

When I asked Mr MS, a 65-year-old retired army sergeant, about the park in February 2012, he said,

> The *Nigam* [MCG] has taken it; they have put some big rocks around the area. I don't really know what they are doing there now. It used to be mostly shrubs and small trees for the cattle, there was a small *jhor* [pond] and plenty of slate and rocks, which the *kumhar* [potter] families mined and sold by the roadside. Women collected fuel wood, or different grasses for fodder after the rains. If we had good rains, we sometimes planted *jaun*, *bajra*, *khadka*, and other such grains. *Kumhars* did not keep cattle but they dug rocks and earth in the *shamalat*.... The *Lohars* also dug rocks, they also did not keep cattle but they worked with Malikan. There was plenty for all us. There were many wild animals and villagers from Aya Nagar, Chakkarpur, and Sikandarpur, sometimes even as far as Jharsa, came here to graze their animals. But, then Ambience Mall bought some of the *shamalat patti* but the money was not shared nor were the claims of the many *gair marusi* (occupants) entertained. Now, we all are fighting court cases. I have three cases in the court right now over that land.[23]

The *shamalat* land was central to all villagers but, like all commons, it was particularly important for smallholders and landless families from the lower castes who constituted almost one-third of the village and relied on the *shamalat* for maintaining their meagre incomes and supplementing their livelihoods. Until recently, some landless potter families kept donkeys and, with the help of small-scale stone contractors, sold rocks and stones and sometimes pottery. Some others built temporary housing structures in the *shamalat* as there was no more room in the village to accommodate the growing population, but the *shamalat* was mostly a space for cattle pasture, storing fodder, or drying cow-dung cakes. Even though lower castes rarely participated in the village council, their usufruct rights were in place. KR, a potter, said:

> We could get the stones and the soil from the *chargah* and made pottery and sold it. My mother and grandmother helped the Yadav families in collecting fodder and the family was given grain in exchange for their labour. Now we can't go there.

Another young man joined in and said:

> They don't want us to keep cattle, or collect stones, they tell us it is the MCG land but what should we do, there are no jobs, the companies don't hire us, we have no land, no cattle, we also have to fill our bellies somehow.
>
> (KR, personal communication, February 2012)

It is in this context of deep mistrust and marginalization that the landless villagers are highly sceptical of any land conversion. One young man, KK, from the potter caste, wryly muttered:

> For us there is no difference between cyber park or bio park, we just know that the land is gone, CLU done, and we have nothing left for us. Some will gain from it, but for us it means more hardship.
>
> (KK, personal communication, February 2012)

Unintended consequences: ambient exclusions

There are ambient tensions between the villages and what the villagers generically call the "DLF" or *sectaran* (planned sectors). The majority of Gurgaon's current population is constituted of middle- and upper-class professionals who have moved into the city over the last two to three decades and live in the *sectaran*. The villagers, depending on their caste and landholdings, have more or less accepted the transition and bought into the prevailing hegemony of urban modernity and economic growth, but they are also acutely aware of the divide that separates the rural from the urban, working classes from the middle classes, and the villagers from the DLF. They complain that they are treated with mistrust in the malls and even disallowed entry, they are not given jobs in the factories, their children are not given admission to private schools, and so on. Typically, middle- and upper-class residents keep their distance from the villages, even though the domestic servants, maids, security guards, and drivers who work in their homes live in the villages.[24] Many new Gurgaon residents have never entered a village and are even unaware of the names of the villages next to their housing complexes. In the general parlance, it is said that the villagers have made a lot of money from selling land and from rental incomes, they are too well off to work, and they are the ones who are behind all of the law-breaking. The DLF residents are quite vocal about their frustration, and one park supporter, as he walked me through the park, said:

> The Park could be even better if we could somehow keep these villagers and their cattle out. They could care less about the park, they just drink and play cards the whole day. These Gujjars are thieves, they do not care what happens to the land, they just know how to steal. They will destroy everything. I have no patience for them.
>
> (JK, personal communication, August 2014)

The double edge of exclusions play out in this context of persistent inequalities and prevailing frictions. The everyday practices of park-making assemble a community of park lovers, mostly from the *sectaran*, and restore the local ecology, but they also materially and symbolically resignify the meanings and social relations of land and nature. These public rituals of urban conservation, caring, and sharing are social-spatial practices that contour the new geographies of land, nature, claim, responsibility, and knowledge and describe what Blomley (2012), in the context of early modern England, has called "disentanglement". According to him, disentangling "is not only a process whereby certain connections, relations and associations are cut. It also, of necessity, entails a process of re-entanglement.... To disentangle requires differently arranged entanglements" (19). He was writing about modern survey techniques and how they reperform property, but in the contemporary context of extensive land conversion and reconfiguration of property regimes, practices in/of urban conservation also disentangle land and property from their local social relations of obligations and reciprocity, and reformat them through different versions of property that belong in the registers of the state, public interest, and eventually commensurate with the familiar logics of private property.

Given the reigning context of speculative urbanism, the concept and practice of private property and ownership have become increasingly normative, and the spaces of the commons are seen as incommensurate and even as anachronistic reminders of an agrarian/rural/"traditional" past. In Western liberal democracies like Canada, Nick Blomley (2004) has argued that property is not only imagined as private property, "with solitary owner exercising exclusionary rights over bounded space" (xiv), but private property is also considered to be positive to the extent that it "fosters valued behaviors, including responsible citizenship, political participation, and economic entrepreneurship" (xv). The commons, on the other hand, are viewed as spaces of "violence and danger" and often associated with persons who are somehow deemed inappropriate to make claims of entitlement (quoted in Blomley 2007, 619). Not only are the commons considered vague and ambiguous spaces with unclear regimes of property, the property that does not *look like* private property is also considered to be marginal, dysfunctional, and vestigial and is treated with ambivalence or suspicion and even hostility. In a place like Gurgaon, where a flood of real estate advertisements and billboards feed the public imagination with vistas of green rolling hills and manicured golf courses, where greenness has become conflated with goodness and cosmopolitanism, the everyday practices of leisure and nature-appreciation work to "clarify" the ambiguity of the commons and, by invoking copious versions of "nature", subtly and slowly disentangle land from its agrarian dynamics and locate it in new registers of value that no longer rest in the realm of agrarian relations, or as a means of livelihood (Mozingo 2011). The park then inadvertently redefines an agrarian land and indexes a critical shift in which the political ecology of common property and agro-pastoral lives are overwritten by certitude of environmental sustainability, moral clarity, state property, and urban propriety.

Relatedly, Kelly (2011) and Paudel (2016) in different contexts have argued that the projects of conservation proliferate despite several critiques because they "create and reproduce the means of capitalist production and, through neoliberal conservation practices, are able to become capital themselves in the form of environmental services, spectacles, and genetic storehouses" (Kelly 2011, 684).[25] They suggest that conservation should be analysed through the concept of primitive accumulation as it can help capture the granular trajectories of accumulation. Primitive accumulation, in theory, entails separating direct producers from their land and enclosing and privatizing the commons and converting them to private property. Public parks, national parks, or sanctuaries are not privately owned but are managed by the state and hence by definition are public property aimed to serve the public good. They do not expropriate resources for private or corporate gain, as is the case with plantations, and in fact, because they pull land out of market relations, they have been described as the "ultimate noncommodity" (Li 2008). But conservation territories nevertheless create the conditions for capital accumulation and can be described as *accumulation by other means*. That is, not accumulation by dispossession but the discourses and rituals of safety, security, expertise, and community facilitate accumulation by reforming and stabilizing the terrain of common property (and danger) and gradually aligning it with the logic of property titles and cleaner boundaries so that it begins to resemble private property. This is not to suggest that the park is a private park, but affective everyday practices like bird watching, tree planting, nature walks, or jogging are an "enactment of property" that create a sense of a quasi-private space for the middle classes. To be clear, the park is not intended to improve the value of local property and it does not directly or immediately contribute to improving the value of property, but it nevertheless creates a context and a replicable model in which certain modes of practices, valuations of land and nature, and importantly notions of property, ownership, and propriety become commonsensical and discursively cultivate the conditions of capitalist accumulation. It is important to note that such modes of indirect accumulation do not replace practices of primitive accumulation or accumulation by dispossession but instead the new regimes of accumulation by other means describe how over time a diverse group of private organizations, individuals, developers, and propertied villagers may benefit from park-making.

It is important to mention that there is no physical exclusion, or eviction, or displacement from the park. As one park supporter, KP, said,

> The Park is open to all. We have nature walks and people from all over the city come but the villagers don't care about the environment, they have no interest in such things. Sometimes, a few people show up. We have put up fences and security guards to stop the cattle, we don't want cows and goats. They can destroy the entire place but otherwise it is open to all.
>
> (KP, personal communication, February 11, 2017)

But, as Hall, Hirsch, and Li (2011) have argued, conservation-inspired initiatives like these are well-intentioned and rest on the goal of achieving common good, but by upholding a moral righteousness they can produce "ambient exclusions" that are not accomplished by force, displacement, or dispossession but that generate an ambient context in which the local villagers feel "out of place", their ways of life are undermined, or their knowledge practices are deemed to be unworthy or rudimentary (60). In a different context, Mollett (2014) has argued that exclusion or displacement does not always involve physical movement but it can be much subtler and can take the "form of constrains on livelihoods and cultural practices and as a result 'displaces futures,' what she describes as 'displacement in place'" (30). Along similar lines, transforming a commons into a park can also inscribe a social geography of class and caste-based exclusion, in which association with the rural and agrarian are devalued and deemed to be out of place.

Engaging contradictions: limits and possibilities

In a context where the additional chief secretary (forest) had recently sanctioned the city's Forest Department to fell trees on a 52-acre plot owned by a real estate firm and located in the Faridabad Aravali,[26] where the Department of Town and Country Planning is resisting declaring the Aravali forests an NCZ and has been trying to dilute the 0.5 per cent construction cap in NCZ areas through the usual strategy of inserting an exception clause, and where recently, in June 2017, Bharti Airtel real estate company cut down 54 acres of Aravali forest to make room for urban projects,[27] it is critical and urgent to support the interventions and actions of the environmentalists who raise their voices against serious environmental damage and undertake conservation projects. To stand up to the powerful nexus of private land developers, investors, politicians, and state authorities is a formidable task and describes the importance of mobilizing at different levels to counter the indomitable forces behind ecological destruction. Yet, as we do so, it is also critical to be aware of the unintended consequences and inherent contradictions that may inform projects of social-environmental improvement. It is therefore critical to revisit and revise familiar practices and discourses of environmental improvement that have over time become standardized and even hegemonic and reflect on the expert discourses and practices, our own subject positions, and the dynamics of class and place that can inscribe a social geography of ambient exclusions. In other words, as the naturalist Dhasmana (2016) notes, we have to learn "to engage with the community in some way" and create the "right kind of engagement", "a strong sense of belonging", and consider ecologies as intimately intertwined with social relations of power and authority. It is certainly not easy to forge such collective projects in which different communities, with their competing standpoints, aspirations, knowledges, and expertise, come together, work together, and collaborate, yet if our attempts to save the ecology and pursue biodiversity conservation are to succeed, we will also have to invent new terrains of urban commons as well as communities in which villagers, migrants, and urban elites can collectively defend the political ecology of the commons. Commons are neither given nor stable entities; they must be worked at, negotiated, and defended as well as practices of commonning invented in order to widen the horizons of our urban communities and commons. In this political-economic conjuncture, it is urgent to move away from the modernist ontology of conservation that inevitably poses nature against humans, pastoralists against farmers, experts against lay people, and state versus communities. Instead, in countries like India, it is imperative to explore the possibilities of reconciling differences and inventing new conservation practices and spaces that acknowledge the centrality of agrarian in making the urban possible.

In thinking about the future of our cities, Harvey (2008) has argued that

> the question of what kind of city we want cannot be divorced from that of what kind of social ties, relationship to nature, lifestyles, technologies and aesthetic values we desire. The right to the city is far more than the individual liberty to access urban resources: it is a right to change ourselves by changing the city. It is, moreover, a common rather than an individual right since this transformation inevitably depends upon the exercise of a collective power to reshape the processes of urbanization.
>
> (23)

I believe this is where the hope and possibilities for our collective ethics and actions for a new commons lies as we grapple with India's urban turn.

Acknowledgements

The earlier versions of the paper were presented in the "Environment of India Conference," University of Michigan, Ann Arbor; Department of Anthropology and Asian Studies Institute, University of Buffalo; International Conference on Blue- Green Boundaries in a Suburbanizing World. FACE-UFMG, Belo Horizonte; Canadian Anthropology Association Meeting (CASCA); American Anthropological Association Meetings, the Annual South Asia Conference; the Royal Geographical Society Conference, London, and at the Grabbing Green conference, University of Toronto. I am grateful to all the conference participants and discussants for their comments and feedback. The research for the paper was partially funded by the SSHRC-MCRI project on "Global Suburbanisms: Governance, Land, and Infrastructure in the 21st Century." I would like to especially thank Sharlene Mollette, Harsh Singh Lohit, Anders Sandberg, and students in my graduate seminar, 'Matters of Nature' 2016 for their very helpful comments and suggestions that helped clarify the argument of the paper.

Notes

1 See "World Urbanization Prospects 2014" (www.un.org/en/development/desa/news/population/world-urbanization-prospects-2014.html).
2 See Simone (2004).
3 See Gururani (2013).
4 See Rademacher and Sivaramakrishnan (2013).
5 See Mawdsley (2004).
6 See Gupta and Nangia (2005) and Narain and Vij (2016).
7 To maintain anonymity, I use pseudonyms for all the women and men whom I cite.
8 See "Gurgaon Lost Five Times More Trees This Year" (www.hindustantimes.com/gurgaon/gurgaon-lost-five-times-more-trees-this-year/story-w06PZms7OxeyMWhCUKgn5H.html).
9 See "Realty Projects to Deplete 15% Gurgaon Forest Cover" (http://realty.economictimes.indiatimes.com/news/industry/realty-projects-to-deplete-15-gurgaon-forest-cover/50157688).

10 See "Gurugram Country's Most Polluted City Again" (http://timesofindia.indiatimes.com/city/gurgaon/gurugram-countrys-most-polluted-city-again/articleshow/57135691.cms).

11 See "Gurgaon Is an Example of How Not to Urbanise India" (www.hindustantimes.com/columns/gurgaon-is-an-example-of-how-not-to-urbanise-india/story-KqAcFBWI8jp62fCvKTEPwK.html).

12 See "Over 9,000 Trees Grounded for Urbanization in Gurgaon, Haryana Could Soon go Forest-Less" (www.planetcustodian.com/2017/02/27/9185/over-9000-trees-grounded-for-urbanization-in-gurgaon-haryana-could-soon-go-forest-less.html).

13 In order to make the park a self-funding project and without relying on government funds, corporate donors like KPMG and Coca-Cola as well as individuals have lent their support for the creation of an amphitheatre, a nursery, and walkways. Generating funds through cultural events held in these locales could then be used towards ecological restoration in the park.

14 See "A Forest Reclaimed" (www.thehindu.com/news/cities/Delhi/a-forest-reclaimed/article5029582.ece).

15 Hall, Hirsch, and Li (2011); Levien (2012); Li (2008); Peluso and Lund (2011); Mollett (2014).

16 See "Builder Profits Soar as Master Plans Proliferate in Gurgaon" (www.thehindu.com/news/national/builder-profits-soar-as-master-plans-proliferate-in-gurgaon/article4753735.ece).

17 Most recently, the 2021 Master Plan introduced 58 new sectors and increased the area under its jurisdiction from 150 sq kms to 300 sq kms; the 2025 Master Plan further added more urban sectors. See Gururani (2013) for a discussion on planning. See Sampat (2013) on land acquisition.

18 Jats and Yadavs are primarily agriculturalists, while Gujjars are agro-pastoral.

19 See Narain and Vij (2016), Massimo (2010), Gidwani and Baviskar (2011) and Linebaugh (2008).

20 See Ostrom (1999) and McCay (2002).

21 See Brara (2006) and Chakravarty-Kaul (1996).

22 See "Haryana Govt to Review Two More Acts for Amendment" (www.dailypioneer.com/STATE-EDITIONS/chandigarh/haryana-govt-to-review-two-more-acts-for-amendment.html).

23 See "Gram Panchayat Nathupur vs Sarupa and Others on 20 March 2009" (https://indiankanoon.org/doc/61463453/).

24 Almost all of these workers are migrants from Jharkhand, Orissa, Bengal, and Bihar and rent accommodation in the villages. The local men and women from the villages do not work in middle-class households.

25 Also see Brockington, Duffy, and Igoe (2008) and Fairhead and Leach (1996).

26 See "Green Tribunal Steps in to Protect Aravalis" (http://timesofindia.indiatimes.com/city/gurgaon/green-tribunal-steps-in-to-protect-aravalis/articleshow/59243280.cms).

27 See "Gurgaon Lost Five Times More Trees This Year" (www.hindustantimes.com/gurgaon/gurgaon-lost-five-times-more-trees-this-year/story-w06PZms7OxeyMWhCUKgn5H.html).

References

Baviskar, Amita. 2003. "Between Violence and Desire: Space, Power, and Identity in the Making of Metropolitan Delhi". *International Social Science Journal* 55(175): 89–98.

Blomley, Nicholas. 2004. "Un-real Estate: Proprietary Space and Public Gardening". *Antipode* 36(4): 614–641.

Blomley, Nicholas. 2007. "Making Private Property: Enclosure, Common Right and the Work of Hedges". *Rural History* 18(1): 1–21.

Blomley, Nicholas. 2012. "Disentangling Property, Making Space". In *Performativity, Politics, and the Production of Social Space*, edited by Michael R. Glass and Reuben Rose-Redwood, 1–43. New York, NY: Routledge. www.academia.edu/2258882/Blomley_N_Disentangling_property_making_space._Per.

Brara, Rita. 2006. *Shifting Landscapes: The Making and Remaking of Village Commons in India*. Delhi: Oxford University Press.

Brockington, Dan, Rose Duffy, and Jim Igoe. 2008. *Nature Unbound: Conservation, Capitalism and the Future of Protected Areas*. London: Earthscan.

Chakravarty-Kaul, Minoti. 1996. *Common Land and Customary Law: Institutional Change in North India over the Past Two Centuries*. Delhi: Oxford University Press.

Dhasmana, Vijay. 2016. "Healing Touch: Aravali Biodiversity Park, Gurgaon". *Landscape Restoration* 48.

De Angelis, Massimo. 2010. "The Production of Commons and the 'Explosion' of the Middle Class". *Antipode* 42(4): 954–977.

Fairhead, James and Melissa Leach. 1996. *Misreading the African Landscape: Society and Ecology in a Forest–Savanna Mosaic*. Cambridge: Cambridge University Press.

Fairhead, James, Melissa Leach, and Ian Scoones. 2012. "Green Grabbing: A New Appropriation of Nature?" *Journal of Peasant Studies* 39(2): 237–261.

Gidwani, Vinay and Amita Baviskar. 2011. "Urban Commons". *Economic and Political Weekly* 46(50): 42–43.

Goldman, Michael. 2001. "Constructing an Environmental State: Eco-governmentality and Other Transnational Practices of a 'Green' World Bank". *Social Problems* 48(4): 499–523.

Goldman, Michael. 2011. "Speculative Urbanism and the Making of the Next World City". *International Journal of Urban and Regional Research* 35(3): 555–581.

Gupta, R. and S. Nangia. 2005. "Population Explosion and Land Use Changes in Gurgaon City, a Satellite of Delhi". Paper presented at the International Union for the Scientific Study of Population XXV International Population Conference, Paris, France, 18–23 July.

Gururani, S. 2013. "Flexible Planning: The Making of India's 'Millennium city,' Gurgaon". In *Ecologies of Urbanism in India: Metropolitan Civility and Sustainability*, edited by A. Rademacher and K. Sivaramakrishnan, 119–143. Hong Kong: Hong Kong University Press.

Hall, Derek, Philip Hirsch, and Tania Li. 2011. *Powers of Exclusion. Land Dilemmas in Southeast Asia*. Singapore: National University of Singapore.

Harvey, David. 2008. "The Right to the City". *New Left Review* 53: 23–40.

Jodhka, S. S. (n.d.). "Caste and Power in the Lands of Agriculture: Revisiting Rural North-West India". Unpublished manuscript. http://sas-space.sas.ac.uk/5649/1/AHRC_1_Jodhka_Northwest_Caste_and_Rural_Power.Shimla.pdf.

Kelly, Alice. B. 2011. "Conservation Practice as Primitive Accumulation". *Journal of Peasant Studies* 38(4): 683–701.

Levien, Michael. 2012. "The Land Question: Special Economic Zones and the Political Economy of Dispossession in India". *The Journal of Peasant Studies* 39(3–4): 933–969.

Li, Tania M. 2008. "Contested Commodifications: Struggles over Nature in a National Park". In *Taking South East Asia to Market: Commodities, Nature and People in the Neoliberal Age*, edited by J. Nevins and N. L. Peluso, 124–139. Ithaca, NY: Cornell University Press.

Linebaugh, Peter. 2008. *The Magna Carta Manifesto: Liberties and Commons for All*. Berkeley and Los Angeles, CA: University of California Press.

Maringanti, Anant. 2011. "No Estoppel: Claiming Right to the City via the Commons". *Economic and Political Weekly* 46(50): 64–70.

Mawdsley, Emma. 2004. "India's Middle Classes and the Environment". *Development and Change* 35(1): 79–103.

McCay, Bonnie. J. 2002. "Emergence of Institutions for the Commons: Contexts, Situations, and Events". In *The Drama of the Commons*, edited by E. Ostrom, T. Dietz, N. Dolsk, P. C. Stern, S. Stonich, and E. U. Weber, 361–402. Washington, DC: The National Academies Press. https://doi.org/10.17226/10287.

Mollett, Sharlene. 2014. "A Modern Paradise: Garifuna Land, Labor, and Displacement-in-Place". *Latin American Perspectives* 41(6): 27–45.

Mozingo, Louise A. 2011. *Pastoral Capitalism: A History of Suburban Corporate Landscapes*. Boston, MA: MIT Press.

Narain, Vishal and Sumit Vij. 2016. "Where Have All the Commons Gone?" *Geoforum* 68: 21–24.

Ostrom, Elinor. 1999. *Governing the Commons: The Evolution of Institutions for Collective Action*. Cambridge: Cambridge University Press.

Paudel, Dinesh. 2016. "Re-inventing the Commons: Community Forestry as Accumulation without Dispossession in Nepal". *The Journal of Peasant Studies* 43(5): 989–1009.

Peluso, Nancy L. and Christian Lund. 2011. "New Frontiers of Land Control: Introduction". *Journal of Peasant Studies* 38(4): 667–681.

Rademacher, A. and K. Sivaramakrishnan. 2013. *Ecologies of Urbanism in India: Metropolitan Civility and Sustainability*. Hong Kong: Hong Kong University Press.

Sampat, Preeti. 2013. "Limits to Absolute Power: Eminent Domain and the Right to Land in India". *Economic and Political Weekly* 48(19): 40–52.

Simone, Abdou Malique. 2004. *For the City yet to Come: Changing African Life in Four Cities*. Durham, NC: Duke University Press.

Sundaresan, Jayraj. 2011. "Planning as Commoning: Transformation of a Bangalore lake". *Economic and Political Weekly* 46(50): 71–79.

Part III

Indigenous territorial struggles

8 Indigeneity, alternative development and conservation

Political ecology of forest and land control in Chittagong Hill Tracts, Bangladesh

Khairul Chowdhury

Introduction

Recently, there has been an explosion of interest in the phenomenon of "land grabbing" as a way to (re)examine the state, neoliberal governmentality, conservation and green development as they shape the lives of millions of the world's poor (e.g., Li 2011; Hall et al. 2011; White et al. 2012). As Mollett points out, notwithstanding their contributions, much of the literature on land grabbing follows political economy perspectives and focuses "on foreign and/or domestic elite investment in large-scale agricultural development and various extractive practices" (Mollett 2016, 413) but fails to consider land grabbing in Indigenous spaces. This chapter contributes to this perceived gap differently, illustrating a case of an Indigenous movement[1] of the hill peoples of Chittagong Hill Tracts (CHT), Bangladesh, and their efforts to push back against the tide of land grabbing that has threatened livelihoods and diminished their territoriality and land control (Adnan 2004).

As in many states and governments in Asia, Bangladesh does not recognize any of its citizens as "Indigenous people" (Barnes 1995). Nevertheless, in Bangladesh the native population of CHT (hereafter, hill peoples), who were labeled "tribes" by the colonial British state, have mobilized under the banner of Indigenous rights to secure recognition and advance claims to land, forest and self-government. Their struggle took the form of an armed insurgency from 1975 to 1997, but after the CHT Treaty of 1997 (hereafter, the Peace Treaty), a more open political climate enabled Indigenous elites and former insurgents to strengthen links with nongovernmental organizations (NGOs) and donors, and begin to articulate Indigenous identity with contemporary neoliberal discourses of development, environmental sustainability, biodiversity conservation and so on. An Indigenous movement led by Taungya,[2] a nongovernmental organization of CHT, for the protection of the so-called "village common forests" (VCF) in CHT is one such example. Founded as an Indigenous movement by Chakma leaders prominent in the Indigenous movement in the early 1990s, Taungya became an NGO following the Peace Treaty of 1997[3] but has remained a distinct type of NGO representing Chakma elites and their positions on Indigenous issues, advocating "alternative" rural development for the protection of Indigenous peoples' customary rights over land and forests. Significantly, since 2003 Taungya has undertaken a series of international donor funded environmental development projects to "protect" the VCFs, including reforming their traditional management (Taungya n.d.). This has initiated a set of related practices similar to those state practices associated with the control over the population and natural resources in Thailand in the late nineteenth century, what Peter Vandergeest and Nancy Peluso call "internal territorialization" (Vandergeest and Peluso 1995, 385) and "political forest" (Peluso and Vandergeest 2001, 762).

Vandergeest and Peluso developed the term "internal territorialization" during the mid-1990s in examining forest management in Thailand. By this term they refer to processes of organizing states' territories both vertically and horizontally into various spatial organizations such villages, regions and provinces on the one hand and, on the other hand, ministries of the government, which were endowed with territorial and functional jurisdiction over population and resources. In particular, they used the term to unravel the processes and strategies of state-making in relation to the land and resources through which the forest emerges as a subject of government and also an object of control, planning and management, separating it from the private domain of agriculture and private property regime (Vandergeest and Peluso 1995, 407–414). In this sense, Peluso and Vandergeest (2001, 762) hold that forests only exist as "political forest," which helped to constitute and were constituted by discourses of state property and "customary rights." Over the years, they have reworked and expanded the analysis of political forests with various analytical and conceptual frameworks, namely customary rights, insurgency and counterinsurgency, to illustrate the ways in which they shape postcolonial forest practice in Southeast Asia (Peluso and Vandergeest 2001, 2011). Most recently, they have made the concept central to write a new "genealogical history" of political forests and their conjunctural transformation in Southeast Asia including recent transformation of political forests by nonstate actors such as NGOs and transnational organizations for conservation (Vandergeest and Peluso 2015). Considering some striking similarities between Southeast Asia and CHT in terms of ecology, colonial history and postcolonial insurgency (Schendel 2002), I find Vandergeest and Peluso's works on political forest in Southeast Asia an important intervention in political ecology for understanding not only the practices of state-making and the making of political forest in both colonial and postcolonial CHT but also the practices of VCFs. As shown by Peluso and Lund (2011), the practices that ran parallel to these past practices of state-making and political forests as well as new practices of forest conservation are "land control" – practices that fix or consolidate forms of access to, claiming over, and at times exclusion from land. Following Peluso and Lund (2011), I hold that, unlike past practices of land control by the state, VFCs represent "new frontiers" of land control that are now being actively created through struggle involving varied local and transnational nonstate actors, contexts and dynamics; they are "sites where authorities, sovereignties, and hegemonies of the recent past have been or are currently being challenged by new enclosures, territorializations, and property regimes" (Peluso and Lund 2011, 668).

As such, this chapter examines the conservation and alternative development projects of Taungya that have recently been implemented to consolidate Indigenous peoples' claims over VFCs in CHT. The chapter has several aims: first, to exemplify a contemporary land struggle in CHT and the ways in which it gets articulated with contemporary neoliberal discourses of environmental sustainability and biodiversity conservation; second, to challenge the dominant, essentialized narratives of common property forests (VCFs), pointing to their economy, spatiality and ethnic dimensions; third, to illustrate strategies and narratives of conservation and the practices of "political forest" and "land control" as well as the risks they entail for livelihood and ecologies; and, finally, to illustrate contradictions and limits of the Indigenous movement that it brings about for the overall Indigenous peoples in CHT. I mainly draw on my ethnographic research with Taungya and their project communities, as well as archival research in the Deputy Commissioner's Library in Rangamati, conducted between July and August 2008. Between January and February 2017, I conducted a further month of research with Taungya and with the Arannyak Foundation, a bilateral organization of the governments of Bangladesh and the United States working on biodiversity and forest conservation in Bangladesh, including VCFs in order to gather facts and documents on recent conservation efforts of VCF by local and national NGOs, including news report and research reports from 2010 to 2015.

In so doing, I also build my approach on critical political ecology perspectives to move beyond romantic, idealized and reified representations of traditional or Indigenous communities and knowledge (Agrawal 1995; Mccay 2001; Tsing 1999). I consider communities or Indigenous communities not as alternatives to market-, state- or growth-oriented development, but rather as part of such development (Li 2001). Following Bebbington (1996), I argue that the Indigenous movement's strategies of forest conservation and alternative development are rather a response to the challenges and promises of "modernization, development displacement and violence" in the region (Schendel et al. 2001). I also argue that the VCF project has been motivated by a number of overlapping political and development agendas other than those of state- or business-led land grabbing or "green grabbing" agendas (e.g., Fairhead et al. 2012). The political objectives are to defend customary control over the remaining common land against market and state forces, showcasing Indigenous forest management against state forestry. The (alternative) development agendas are to reform the management, customary rights and practices of VCFs to improve gender equity, conservation and rural livelihoods, although the latter two goals (conservation and rural livelihoods) are often in conflict. Both the political and alternative developmental agendas assume, as they serve to produce: (1) the indigeneity of the hill peoples; (2) the hill peoples' cultural differences with Bengalis (the majority group) and the state; and (3) to some degree, the hill peoples' social and political autonomy. Nonetheless, a potential outcome of the Indigenous movement is new political forests and land control leading to the strengthening of locally enforced forest exclusion, at the expense of traditional livelihoods based on *jhum* (slash-and-burn cultivation). I explore these tensions through a close examination of the origins and deployment of the concept of the VFC. In turn, I address the cultural logic and emerging limits of conservation of VCFs in CHT.

The context: cultural geography of CHT

Unlike the flood-plain land in the rest of Bangladesh, CHT primarily comprises chains of hill ranges interspersed by valleys and river drainage systems, and is one of the most forested regions in Bangladesh. The forests of CHT emerged as "political forests" in the late nineteenth century as part of the processes of internal territorialization and state-making in the region after it was annexed and became a district in the British Indian Empire in 1860 (Sivaramakrishnan 1999; Chowdhury 2014). This resulted in the creation of large areas of "reserved forests" under the authority of the Forest Department (see Figure 8.1).[4] The remaining areas were "open forest" and included cultivable plain land; these areas were labeled "Unclassed State Forest" (USF) and were designated for meeting the agricultural needs of the population, retaining ownership and control for the state (Chowdhury 2014, 78–95).

The entire CHT was and still is considered forest and therefore all the lands belong to the state (or *Khas land*). At present, almost one-third is reserved forests;[5] meanwhile, much of the USF land, which had been the common property of the hill peoples, has been alienated for counterinsurgency development programs including Bengali settlements, industrial rubber lease to Bengali business, and forest extension. In turn, there emerged in USF an individual property rights regimes on the one hand and state property of forest on the other hand, resulting in a large number of the hill peoples as internal refuges, who were forced to live in reserved forests under the military (Chowdhury 2014, 179–259).

Eleven ethnic groups who collectively call themselves "Jumma" or at times "Pahari," meaning hill people, inhabit the region. Of these hill peoples, the Chakma, Marma and Tripura are numerically dominant groups; the other groups number a few thousand and include the Tanchangya, Mro, Bawm, Pankho, Khumi, Khyang, Chak and Mizo. *Jhum* has remained the main livelihood strategy for most of the rural hill peoples, although residents of the valleys and plains use more intensive cultivation techniques, and the educated elite – especially members of the Chakma group – are increasingly detached from farming (Roy 2000a; Tripura and Harun 2003).

CHT is currently divided into three administrative districts: Bandarban, Khagrachhari and Rangamati. These are further divided into 25 subdistricts or *Upazilas* and into 110 union councils for local government under the bureaucracy (Figure 8.1). CHT also has an overlapping local government system for each district called Hill District Councils, dominated by Indigenous political elites, and a

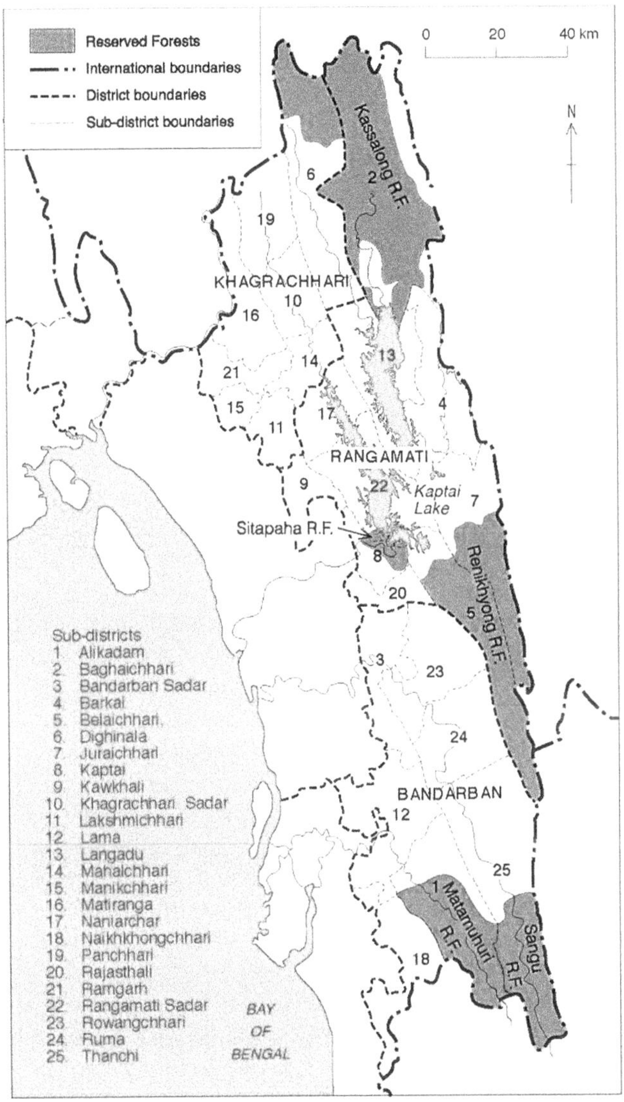

Figure 8.1 Districts, sub-districts and reserved forests in Chittagong Hill Tracts.

Source: Bangladesh Bureau of Statistics 1986. Copyright: © Khairul Chowdhury.

Regional Council for coordinating the functions of Hill District Councils (Mohsin 2003). In addition, CHT has an exceptional traditional administration and revenue system called "circles," which have existed since the 1880s but were only formalized by the Regulation of 1900, which has remained the main law for the civil and judicial administration of CHT. A traditional chief or *Raja* heads each circle under the bureaucracy (Schendel et al. 2001), which is further divided into revenue units *or Mouza* under headmen. *Mouzas* are conventionally comprised of several villages with a village headman (*Karbari*) for each (Hutchinson 1909).

The origins of VCFs: Indigenous invention vs. state regulation

In mid-July 2008, I participated in a day-long training and workshop session for Taungya's staff at Taungya's head office in Rangamati. The agenda of the workshop included a screening and discussion of the English version of the documentary film *Saving the Village Common Forests in the Chittagong Hill Tracts*.[6] The documentary begins with a scene portraying the life of rural villages of hill peoples, and then moves to selected presentations of historical narratives of CHT, which describe the birth of VCFs in the early twentieth century as an "innovation by indigenous elders." In this section, I problematize this claim to situate VCFs in their economy, ethnicity and spatial dimensions, and show that VCFs mostly exist in Chakma villages in the territory of the Chakma chief and have largely been shaped by the Kaptai Hydroelectric Dam as well as by the insurgency and counterinsurgency in CHT.

In its most common usage, the term VCFs refers to small patches of common land in USF. Generally, VCFs hold some forest cover and have remained common property, not alienated or settled by individuals, businesses or state agencies. They are managed traditionally by headmen and at times by village headmen for everyday use as sources of fuel or other household necessities.

However, until recently, the existence of VCFs had been little known beyond CHT. They first became public knowledge briefly in the 1998 Rangamati Declaration (Gain 2002), and then later in 2001 when an elaborate account of VCFs was co-authored by Chakma chief Raja Roy (Roy and Halim 2001). In fact, the leadership of Raja Roy played an instrumental role in bringing awareness of VCFs not only to the wider public but also to urban Indigenous activists of the hill peoples. Asish Chakma (a pseudonym), 35, who worked with Taungya from 1998 to 2005 in various capacities including as a field supervisor of VCF projects, explains this as he described to me his own surprise on discovering the VCFs:

KHAIRUL: How and when did you come to know VCFs?

ASISH: In early 1998. Rajababu (Chakma chief Raja Devasish Roy) told me about it.

KHAIRUL: What did Raja Roy tell you and why?

ASISH: I was the founding member of Taungya and Rajababu was my boss. So he told me to visit Beganachari village in Barkal Upazila and talked to a local Union Council's Chairman for assistance for video recording a VCF and village elders. I did not know what a VCF was. Rajababu explained it with few words and told me to see it with my own eyes. So I went to Shuvolong and met the local Chairman and then to Beganachari. We [taped] the VCF in Beganchari and interviewed the village elders in their seventies. The elders called the VCF reserved or *rajdhani*, and they said they had had it for a long time: "parents or grandparents must have kept it in the way it is now; we take bamboo and at times trees when one needs them." They knew it was not a government reserved forest, and I was very shocked that I did not know much of our own people and culture!

KHAIRUL: Could you tell a bit more about why you taped the VCF and interviewed elders?

ASISH: Oh yes! I do not know for sure but I think a Danish ambassador came to CHT after the Peace Treaty. Rajababu must have talked to him about VCFs. I believe the video tape was meant for the ambassador.

KHAIRUL: Do you know how Raja Roy came to know about VCFs?

ASISH: No, I do not know. But I think he must have known everything in his area, should he not? You know there is a standing order [of the Deputy Commissioner] of the 1960s and Rajababu knew it, and the [political] environment has not been conducive for him to work until now.

(Interview, July 28, 2008)

"Village common forest" (VCF) is a neologism. The terms usually used by the Chakma to refer to these lands are *service bon* or *rajdhani*. *Service bon* is a hybrid term of the English word *service* and Bengali word *bon*, meaning forests. *Service bon* literally means forests for service. The name derives from the practice of privileges for headmen, the service holders of the traditional administration who were allowed by the Regulation of 1900 to keep certain areas of USF as forest common lands in their *Mouzas*. On this consideration, *service bon* is a forest area in USF under headmen or at times under village headmen for their service to the government, and is not taxable. The term *rajdhani* is a Bengali word meaning the capital city. The appropriation of the term *rajdhani* to refer to "common forest" underscores, first of all, the centrality of this resource to the community and, importantly, the position and power of headmen or village headmen who control it. Both local names for this land signify that it is a place of resource whose meaning depends upon the traditional authorities' control of the resource.

The textual origins of the VCFs, or the appearance of them in written language, can be identified with precision to the amendment of Rule 41 of the Regulation of 1900 in 1939. The amendment, Rule 41A, was intended to empower the deputy commissioner of CHT to regulate and control *jhum* cultivation and the migration of *jhum* cultivators from one *Mouza* to another. Rule 41A also included provisions to empower headmen to keep some areas of common USF land as a *Mouza* reserve of bamboo, timber and other forest products. The detailed provisions of the rule and the deputy commissioner's annual report of 1939–40 suggest that the provisions were meant as a regulatory instrument aimed to encourage headmen to take care of the future domestic needs of the hill peoples of their *Mouza* (GOB 1941, 11). A subsequent text to this rule was a

1965 executive order of the deputy commissioner under Rule 7 of the Regulation of 1900. In part, the order clarifies the status of VCFs in the past, while providing specific directives to all headmen to maintain village common forest in their *Mouza*. This order was issued following the mass displacement of the hill peoples caused by the Kaptai Hydroelectric Dam in the early 1960s and subsequent resettlement of the displaced hill peoples. I would argue that the Kaptai Dam marked a significant shift in the practices of the VCF. No longer were VCFs to be conserved for use by the hill people according to their traditional practices; rather, they became a political resource to be controlled by traditional elites. As I show in the next section, Tanugya's effort to reform traditional management is a response to this development.

According to the 2003 Taungya inventory report, there are about 127 VCFs in CHT; most of these are in Rangamati district, with as many as five in Khagarchhari district and eight in Bandarban district. However, the inventory could only report details of 88 VCFs in Rangamati and Khagarchhari districts, of which only one came into existence before 1941 and as many as 10 from 1940 to 1950, but the overwhelming majority (51) during the 1960s, immediately after the Kaptai Dam.[7] The remaining have been established only recently, since the late 1970s. Looking below the district level at the mid-level civil administrative units, we find that in Rangamati the VCFs are located only in four out of the district's 10 subdistricts. Furthermore, more than half (47) of these VCFs are concentrated in the single subdistrict of Barkal. The VCFs of Khagarchhari district belongs to Dighinala *Upazila*, one of the district's seven subdistricts. An important common pattern is that all of the VCFs fall within the boundary of the Chakma chief's circle; all are reported as being inhabited by members of the Chakma community, as I found in Beganachari and Nahbhanga villages of Barkal *Upazila* during my fieldwork.

So why do VCFs occur only among the Chakma in specific locales within the territory of the Chakma chief's circle? I argue that the conjuncture relates to the effects of two historic and tragic events in the history of CHT: the first is the construction of Kaptai Dam and the subsequent displacement and resettlement programs affecting the hill peoples, primarily the Chakma. Completed in the early 1960s, the Kaptai Dam submerged 256 square miles in the valleys of the Karnaphuli River and all its tributaries to the north and northeast of the CHT. This included 54,000 acres or 40 percent of the plowland of the district and thousands of acres of USF lands in the Chakma chief's circle, and in turn uprooted 100,000 people of 18,000 families (which was one-fourth of the total population of the district) (East Pakistan Agricultural Development Corporation, n.d., 2). The Chakma represented 90 percent of the displaced hill peoples (Sopher 1963). It is, therefore, no surprise that, as the Chakma reorganized their lives and communities after the displacement in and around the upland in the vicinity of Kaptai Dam, they began to keep VCFs in their communities to meet the ensuing resource crisis.

The second and interrelated factor behind the continuation of the practice of VCFs in specific localities is the strategic positioning of these localities from the standpoint of the insurgency movement and counterinsurgency programs. Space does not allow for details, but it is important to note that of these subdistricts Barkal *Upazila* to the east and Dighinala *Upazila* to the north of CHT were considered to be frontier base camps of insurgents bordering the Indian states of Mizoram and Tripura respectively, and were connected by the Karnaphuli River and its tributaries (see Figure 8.1). They had also been major sites of insurgency and counterinsurgency violence as well as alleged genocide (see Levene 1999). This was also due to the fact that the Chakma predominantly inhabited Rangamati and Khagarchhari districts and overwhelmingly participated in the insurgency (Schendel 1995).

These observations are not, however, meant to deny or to reject Indigenous agency in the origins and practice of VCFs. Regarding the origins of VCFs and the agency of Indigenous communities, it is rather pertinent to ask whether or not the state regulation and the existing practice of VCFs have some basis in the previously existing Indigenous customs of the hill peoples. As Hall (1990) reminds us, cultural practices (broadly defined) always come from something; they always have their own history.[8] The oral testimonies that I gathered during fieldwork with the Mro and the Marma forest villagers in Matamuhuri Reserved Forest, as well as with the Tripura community of "Golden River" in Bandarban district, suggested that both communities had the tradition of "community forests," but their purpose was to conserve forest products for domestic use, not for conservation as such. The forests were generally kept near settlement areas for their immediate needs for bamboo and other forest products. However, as the communities moved out for new settlements after some time, the forests were cut down and burned for *jhum* cultivation.

In sum, VCFs at present are mainly a Chakma institution. The origins of the VCFs among hill peoples is a complex story that cannot be simply attributed to the sovereign will of some "Indigenous elders." VCFs apparently had some basis in the Indigenous customs of some hill peoples' groups, but they are part of colonial state-making, constituted at the intersection of multiple political and economic interests.

VCF projects: a new discourse of political forests and land control

Taungya has undertaken several programs and strategies since 2003 to protect the VCFs, including reforming their traditional management. The project titled "A Pilot Project on the Protection of Village Common Forest in the Chittagong Hill Tracts: A Project on Watershed Management" (hereafter, the pilot project), funded by the Human Rights and Good Governance Program Support Unit of the Danish International Development Agency, Dhaka, was completed in 2005. This pilot project is considered to be a successful program and strategy and is now widely adopted by other NGOs and organizations for similar projects (see the next section). In this section, I examine the discourses of the pilot project, its programs of making and unmaking of VCFs, and the strategies of land control to illustrate the new practices of political forest and land control in CHT.

The key concept that informed the project's rationales was the "protection" of VCFs and their biodiversity. The project plan argued that:

> the management of VCFs provides an important role to rural communities in environmentally sound watershed management, which is extremely necessary to combat deforestation, harmful monoculture plantation, environmental degradation and resource scarcity. Thus, better protected VCFs would in turn lead to: (i) maintenance of forest cover; (ii) maintenance of biodiversity; (iii) protection of headwater streams; (iv) maintenance of herbaria; and (v) preservation of cultural and religious tradition of indigenous communities related to forests.
>
> (Taungya 2002, 13–14)

The plan to protect the VCF was predicated on analyses of a number of interrelated social, political and environmental problems in CHT by the experts and activists of Taungya, namely Raja Debasish Roy and Dr. Sadeka Halim. According to Roy and Halim (2001), as VCFs are formed from parts of USF land and the state only recognizes usufruct rights of the communities over the VCFs land, legal access to the VCF lands remains wide open for state acquisition or market forces. Roy and Halim (2001) argue that the absence of land tenure over VCFs has had a severe impact on the remaining VCFs and requires protection not only from external processes of state, market and Bengali business, but also from affluent and urban members of Indigenous hill peoples' communities. They conclude that "indigenous forest management perspectives on [forest land tenure] have differed radically from the conventional industrial-capitalist concepts influenced by colonial legislative regimes [and] need to be accounted for and acknowledged to ensure sustainability of the VCFs" (Roy and Halim 2001, 28). Nevertheless, they concede that various regimes of local customary management also present a major problem for the sustainability of the VCFs as they are mostly governed by headmen or village headmen, lacking uniform rules or any rule, depending on the particular power relations between VCF communities and the traditional elites.

As these analyses inform Taungya's political agendas with respect to land and forest, the pilot project turned them into a technical problem of "protection and preservation" of the VCFs. In so doing, the pilot project took the local VCF communities as its primary targets of intervention, where it could maximize the effects of achieving its goals, while the state and its bureaucracy were secondary targets for liaison and advocacy for collective rights over the VCF land. It selected 12 VCFs covering three subdistricts of Rangamati district, namely Barkal, Langadu and Rangamati Sadar. At the community level, the project planner proposed a policy of "limited intervention" in the spirit of a "bottom up" approach to community development. The plan had two main programs: (1) reforming the existing unstructured or semi-structured local management of VCFs, and (2) raising community awareness about VCFs in relation to biodiversity, environment and watershed protection.

Several ideologies and development agendas informed the pilot project's programs, which are aligned with the contemporary neoliberal discourse of community and environmental development. What is new, however, is the way that Taungya translated the discourse of community and environmental development to shape the practice of common property forest management on the ground. Under the reform program, 11 VCFs were brought under a management committee (with one-third women participants) elected by the respective VCF villagers for a two-year period. The community of Noapara VCF opted out of the project because it had to open its VCF area for *jhum* cultivation owing to a shortage of cultivable lands; I take up this tension between *jhum* land and VCFs in the next section. The management committee was given sole responsibilities for: (1) safeguarding the VCF land and resources from jhum cultivation, fire, hunting and unauthorized logging or "thieves"; (2) regulating the community use of VCF through a policy of equal access to all villagers; (3) determining the harvesting period of bamboo on a sustainable basis, and the sale of the harvest; and (4) distribution of income from the VCFs. Accordingly, each of the VCF communities set new rules for community members' usage and access rights over VCF resources, including the harvesting schedule, sale of VCFs, and distribution of the income from VCFs. In the Beganachari VCF, the following are the provisional rules agreed to by the villagers:

I To be considered a member of the VCF, every household of the village community should join the VCF community, paying Taka (Tk.) 5.00 every month.

II No person from other than the member's household will be allowed access rights over the VCF land and forest produce.

III The member household will be allowed to collect fuel, fodder and vegetables other than bamboo roots from the VCF, but hunting, trapping and any form of cultivation will be prohibited.

IV Each member household that needs bamboo for personal use or household repairs should purchase bamboo for Tk.3.00 each by the permission of the committee.

V The harvesting and sales period for bamboo will be five years, while timber trees will be preserved.

VI In the case of a newcomer to the village community, she/he cannot be a member of the VCF community; if she/he resides in the village for a minimum of two years and is willing to live in the village permanently, the committee will decide his/her membership if she/he wishes to join the VCF community.

The rules of Beganachari appear to be typical of the way that VCFs have been reorganized as the collective property of resource users or what can be called a form of "community forestry."

To supervise and assist the activities of the committees in their respective subdistricts, Taungya hired and trained three VCF community members from each subdistrict in the position of "community organizer." The major responsibilities of the community organizers were to guide the management committees and VCF village communities through the following: participatory assessments of community resources (schools, clubs, agricultural activities) and VCF resources (flora and fauna); problem analysis; preparation of development proposals; budget funding; and use of the income from community memberships and the VCF. Over the project period, the members of the management committees were brought to Rangamati to join in a series of workshops and seminars designed to address the question of Indigenous land rights and forests, which opened up an opportunity for the VCF communities to meet and speak directly to state functionaries, headmen and Indigenous activists. Meanwhile, the communities were visited by Taungya's members for similar kinds of training and community meeting.

The assumptions that underlie the action of community organizers and the training of members of the VCF committees is that hill people villagers need to be reminded of their customs and traditions because these have been either lost or increasingly ignored owing to the insurgency and war as well as resulting economic, political and social crises.[9] There was also a hope that the training would make the functionaries and resource users in VCF village communities into collective environmental subjects who would plan, reach consensus and think of the village population in relation to the natural resources to be managed. The story of Rena Chakma appeared in the blog of the Chittagong Hill Tracts Development Facility (CHTDF), a multidimensional development program of the United Nations Development Programme (UNDP), is a good illustration of this. Rena was a member of Beganachari VCF, one of the VCFs of the pilot project, and was among 27 participants who participated in the Community Mobilization and Participatory Rural Appraisal, training organized by the office of the traditional chiefs of CHT as part of their projects to reform the traditional administration of 55 VCFs for the period 2014–17 supported by the CHTDF. Rena is quoted as saying the following:

> With the new responsibility since joining the Chakma Circle, I was not confident enough about my abilities to mobilize communities and conduct situational assessments of VCF. This training has boosted my confidence. I have learnt communication skills and techniques to assess community needs and plan efforts to resolve issues related to natural resource management.
>
> (UNDP 2016)

Further, these actions created a new network of VCF communities, the Chittagong Hill Tracts Association of *Mouza* Reserve, to coordinate these VCF communities at the regional level of CHT with the aim of achieving legal and political recognition of VCFs as the collective property of village communities. In 2016, CHTDF has financed more than Tk.11 million to three local NGOs including Taungya to strengthen the network across CHT (ZKS 2016).

In sum, the pilot project brought about a new form of "community forestry" in CHT that mobilized a large group of rural men and women of the hill peoples in the project villages and turned them into corporate bodies of resource users. In turn, the project implemented contributes to (re)making "political forests" in CHT that not only risks the exclusion of the hill peoples' customary access to forest resources in *Mouzas* but also threatens the livelihoods of rural Chakma.

Implications

There has been increased interest in VCFs among conservationist national and international NGOs, policy planners, academics and Indigenous activists. In 2011, UNDP recognized VCF as one of the good practices for sustainable management of natural resources (ZKS 2016). In 2008, a VCF community of Taungya's pilot project received the Prime Minister Award for an outstanding forest conservation effort. Currently, in addition to Taungya and the office of the three chiefs, a number of national and international NGOs are running VCF projects for biodiversity conservation and rural development in CHT. For example, between 2009 and 2016 the Arannayk Foundation financed several national and local NGOs to bring 17 VCF communities under their conservation and livelihood support projects (AF 2015; pers. comm. 2017). These interventions have not only appropriated Taungya's model of interventions but also exaggerated Taungya's popular narratives of VCFs. For example, Friends of the Earth International, in its 2009 annual report, claims VCFs are an "ancient system of forest use and management," practiced by the communities living in CHT (Friends of the Earth International 2009). In fact, Taungya's popular narratives of VCFs have now saturated most of the common sense, regularly appeared in newspaper columns (Baten 2010), think tank reports (Baten et al. 2010) and academic publications (Nath et al. 2016).

Considering the ecology, economy and history of land conflict in CHT (Roy 2002b; Halim and Chowdhury 2015), the articulation of indigeneity and forest conservation raises a serious concern about the possible effect of VCFs on hill peoples in general and on *jhum* cultivation in particular. The project completion report of the pilot project provides clear evidence that there are long, drawn-out conflicts over VCF land, including conflicts between conservation and *jhum* cultivation in all the project villages (Taungya 2006). It seems that the pilot project has not only further exacerbated such conflicts but also to have coerced hill people into giving up their common land and at times private land for the expansion of VCFs. For example, let us consider the following local stories regarding three VCFs of the pilot project that I have constructed from the final report of the pilot project, and my field notes from the office reports of the community organizers.

The first is the Duluchari VCF, one of the primary project areas of the pilot project. The community of Duluchari VCF consists of a village with 74 households, mainly *jhum*-cultivating peasant families, and a Buddhist monastery. The land area of the VCF was reported in different office reports of Taungya to be between 120 and 500 acres. The final report of the pilot project put the land area at about 200 acres at the outset; however, in describing details about the current management of VCF the report contradicted itself, saying that the size of the VCF was approximately 120 acres. Most interestingly, it further suggests that the land area was initially "half of the present size" of 120 acres and that the additional land came in 1991 from the villagers' donation of their privately owned registered and unregistered land to the Buddhist monastery in the village, which is part of the VCF.

Second, the Madyachar VCF, another primary project area of the pilot project. The VCF, according to the final report, was established in 1956 and was about 200 acres. In 2003, when it came under the project, the land area was 100 acres and was claimed by nine villages of about 500 households. The reports of the community organizers suggest that the land area of the VCF grew to 500 acres in 2004 after the *jhum* harvest of that year. The major problems of the management of the VCF, as noted in the final report, were: (1) no clear demarcation of the boundary; (2) conflicts about the number of villages having claims over the VCF; (3) conflicts over *jhum* land and VCF land; (4) conflicts over claims to private land in VCF; and (5) fire from *jhum*.

Finally, the Bagchari VCF. This VCF was reported to have been formed jointly by Bagchari and Rangdakaba villages in 1965. In 2001, Rangdakaba villagers wanted the VCF for *jhum* cultivation but Bagchari villagers denied them. Thus, the VCF was divided between the villages, and Rangdakaba villagers did *jhum* on their part. In 2003, when the villagers of Bagchari joined the pilot project, they formally complained to the Chakma chief against the local headmen for giving Rangdakaba more than their half of the share in the VCF. The intervention of the Chakma chief helped Bagchari villagers to recover their share of the land. Interestingly, the Bagchari community also expressed their desire to increase their area of the VCF because they claimed Rangdakaba had formed a new VCF that was bigger in area than Bagchari's.

Beyond Taungya's pilot project's communities, Kamalchari VCF is the most illustrative story of conflict over VCF. As it appeared in the Arannayk Foundation's annual report of 2015, the story goes like this. Kamalchari VCF belongs to a Chakma community, living in Kamalchari village in Khagrachari subdistrict and is about 127 hectares in term of land area. Located at distance about two kilometers from the Kamalchari village, the VCF was regularly access over by two adjacent Tripura villages, Jadurampara and Thana Chandrapara. In order to prevent Tripura villagers from accessing the VCF, the Chakma villagers settled 25 villagers inside the VCF with rights to *jhum* cultivation, but the strategy failed as the settler families found it hard to make a living with limited access to VCF land. At one point, the community decided to sell the VCF forest to brickfield, and it was at this point that the Arannayk Foundation intervened to save the VCF with their conservation and livelihood support programs for both the VCF community and VCF dependent Tripura communities (AF 2015, 35). In sum, I concede that, while these stories are no doubt a partial account, they do provide evidence of the possible risk of land control that VCFs pose to *jhum* cultivation in the project areas and also point to complex nature of emerging land conflict in CHT among NGOs, Indigenous elites and local communities.

Conclusion

This chapter examined an Indigenous movement of the hill peoples of Chittagong Hill Tracts (CHT) led by Taungya, a local NGO of CHT, and their strategy to protect VCFs for customary control over the remaining common property resources in the region. Drawing upon nonessentialist and critical political ecology perspectives, I have challenged the movement's VCF "origin story" – its argument that VCF is an Indigenous invention – suggesting instead that VCFs have multiple origins, formalized through state intervention and laws. I have shown that VCFs have an ethnic and spatial dimension; at present, they mostly exist in Chakma villages, in specific locales in the territory of the Chakma chief, and have largely been shaped by the Kaptai Hydroelectric Dam as well as by the insurgency and counter-insurgency in CHT. Evidently, hill peoples' interest in the conservation of VCFs arises in part as a means to reclaim customary land rights, and has several political and development agendas, including the reform of the traditional management of VCF in favor of a decentralization of power and gender equity, but presents a serious risk to the livelihood of CHT rural communities. The VCF rules also show some striking similarities with the political forest and land control by the state in the past and the criminalization and disciplining of *jhum* cultivation (Sivaramakrishnan 1999). However, the main success of the movement led by Taungya is not the protection and reformation of VCFs; rather, it is the mobilization of large groups of grassroots actors and educated young men and women who desire to help their rural cousins against forces of the state, market and business in order to prevent dispossession and land alienation.

Put differently, this chapter has presented a contemporary South Asian Indigenous movement and their struggle for land rights and the ways which it articulates Indigenous identity and issues with forest conservation and alternative development. In particular, I have illustrated how discourses of forest conversation, alternative development and Indigenous identity in CHT are now articulated by Chakma elites through practices of the conservation of VCFs to assert customary control over these common property natural resources, and how these discourses have promoted the (re)invention of VCF and expansion of political forests, resulting in land control and social exclusions, conflicts and corporatization of common property forest resources. Following Franz Fanon's (1967) arguments with regard to the relationship between anticolonial national struggles and national cultures, I concede that Indigenous peoples' struggles for power and resources take on different forms and meanings through the discourses of Indigenous identity and Indigenous environmental values. However, I argue that whether it is a strategy or a movement for Indigenous identity and land rights, conservation of VCFs not only risks the livelihood of CHT rural communities but has limited purchase. First of all, if the VCF movement becomes successful, it will further marginalize the remaining *jhum* land or *jhum* cultivation, something the state has tried and failed to do so since the British. The loss of *jhum* cultivation would mean the loss of the rural way life of the hill peoples, and for some hill peoples it would certainly cause poverty or the loss of entitlement to livelihood security, particularly for marginal *jhum*-cultivating peasants among the Chakma. Significantly, there are hardly enough USF common lands for the entire rural hill peoples' groups to have VCFs of their own. Given that VCFs exist mainly among the Chakma villages in the Chakma chief's territory, the problem is clearly the conceptual justification of the Indigenous identity that the VCFs try to articulate in the first place. To conclude, the practice of VCF conservation not only risks exacerbating class differentiation among the project communities, in terms of their access to USF and VCF resources, but also portends the development of a new Indigenous identity as one ethnic group seems to be redefining hill peoples' indigeneity itself.

Acknowledgment

I am indebted to Professors Shubhra Gururani, Peter Vandergeest and Malcolm Blincow of York University, Toronto, and especially to Professor Tania Li of the University of Toronto, for their comments on various drafts of this chapter. I would also like to express my sincere thanks to the editors, Sharlene Mollett and Thembela Kepe, for their time and review of the chapter. The research of this chapter was part of my PhD dissertation and was facilitated by financial assistance I received from the International Development Research Centre (Doctoral Research Award), Canada, and from the Faculty of Graduate Studies (Fieldwork Cost Fund) of York University. I am grateful to the International Development Research Centre and York University for their financial assistance.

Notes

1 Several Indigenous networks and movements exist in Bangladesh (Chowdhury 2008; Bleie 2005).
2 Taungya is also the name of an agro-silviculture technique for forest plantation (Bryant 1994).
3 Taungya was first established in 1995 by traditional Indigenous elites in CHT including Raja Devasish Roy, the sitting Chakma chief, and was called "The Committee for the Protection of Indigenous Culture." In 1996, the committee changed its name to Taungya as part of its claim to represent the Indigenous culture of *jhum* (slash-and-burn) cultivators and their relations to forests, on the assumption that the agro-silviculture technique taungya cultivation is an Indigenous tradition. Taungya registered as a nongovernmental organization (NGO) with the Department of Social Welfare in 1998, and afterwards with the NGO Affairs Bureau in 2001 (Taungya n.d.).
4 This includes four compact reserved forests on the borders of CHT, separating the region from Arakan (Myanmar), Lushai Hill (Indian State of Mizoram), Hill Tripura (Indian State of Tripura), and small areas on the banks of the Karanphuli River in the center of the region.
5 This estimation is based on fieldwork data: at present, the land area of the reserved forests is 1,598 square miles; this includes 1,253 square miles of old reserved forests that were created during British rule and 345 square miles that were created recently as part of the counterinsurgency.

6 Taungya produced the documentary in 2004 and it is also available in the Bengali and Chakma languages.
7 The inventory was conducted for Taungya by its Indigenous staff during 2002–03 with financial assistance from the International Center for Integrated Mountain Development. I read this report in Taungya's office file. It is worth mentioning that the inventory is the only reliable data about the currently existing VCF, though a new VCF project proposal by a local NGO put the number much higher, the validity of which I could not ascertain (see ZKS 2016).
8 In fact, Hall refers to cultural identity in the quoted passage, but I see his point as equally valid with respect to cultural practices (compare Li 2000, 152).
9 The statement is based on interview with Parosh Kisha, a physician and general secretary of Taungya, July 4–6, 2008.

References

Adnan, Shapan. *Migration, Land Alienation and Ethnic Conflict: Causes of Poverty in the Chittagong Hill Tracts of Bangladesh*. Dhaka: Research and Advisory Services, 2004.

Agrawal, Arun. "Dismantling the Divide between Indigenous and Scientific Knowledge." *Development and Change* 26 (1995): 413–439.

AF (Arannayk Foundation). *Annual Report 2015: Seeding Hopes in the Coast, Hills and Haors*. Dhaka: AF, 2016.

Baten, Mohammed A. "VCF in CHT: A Sustainable Model of Forest Management." *The Daily Star*. February 13, 2010. www.thedailystar.net/news-detail-126019 (accessed January 3, 2017), 2010.

Baten, Mohammed A., Niaz A. Khan, Ronju Ahammad and Khaled Missbahuzzaman. *Village Common Forests in Chittagong Hill Tracts, Bangladesh: Balance between Conservation and Exploitation*. Dhaka: Unnayan Onneshan, 2010.

Barnes, R. H. "Introduction." In *Indigenous Peoples of Asia*, edited by Robert H. Barnes, Andrew Gray and Benedict Kingsbury, 1–12. Ann Arbor, MI: The Association for Asian Studies, 1995.

Bangladesh Bureau of Statistics. Area Atlas of Bangladesh: Mauzas and Mahallas of Chittagong H. T. District. Dhaka: Statistic Division, Ministry of Planning, 1986.

Bebbington, Anthony. "Movements, Modernizations, and Markets: Indigenous Organizations and Agrarian Strategies in Ecuador." In *Liberation Ecologies: Environment, Development, Social Movements*, edited by Richard Peet and Michael Watts, 86–119. London and New York, NY: Routledge, 1996.

Bleie, Tone. *Tribal Peoples, Nationalism and the Human Rights Challenge: The Adivasis of Bangladesh*. Dkaha: University Press, 2005.

Bryant, Raymond L. "Shifting the Cultivator: The Politics of Teak Generation in Colonial Burma." *Modern Asian Studies* 28, no. 2 (1994): 225–250.

Chowdhury, K. "Politics of Identities and Resources in Chittagong Hill Tracts, Bangladesh: Ethnonationalism and/or Indigenous Identity." *Asian Journal of Social Science* 36, no. 1 (2008): 57–78.

Chowdhury, Khairul. "The Making of Political Forests in the Chittagong Hill Tracts, Bangladesh: the State, Development and Indigeneity." Unpublished doctoral dissertation, York University, Toronto, Canada, 2014.

East Pakistan Agricultural Development Corporation. Master Plan for the Chittagong Hill Tracts Development Project. Dhaka: East Pakistan Agricultural Development Corporation, n.d.

Fairhead, James, Melissa Leach, and Ian Scoones. "Green Grabbing: A New Appropriation of Nature?" *Journal of Peasant Studies* 39, no. 2 (2012): 237–261.

Fanon, Frantz. *Black Skin, White Masks*. New York, NY: Grove Press, 1967.

Friends of the Earth International. *Annual Report 2009: 16, Bangladesh: Assessing Village Common Forest*. www.foei.org/wp-content/uploads/2014/02/final-foei-annual-report-lr.pdf (accessed February 24, 2017), 2009.

Gain, Phillip. *The Last Forest of Bangladesh*. Dhaka: SEHD, 2002.

GOB (Government of Bengal). Report of the Land Revenue Administration of the Chittagong Hill Tracts for the Year 1939–40. Alipore: Bengal Government Press, 1941.

Halim, Sadeka and Kharuil Chowdhury. *The Land Problem in the Chittagong Hill Tracts: A Human Rights Anatomy*. Dhaka: National Human Rights Commission, 2015.

Hall, Stuart. "Cultural Identity and Diaspora." In *Identity: Community, Culture, and Difference*, edited by Jonathan Rutherford, 222–237. London: Lawrence and Wishart, 1990.

Hall, Derek, Philip Hirsch and Tiana M. Li. *Powers of Exclusion: Land Dilemmas in Southeast Asia*. Singapore and Honolulu, HI: National University of Singapore Press/ University of Hawaii Press, 2011.

Hutchinson, R. H. S. *Eastern Bengal and Assam District Gazetteers: Chittagong Hill Tracts*. Allahabad: Pioneer Press, 1909.

Levene, Mark. "The Chittagong Hill Tracts: A Study in the Political Economy of 'Creeping Genocide.'" *Third World Quarterly* 2, no. 2 (1999): 339–369.

Li, Tiana M. "Articulating Indigenous Identity in Indonesia: Resource Politics and the Tribal Slot." *Comparative Studies in Society and History* 42, no. 1 (2000): 149–179.

Li, Tiana M. "Boundary Work: Community, Market, and State Reconsidered." In *Communities and the Environment: Ethnicity, Gender, and the State in Community-Based Conservation*, edited by Arun Agrawal and Clark C. Gibson, 157–179. New Brunswick, NJ: Rutgers University Press, 2001.

Li, Tiana M. "Centering Labor in the Land Grab Debate." *The Journal of Peasant Studies* 38, no. 2 (2011): 281–298.

Mccay, Bonnie J. "Community and the Commons: Romantic and Other Views." In *Communities and the Environment: Ethnicity, Gender, and the State in Community-Based Conservation*, edited by Arun Agrawal and Clark C. Gibson, 180–191. New Brunswick, NJ, and London: Rutgers University Press, 2001.

Mohsin, Amena. *The Chittagong Hill Tracts, Bangladesh: on the Difficult Road to Peace*. London: Lynne Rienner, 2003.

Mollett, Sharlene. "The Power to Plunder: Rethinking Land Grabbing in Latin America." *Antipode* 48, no. 2 (2016): 412–432.

Nath, Tapan Kumar, Mohammed Jashimuddin, and Makoto Inoue. "The Village Common Forest (VCF): Community-Driven Forest Conservation in Chittagong Hill Tracts." In *Community-Based Forest Management (CBFM) in Bangladesh*, 155–167. Switzerland: Springer, 2016.

Peluso, Nancy Lee, and Christian Lund. "New Frontiers of Land Control: Introduction." *Journal of Peasant Studies* 38, no. 4 (2011): 667–681.

Peluso, Nancy Lee, and Peter Vandergeest. "Political Ecologies of War and Forests: Counterinsurgencies and the Making of National Natures." *Annals of the Association of American Geographers* 101, no. 3 (2011): 587–608.

Peluso, Nancy Lee, and Peter Vandergeest. "Genealogies of the Political Forest and Customary Rights in Indonesia, Malaysia, and Thailand." *The Journal of Asian Studies* 60, no. 3 (2001): 761–812.

Roy, Raja D. "Occupation and Economy in Transitions: A Case Study of the Chittagong Hill Tracts." In *Traditional Occupation of Indigenous and Tribal Peoples: Emerging Trends*, 73–124. Geneva: ILO, 2000a.

Roy, Rajkumari C. K. *Land Rights of the Indigenous Peoples of the Chittagong Hill Tracts, Bangladesh (No. 99)*. Copenhagen: IWGIA, 2000b.

Roy, Raja D., and Sadeka Halim. "Valuing Village Commons in Forestry: A Case from the Chittagong Hill Tracts." In *Chittagong Hill Tracts: State of the Environment*, edited by Quamrul I. Chowdhury, 11–44. Dhaka: Forum of Environmental Journalists of Bangladesh, 2001.

Schendel, Willem Van. "The Invention of the 'Jummas': State Formation and Ethnicity in Southeastern Bangladesh." In *Indigenous Peoples of Asia*, edited by Robert H. Barnes, Andrew Gray, and Benedict Kingsbury, 121–144, 409–422 and 459–466. Ann Arbor, MI: Association for Asian Studies, 1995.

Schendel Willem Van, Wolfang Mey and Aditya Kumer Dewan. *Chittagong Hill Tracts: Living in a Borderland*. Dhaka: University Press Limited, 2001.

Schendel, Willem Van. "Geographies of Knowing, Geographies of Ignorance: Jumping Scale in Southeast Asia." *Environment and Planning D: Society and Space* 20, no. 6 (2002): 647–668.

Sivaramakrishnan, K. *Modern Forestry: Statemaking and Environment in Eastern Colonial India*. Stanford, CA: Stanford University Press, 1999.

Sopher, David E. "Population Dislocation in the Chittagong Hills." *Geographical Review* 53, no. 3 (1963): 337–362.

Taungya. "About Us." www.taungya.org.bd/AboutUs.aspx. (accessed September 27, 2013), n.d.

Taungya. *A Pilot Project on Protection of Village Common Forests in the Chittagong Hill Tracts: A Project on Sustainable Watershed Management*. Rangamati: Taungya, 2002.

Taungya. *Final Report on the Project Village Common Forest (VCF) in the Chittagong Hill Tracts*. Rangamati: Taungya, 2006.

Tripura, P., and Abantee Harun. *Parbattya Chotograme Jhum Chash* [*Swidden Agriculture in the Chittagong Hill Tracts*]. Dhaka: SEHD, 2003.

Tsing, Anna. L. "Becoming a Tribal Elder, and Other Green Development Fantasies." In *Transforming the Indonesian Uplands: Marginality, Power and Production*, edited by Tania Li, 159. London: Routledge, 1999.

United Nations Development Programme. *How to Revive a Village Common Forest: With Passion, Commitment and Community*. www.bd.undp.org/content/bangladesh/en/home/operations/projects/crisis_prevention_and_recovery/chittagong-hill-tracts-development-facility/how-to-revive-a-village-common-forest-with-passion-commitment-.html (accessed February 24, 2017), 2016.

Vandergeest, Peter, and Nancy Lee Peluso. "Territorialization and State Power in Thailand." *Theory and Society* 24, no. 3 (1995): 385–426.

Vandergeest, Peter, and Nancy Lee Peluso. "12. Political forests." In *The International Handbook of Political Ecology*, edited by Raymond L. Bryant, 162–175. Cheltenham: Edward Edgar, 2015.

White, Ben, Saturnino M. Borras, Ruth Hall, Ian Scoones and Wendy Wolford. "The New Enclosures: Critical Perspectives on Corporate Land Deals." *Journal of Peasant Studies* 39, no. 3–4 (2012): 619–647.

ZKS (Zabarang Kalyan Samity). *Project Proposal: Promoting a Network of Village Common Forests (VCFs) and Building Capacity of the Network Members in Chittagong Hill Tracts*. Khagrachari: ZKS, 2016.

9 Wapichan Wiizi

Conservation politics in the Rupununi (Guyana)

Katherine MacDonald

Indigenous peoples are often viewed by ecologists and conservationists as incompatible with conservation efforts and are presumed to be destroyers and exploiters of the environment, unable to manage their resources (Blaser, Feit, and McRae 2004; Mollett 2011; 2013). These same scientists provide evidence of rapidly devolving traditional practices[1] and Indigenous-led adoption of market-oriented approaches to the environment, seemingly out of place with conservation (Peres 1994). Of course, such environmental imaginaries are constructed within complex and often ambivalent relations of political power and power structures that operate effectively within neocolonial hegemonic patterns that often marginalize and epistemically erase Indigenous cultures from ecological histories and continuing geographies (Braun 2002; Hecht 2011; Li 2004; Sundberg 2008). Within Guyana, national and regional hegemonic decisions continue to contribute to the silencing of Indigenous voices, as current legislation acts to remove Indigenous populations from state ideology in concurrence with foreign expectations and domination patterns. The situation of Indigenous peoples even today is reminiscent of the colonial experience (Bulkan and Bulkan 2006), and "a deafening silence can be intuited from within dominant society on the subject of an applicable value to modernity from Indigenous Amerindian knowledge" (Mentore 2007, 58).[2]

The Government of Guyana recently embraced conservation ecology as a matter of national policy, and is actively engaged in promoting the country and various regions as examples of advanced environmental stewardship. Nationally, the Government of Guyana has partnered with the Government of Norway and the World Bank in the internationally supported climate change mitigation program intended to reduce deforestation in Guyana's hinterland regions through the provision of substantial grant aid through a global carbon market scheme entitled the Low Carbon Development Strategy (LCDS). Regionally, Conservation International Guyana, at the request of the Government of Guyana and in collaboration with the Ministry of Indigenous Peoples' Affairs (MIPA) and the Environmental Protection Agency (EPA), is involved in the establishment of the Kanuku Mountains Protected Area (KMPA) in the Rupununi, one of the most ecologically diverse areas of the country. However, this shift in conservation policies, toward an approach that sees "development needs of local populations as compatible with and complementary to the achievement of conservation goals" (Anthias and Radcliffe 2015, 260) proceeded with disregard for the populations it presumes to speak for. Problematically, for neither of these conservation proposals do the Indigenous peoples believe they were consulted, nor do they believe their traditional and customary practices, including their traditional Indigenous knowledges, were acknowledged or respected.

Consequently, the complex eco-political landscape that emerged from these processes was shaped solely by national and international policies and programs implemented by the state, foreign powers, and international environmental non-governmental organizations. The implicit marginalization of Indigenous knowledge in the proposal, creation, development, and execution of these protected areas is causing fragmentation of Indigenous ontologies, often resulting in the complete silencing of Indigenous voices. Disciplined by a colonial system of territorial governance that fails to acknowledge Indigenous ontologies, the Rupununi as a territory collapses into mere land, divisible through the Western concept of property.

In contrast, the Wapishana peoples of the South Rupununi initiated a customary management plan from within their communities entitled *Baokopa'o Wa Di'itinpan Wadauniinao Ati'o Nii: Kaimanamana'o, wa zaamatapan, wa di'itapan na'apamnii wa sha'apatan Wapichan wiizi Guyana'ao raza* (Thinking Together For Those Coming Behind Us: An outline plan for the care of Wapichan territory in Guyana) (2012). This document is based on extensive consultations over a period of four years within the 17 communities that occupy the South Rupununi, and was written and published with the support of Wapishana leaders, the South Central and South Rupununi Districts Toshaos Councils (DTCs). Instead of "conservation" policies and practices initiated and developed outside of the region, the Wapishana perceive the proposal as "a general framework for land management and self-determined development based on consensus among our communities on land use issues and measures needed to protect our rights and continue our way of life" (South Central and South Rupununi Districts Toshaos Councils 2012, iv).

By arguing against Western conservation and instead presenting a customary use management plan for the region, the Wapishana are reterritorializing the Rupununi, insisting on the recognition of Indigenous ontologies, while demanding a strategic "protection of a 'life' within a struggle for 'territory'" (Baletti 2012, 575). In what follows here, I explore Indigenous and environmental concepts of territory, territorialization, and territorialities to theorize the Rupununi as a site of ontological shift, where territory as "spaces of life" (Escobar 2008) is overcoming the regional dominance of colonial conservation practices.

Methods

This study is based on 18 months of field research in the Rupununi, carried out in four fieldwork sessions between 2010 and 2016. During this period, I worked with five Rupununi villages, including Shulinab, Aishalton, St. Ignatius, Karasabai, and Annai Central, each representing one subdistrict of the Rupununi in order to gain a broad overview of perspectives from the region. The majority of those living within the region continue to employ a subsistence mode of production, relying on hunting with bows and arrows, fishing with cast nets, fish traps, and ethnocultural fish poisons, gathering of forest products for construction and craft materials, bush medicines, and *bina* (charms), and rotational agriculture, with bitter cassava (*Manihot esculenta*) being the principal crop (South Central and South Rupununi District Toshaos Council 2012), although this lifestyle is changing. The five villages were chosen in consultation with local Indigenous organizations identified by the communities, including the North Rupununi District Development Board (NRDDB), the South Central Peoples' Development Association (SCPDA), and the DTCs, and, in addition to representing each of the five subdistricts of the Rupununi, these five villages together suggest a broad representation of other differences within the Rupununi. Two of the villages (Annai Central and Karasabai) are dominantly Makushi, and one village (Aishalton) is dominantly Wapishana. Shulinab is a traditionally mixed village (Makushi–Wapishana), while St. Ignatius is a village that has recently undergone significant demographic change and is now recognized as a mixed village (Makushi–Wapishana). The villages range in size from comparatively small (Shulinab, with a population of 545, is one of the smaller villages in the region) to comparatively large (Karasabai, with an approximate population of 1,600, is one of the largest villages in the region). Additionally, the NRDDB, SCPDA, and the Deep South DTC headquarters are located in three of these villages (Annai Central, Shulinab, and Aishalton, respectively), thereby heightening their importance for inclusion.

The research entailed long-term observation and informal conversations in addition to 107 semistructured interviews with residents of these Makushi and Wapishana communities, as well as observations of community consultations, events, and meetings, and interviews with local (Indigenous) NGOs and local (Indigenous) government representatives. Additionally, two research return visits, including one three-month feedback session, and one two-month feedback session were conducted in cooperation with all five villages in recognition of the importance of knowledge exchange to ethical research. Koster et al. (2012) believe that sharing results in meaningful ways helps maintain research honesty and increases the utility of the research, in addition to validating the research findings in organized community settings, allowing for both review and confirmation, as well as criticism and suggestions for improvement. Engaging in research with Indigenous peoples is historically fraught with notions of cultural appropriation and exploitation of Indigenous Knowledge through Western paradigms of positivist, essentialist, imperialist methodologies and the classic Orientalist division between "us" and the "other." By validating the research through this feedback and validation mechanism, respect for Indigenous perspectives traditionally silenced was further protected, arguably resulting in a more ethical process.

Territories, territoriaizations, territorialities

Territory is typically defined as a "unit of contiguous space that is used, organized, and managed by a social group, individual person, or institution to restrict and control access to people and places," and the dominant usage has always been political, involving implied power relations between peoples and/or places (Agnew 2009, 746). In allowing individuals, groups, or otherwise the possibility of claiming geographic space, the bounding of that space is implied, which necessarily entails a division between an "inside" and an "outside" (Delaney 2005; Samers 2010). With this definition, territorialization is understood as "an effort to 'governmentalize' space, necessarily creating an hierarchical relationship" (Baletti 2012, 577) between individuals or communities and relevant authorities involved in regulating their activities, including resource use, in a given area (Peluso and Lund 2011).

However, this definition of territory is problematic, as it implies that "the idea of territorial struggle can only be understood as a struggle over the terms of incorporation into the state," and recent research is challenging this idea of territory as a "fixed, bounded, spatially coherent entity" (Baletti 2012, 577). Whereas previously political power was concentrated in the state, more recently a redistribution of power between nonstate actors, including local organizations and communities, gives "rise to a world whose territorial compartments are … multidimensional" (Newman 2008, 133), a situation that has a significant impact at the local level. In particular, this rethinking of territory, as a subject-making practice but also as a space produced by the people within it, allows for a relationality of place, people, and practices (Baletti 2012; see also Bryan 2012; Escobar 2008; Kuper 2003; Reyes 2012, Reyes and Kaufman 2011).

The acceptance of relationality also makes apparent the arbitrariness of the spatial orders deployed in geography through definitions of territory, generally along political lines. Indeed, a place perspective "stresses the always open and contingent nature of this relation, and the multiple ways in which resistances are acted out in particular places" (Oslender 2004, 981). This reimagining of territories as "non-liberal territorialities" (Escobar 2010, 42), which recognize collective territories and collective rights, shifting toward relational understandings of territory, allows for a recognition of "multiple territories (physical spaces), territorializations (ways of taking hold of that space), and territorialities (subjectivities made in taking hold of space)" and their coexistence "both in practice and in potentiality" (Baletti 2012, 578).

In the Rupununi, the politics of territory has a long and complicated history of colonial dispossession, unfulfilled land claims, and deliberate misinterpretation of understood customary land uses. Originally British law assumed that all lands not already allocated to settlers could be treated as crown lands, owned and administered by the colonial power (Colchester 2005). At first they conceded special status to the "Aboriginal Indians of the colony" by recognizing their "traditional rights and privileges"; however, as competing interests began to move into the interior, these rights were progressively curtailed (ibid., 279). Yet, as a condition of independence, the colonial British government insisted that Indigenous peoples of the country should be granted:

> legal ownership or rights of occupancy over areas and reservations or parts thereof where any tribe or community of Amerindians is now ordinarily

> resident or settled and other legal rights, such as rights of passage, in respect of any other lands where they now by tradition or custom de facto enjoy freedoms and permissions corresponding to rights of that nature.
>
> (British Guiana Independence Conference Report 1965)

In partial fulfillment of this legal obligation given to Guyana at independence, the Amerindian Lands Commission was established in 1966, which attempted a comprehensive review of the Indigenous peoples' land situations and documented Indigenous land claims (Colchester 2005). However, extensive delays in the granting of customary lands continue until today. When community titling did eventually begin in the Rupununi, the Commission recommended areas substantially smaller than the territorial claims made by the peoples of the area to the Commission (ibid.). Because of this rejection of title, wherein Indigenous peoples claim that the territory has been a part of their lives from time immemorial, La Rose (2004) notes that Guyana's Indigenous peoples continue to exist within a political context of racial exclusion as marginalized communities, actualized through formalized displacement, or land grabs.

Territories of environmentalism

Recent scholarship has focused on the trend of land grabs noted above, which entail large-scale land and/or resource acquisitions, primarily aimed at securing agricultural land for increased development (Lunstrum 2016; see also De Schutter 2011; Lazarus 2014; Ojeda 2012; Zoomers 2010). Land grabbing is operationalized through the state (Mollett 2016) and is a process that is perceived as the "foreignization of space" (Zoomers 2010) through the enclosure of common spaces generally via transnational commercial transfers (Borras and Franco 2012).

The more specific "green grab" experience focuses on the expropriation of land and/or resources specifically for environmental purposes (Lunstrum 2016), increasingly by international development and/or environment organizations. These green grabs generally involve "forms of enclose that operate under the guise of addressing the global environmental crisis" (Corson and MacDonald 2012, 263), including the development of protected areas, payment for ecosystem services, and/or projects aimed at biodiversity conservation or mitigating the impacts of climate change (Baletti 2012; Corson and MacDonald 2012; Fairhead, Leach, and Scoones 2012; Zoomers 2010).

Importantly, these emergent "green" enclosures involve not only physical land grabs but also the "privatization of rights to nature, the creation of new commodities, and markets [for exchange of these rights and commodities] from nature" (Corson and MacDonald 2012, 264). With "green credentials" justifying these various types of land and/or resource expropriation (Corson, MacDonald, and Neimark 2013, 1), historically influential development and conservation organizations' actions are increasingly labeled environmental accumulation (MacDonald 2013), green capitalism (Baletti 2012), or neoliberal conservation

(Hackett 2015, 2016), and thus green grabs are seen as "the dark side of the green economy" (Corson, MacDonald, and Neimark 2013, 3; see also Borras et al. 2010).

This is particularly so when considering the local communities involved in these environmental land grabs, many of whom find themselves displaced from their lands and/or the resources upon which they depend by the appropriation of exactly these lands and/or resources by the green economy. When large tracts of land are repurposed for ecological ends, green grabs can "incite complex and troubling patterns of displacement" largely for the benefit of private investors, increasing inequality and reinforcing colonial patterns (Lunstrum 2016, 142; see also Lunstrum et al. 2016; Mollett 2013, 2016; Ybarra 2012).

The Government of Guyana, in what it posits as an "innovative and creative" policy, has indicated that it is willing to put "virtually [its] entire rainforest, which is about the size of England, under long term protection if the right economic incentives were created" (Then-President Jagdeo, cited in Office of the President 2010, 5), as a leading example of international carbon trading. Deforestation and forest degradation are credited with contributing an estimated 17 percent of the world's greenhouse gases through carbon emissions, therefore REDD (reduced emissions from deforestation and forest degradation) strategies are posited as an essential component of any climate change mitigation strategy (Dow et al. 2009; Office of the President, 2010). However, the feasibility of the scheme, the environmental sustainability of the benefits proposed, and most importantly the social and environmental consequences and impacts of the strategy upon the Indigenous peoples of Guyana as the primary inhabitants of the interior forest communities are questions that require further investigation (Colchester et al. 2002; Forte 1996).

According to the LCDS, in alignment with the principles of free, prior and informed consent, Indigenous communities will not be required to participate in REDD/+ and the LCDS unless they choose to do so, and no deadline will be set for whether and how they can opt in (Office of the President 2010). At issue with this declaration is the fact that, as noted above, many Indigenous land titles are unsettled, with some left outstanding since independence (1966) (Bulkan and Palmer 2016; FPP 2009). Amendments to the Amerindian Act in 1976 and 1991 provided land title for 64 Indigenous communities, bringing the total number of communities with title and demarcated lands to 97 (Bulkan 2009a; Office of the President 2010). In 2006, a further review process was undertaken to amend the Amerindian Act under the guidance of the World Bank and the Inter-American Development Bank. However, the revisions enacted by the government were regressive in some instances, and against international agreement in others. The Forest Peoples' Programme (FPP) and the Amerindian Peoples' Association (APA) submitted a complaint to the United Nations Committee on the Elimination of Racial Discrimination under its urgent action/early warning procedure, alleging that the Act was contrary to the rights of Indigenous peoples (Colchester and La Rose 2010).

However, despite this, 42 communities throughout the country are still without title, indicating that successive postindependence governments of

Guyana have not yet complied with the legal obligation in the independence agreement with the United Kingdom to "provide title to the communities for the lands which they occupied and used at the moment of independence" (Bulkan 2009a, n.p.).

The problem of untitled lands arises within the LCDS when the government refers to all land not currently under land title as "state forest," and the option for Indigenous peoples to opt in disintegrates in the face of title disputes. One Indigenous community member working with the APA noted that:

> the state is claiming most forest lands in the country and saying only fourteen percent belongs to Amerindians, yet under our customary laws we own much more traditional land and we do not accept that these ancestral lands are "state forests."

Another echoes this sentiment, asking:

> what about our untitled lands and our territorial lands? It seems as if the government is saying that all the forests outside our existing titles which are untitled belong to them: this is not fair, and is unjust. The only way we can work on this is if we look at Indigenous peoples' rightful land claims.
>
> (Cited in APA 2009, 17–18)

A further problem concerning Guyana's Indigenous populations revolves around what activities will be permitted within LCDS protected areas, under either state or Indigenous title. The concern originally arose from the Readiness Plan (R-Plan), a document required for REDD policies to help organize a country's framework, schedule, and budget, and to in part determine if a country is sufficiently able to proceed, published in 2009, which indicated that Guyana was seeking to reduce the practice of traditional rotational agriculture in Indigenous communities and reduce the expansion of farming (FPP 2009). This was further supported in a speech given by then-President Jagdeo, where he publicly stated that one major goal of a national REDD strategy would be to "make Amerindian peoples less dependent on traditional crops and forest lands and resources" (cited in FPP 2009, 4). During community consultations, the issue of traditional Indigenous practices of rotational farming by forest-dependent peoples was raised in nearly all of the consultations (Dow et al. 2009) and it was noted that Indigenous peoples did not agree that their traditional farming practices should be classified as deforestation or degradation (APA 2009). The LCDS multi-stakeholder consultation steering committee agreed on June 23, 2009, that traditional rotational agriculture is *not* deforestation or degradation and should be safeguarded within the LCDS–REDD program (Bulkan 2009b; Dow et al. 2009). However, problematically, in the latest draft of the LCDS, the government has left the future legality of traditional farming practices ambiguous by stating, "when communities decide to opt in, they will need to determine what, if any, action they wish to take on the use of traditional rotational farming methods" (Office of the

President 2010, 35). Local communities continue to be nervous about these future LCDS implications, as one Toshao explained to me:

> about the LCDS people were asking these questions, will we continue to do our farming in the forest? Will we continue to do our farming in the bush islands? Will we be allowed to go and extract materials the way we used to do, free of cost and those kinds of things, so they are, very sceptical about these, yeah.
>
> (Interview, December 5, 2011)[3]

Guyana's Indigenous communities are unlikely to receive significant direct benefits from the LCDS and Guyana's REDD policy where they do not have secure ownership rights over their traditional lands, and, indeed, Indigenous peoples must face the precedented history of loss of territory in preference for ecological conservation policies and practices (Cronon 1995; Li 2007; Lowe 2006; Lunstrum 2011; Pandian and Kosek 2003). The APA and many communities continue to be hesitant to trust the government, claiming that state proposals for LCDS and REDD are vague, and the potential risks, costs, and benefits are undefined (Griffiths and Anselmo 2010; FPP 2009; La Rose et al. 2012), particularly where traditional Indigenous practices are concerned. Finally, Guyana's Indigenous peoples were effectively absent from the proposal, creation, and development of the LCDS, leading to an erasure of Indigenous perspectives, a silencing of Indigenous voices, and a dismissal of Indigenous epistemologies, customary management, and traditional land practices at the national level.

Similar concerns exist on the regional scale. The Kanuku Mountains, located in the heart of the Rupununi savannahs in the south of Guyana, encompass an area of approximately 5,000 square kilometers. The Government of Guyana requested that Conservation International Guyana work together with the Ministry of Amerindian Affairs (MoAA) and the EPA to develop the KMPA. To balance this bureaucratic management, the Kanuku Mountain Community Representative Group (KMCRG) was formed in 2003 in order to facilitate communication and collaboration within the 11 communities and seven satellite communities that will be impacted by the creation of the KMPA.[4]

Unfortunately, many of the same issues that arose with the LCDS emerged during the proposal, creation, and development of the KMPA. The issue of land title was highlighted as a primary concern, as most of the villages surrounding the KMPA have unsettled land claims and land claim extensions submitted to the MIPA and the courts of Guyana. As with the LCDS, the problem of untitled lands arises when the government refers to all land not currently under land title as "state forest" and the concerns of Indigenous peoples vanish in the face of title disputes.

Indeed, one SCPDA board member noted that, in creating the KMPA, Conservation International, the MoAA, and the EPA were mandated to delineate the title boundaries; however, as he noted, the KMPA is

> A huge area, huge area. Right, so they delineated that part, right? And part of the management plan of the protected area, was that we here from Shulinab, from other communities too [we] said that we would like this line here, whenever the protected area becomes a protected area, [we] must be able to flex to accommodate our extensions. Right? This line here mustn't be built in stone, but must be able to flex, because one of the things we wanted was to deal with our land issues first. Give our Amerindian communities their lands, their extensions, and then you know, go into dealing with the protected area.
>
> (Interview, November 16, 2011)

This request, however, was not honored, as the KMPA became a legally protected area in Guyana in 2012, while none of the surrounding territorial claims submitted was settled, nor were clauses included to provide for this requested flexibility.

Furthermore, the territorial status of the protected area has been left uncertain for the Makushi and Wapishana of the region. The then-president of the KMCRG reflected that,

> [a]ccording to the Government of Guyana, it's a separate area; according to the Indigenous people, it's lands that are theirs by customary use. Part of that land was given to the communities, as part of their customary and traditional lands [it] was given to them. But now the entire area is one thing, that is a protected area, so that in itself, [while it] is still a part of those customary and traditional lands, it is going to be state property of the Government of Guyana.
>
> (Interview, March 5, 2012)

This confusion is exacerbated by the customary use patterns of the Makushi and Wapishana of the Kanuku Mountains area, since the mountains are a principal farming area for several villages and an important hunting area for others. The APA argued against the development of protected areas, and with reference to KMPA stated, "The Indigenous peoples were promised that they can still carry out their traditional activities. When reality stepped in, they were told that they cannot do as they want or else they will be charged for breaking the laws" (Kukuigok 2011, n.p.). Community leaders and villagers are unclear as to what the status of the protected area is in terms of these traditional practices. One village elder argued that most people in the region were against the creation of the protected area, maintaining that the suggested area is,

> Their farming area, and they will have to hunt farther, and all these things, they have to pick up whatever resources then, you know. A lot of resources were up in the mountain then.... Where are we going to hunt after when we have this, and all sort of things too.... They stop them from hunting, stop them from this, stop them from everything.
>
> (Interview, March 6, 2012)

A Toshao from a different village expressed his concern about the implementation of the KMPA, stating that:

> [i]t is impacting, it is a problem, because these protected areas, people are very worried because we are living without our Kanuku Mountains, we are living out from our Mountains, back from our Kanuku Mountains, because not that we don't make use of it, we Sawariwao use it in a way, so people are very afraid, will they allow us to continue to do our traditional practices, and those kinds of things.
>
> (Interview, December 5, 2011)

And one regional leader noted that:

> what I don't like about it, I can't do my own thing in my own trees, or own creek, or own fish, or own bird, or you name it. If I go away and I see a fish down there, I can't catch it. It's, because it's being conserved.
>
> (Interview, March 16, 2012)

This aversion to "conservation" can be directly traced to Indigenous epistemologies, since it is widely known that it is primarily because of their customary land management that the Kanuku Mountains area is worthy of "protection"; as the then-leader of the NRDDB stated, "we've been protecting these things for ages" (interview, April 4, 2012), which one village Toshao echoed when he said "because, I mean we have been living like this for years.... Yeah, that's why we still have the forests" (interview, April 5, 2012).

From land to territory

Indigenous organizations increasingly indicate that

> land rights offered, or even granted, within the state territorial framework often diverge significantly from their actual claims or demands, providing a partial granting of rights that does not meet their visions for self-determination and the reproduction of their forms of life.
>
> (Baletti 2012, 589)

In response, Indigenous communities are beginning to frame their territorial demands outside of classical political economy debates for land, and are instead arguing for the protection of their ontologies, or world views, "in defense of life and culture that demands territory instead of land – self-determination instead of property" (ibid., 593; see also Bryan 2012). Indeed, decolonizing territory would entail "exposing the ontological violence authorized by Eurocentric epistemologies" (Sundberg 2014, 34).

From this perspective, the shift to territory as "spaces of life," as opposed to land as property, is grounded in the acceptance of Indigenous ontologies that view the nonhuman world relationally (Escobar 2008; see also Blaser 2009, 2013, 2014; de la Cadena 2010, 2015; Escobar 2010; Viveiros de Castro 1998, 2005), in stark opposition to the Western political economy wherein land use is defined by productivity (Baletti 2012). These "spaces of life," wherein space, place, and society "mutually constitute and impact on one another" (Oslender 2004, 960), provide a "place-based framework linking history, culture, environment, and social life" (Escobar 2008, 62), where places are seen as multiple, political, and collective (Bryan 2012). By valuing "territory" as "spaces of life," where "the environment" is perceived to be a relation as opposed to a resource to be exploited or conserved, Indigenous ontologies are prioritized, which allows for a restructuring of the inherent power dynamics involved in land and/or green grabs (Baletti 2012), as well as an "*economic, ecological, and cultural conversion*, a reconfiguration of the biophysical and cultural landscape" (Escobar 2008, 64, emphasis original).

For the Wapishana, territory plays a significant role in the way in which their identity is expressed. Within the Rupununi, political designations have begun to appear within Indigenous place references as part of the process of reclaiming customary lands from the state, where "lands" have become "territories" through interactions with colonial and (post)colonial governments. Places previously referred to as collective, or customary lands are becoming "territory" through political maneuvers, including the use of Indigenous language to imply "authenticity" (Graham 2002). Furthermore, the Wapishana are using the term "ancestral territory" politically as a means of reference, even though the traditional definitions of territory above do not fully apply in Indigenous ontological perspectives.

Indeed, many peoples of the Rupununi have not forgotten their traditional territories, and are still fighting to claim what their grandparents left them. The region's Indigenous peoples submitted joint claims by several villages for collective ownership over a continuous territory, encompassing all the villages, as well as all the space between villages. As it was explained to me by one SCPDA leader,

> What we want to do is that we must have no space between our titles. So all will be a whole territory, and that's what the government don't want, and that's what we're fighting for. That's what it should have been originally. That's what the old Chiefs wanted, and that's what we're fighting for. To make it one big territory.
>
> (Interview, November 10, 2011)

But the Amerindian Land Commissioners did not accept their claim, as they considered it was excessive and beyond the ability of the residents to successfully administrate and develop. Indeed, state claims of "empty" and "uninhabited" lands, or the abuse of those lands through "unsuitable (i.e.: Native) land use practices" and "pejorative representations of Indigenous peoples … customary and collective tenure arrangements" are common patterns of imperialist thinking that continues today (Mollett 2016, 414–415; see also Sundberg 2006). In the Rupununi, one SCPDA board member explained to me what was said at a meeting of the President of Guyana and the District Toshaos Council:

> When the President said "why you want so much of land?" He said, "all right, y'all want the land", because we were talking about the same 1967 land claim right? He said "if y'all want the land, show me what you will do with this land, and then we will see what will happen. Show me what you need this for."
>
> (Interview, November 16, 2011)

Thus began the territory mapping project, followed by a community-based research project documenting traditional practices and customary use, *Wa Wiizi, Wa Kaduzu* (David et al. 2006), which led to the creation of the territorial management plan, *Baokopa'o Wa Di'itinpan Wadauniinao Ati'o Nii* (South Central and South Rupununi Districts Toshaos Councils 2012). In contrast with the LCDS and KMPA projects, the Wapishana customary use and traditional practices documents were developed through extensive community consultations, with villagers, elders, traditional and specialist knowledge holders, community leaders, regional Indigenous organizations, and with the recognition, support, and assistance of the DTCs.

Rather than excluding traditional Indigenous Knowledge, these documents and the plans they describe are deeply linked to Indigenous epistemologies, acknowledging ancestors, spirit masters, and forest and savannah animals and plants as integral to Wapishana ontologies. Indigenous peoples, including the Wapishana, often live in a different ontological reality, and their holistic perspective is frequently overlooked or disregarded in the design of conservation zones or protected areas (Brockington and Duffy 2010; Graddy 2013; MacDonald 2010). With reference to the KMPA, one Wapishana villager commented to me:

> So, I think if Kanuku, KMPA then could be, could be drawn on a something, and show them to be, like argue what happen between these two protected areas doesn't matter. You know? You telling me the creeks that connect these two protected areas don't matter, what are you saying? Because I asked about these, I asked the same fellow the same question, you know? You have rivers running through the Kanukus and they're mining up, upstream, and granting concessions. And then there was the director of CI sitting there too, yeah man. Yeah, they don't care man, they're just like looking at this area.
>
> (Interview, December 12, 2011)

As articulated by the Wapishana villager above, mainstream conservation practices fail to see the ecosystem as a whole entity, comprised of multiple overlapping ecologies. And, rather than relying upon the Wapishana knowledges and practices that have kept Rupununi lands intact, the Government of Guyana is looking to external organizations, such as the World Bank and Conservation International, for guidance on how to best manage their ecology. These external environmental imaginaries invite imbalance into political power relations as repeatedly Indigenous peoples' perspectives, knowledges, and experiences are marginalized and their voices and contributions are epistemically and materially erased from ecological histories and continuing geographies.

Through the failure to acknowledge traditional territories, the suspension of traditional practices, and the lack of consultation with Indigenous peoples, national and regional hegemonic decisions continue to contribute to the silencing of Indigenous voices within Guyana, and current legislation removes Indigenous populations from state ideology in concurrence with foreign expectations and domination patterns. The Wapishana territorial mapping project, the community-based research project documenting traditional practices and customary use, *Wa Wiizi, Wa Kaduzu*, and especially the customary management plan, *Baokopa'o Wa Di'itinpan Wadauniinao Ati'o Nii*, are offered as an alternative to ongoing colonial domination, as part of a conscientization movement aiming to free the Wapishana from oppression, marginalization, and neglect, and to further their goal of self-determination while "conserving" their traditional territory through customary practices and their Indigenous Knowledges.

Notes

1 Guyana currently recognizes nine distinct Indigenous populations: Akawaio, Arawak, Arekuna, Carib, Makushi, Patamona, Wai Wai, Wapishana, and Warao. The peoples of the Rupununi today include the Makushi, the Wapishana, and the Wai Wai, although they acknowledge that the peoples are more multiple than this, stating that "Our grandfathers tell us that long ago the Rupununi was home to a variety of Indigenous peoples. These peoples included the Atoradnao, Daozai, Tarabainao, Chiibizai dinnao, Arokonnao, Parau yannao, Paowishiyannao, Maoyanao, Karapunnao, Taromnao, Nikanikarunao, Burokotonao and Macushi peoples, as well as our own people: the Wapichannao" (David et al., 2006:9). It is not my intention to homogenize these voices in this paper; the multiplicity of populations and perspectives should be understood as implicit from my use of 'peoples.'

2 In 2015, Guyana officially adopted the term Indigenous, rather than Amerindian, with consequent changes to all government institutions, including the Ministry of Indigenous Peoples' Affairs. Since the majority (but certainly not all) of the people with whom I spoke concurred with this internationally recognized terminology, I chose to use "Indigenous" for this study.

3 Traditional research ethics call for protection of sources and confidentiality of information, and when I submitted my research proposal for Ethics Approval, this is what I promised, thus community members are only identified by their role in the village or the region in this paper. However, I have come to understand that many people, when they give knowledge, would prefer that it be acknowledged as theirs (Castleden, et al., 2012).

I have chosen to retain the dialect and vocabulary of the Makushi and Wapishana to emphasize the methodological approach of this project, which specifically aims to highlight Indigenous voices. This is meant to be a sign of respect, not a means of 'othering' the Makushi and Wapishana.

4 The official number of satellites is seven, however, the KMCRG list nine satellite communities.Katoka, Yupukari (Kaicumbay is listed but there is also Quatata and Fly Hill), Nappi (Hiowa and Parishara), Moco Moco, St. Ignatius (Kumu and Quarrie), Parikwarunawa, Shulinab (Meri Wau and Quiko), Sand Creek, Rupunau, Shea and Maruranau (KMCRG, 2012).

References

Agnew, John. "Territory." In *The Dictionary of Human* Geography, edited by D. Gregory, R. Johnston, G. Pratt, M. J. Watts, and S. Whatmore, 5th edn. Oxford: Wiley-Blackwell, 746–747, 2009.

Amerindian Peoples Association and Forest Peoples Program. *Indigenous Peoples' Rights, REDD and the Draft Low Carbon Development Strategy (Guyana).* A summary report of a workshop held in the Regency Suites, Georgetown, 24–26, 2009.

Anthias, Penelope and Sarah A. Radcliffe. "The Ethno-Environmental Fix and its Limits: Indigenous Land Titling and the Production of Not-Quite-Liberal Natures in Bolivia." *Geoforum* 64 (2015): 257–269.

Baletti, Brenda. "Ordenamento Territorial: Neo-developmentalism and the Struggle for Territory in the Lower Brazilian Amazon." *The Journal of Peasant Studies* 39, no. 2 (2012): 573–598.

Blaser, Mario. "Ontology and Indigeneity: On the Political Ontology of Heterogeneous Assemblages." *Cultural Geographies* 21, no. 1 (2014): 49–58.

Blaser, Mario. "Notes Towards a Political Ontology of 'Environmental' Conflicts." In *Contested Ecologies: Nature and Knowledge*, edited by L. Green. Cape Town: HSRC Press, 13–27, 2013.

Blaser, Mario. "The Threat of the Yrmo: The Political Ontology of a Sustainable Hunting Program." *American Anthropologist* 111, no. 1 (2009): 10–20.

Blaser, Mario, Harvey A. Feit, and Glen McRae. *In the Way of Development: Indigenous Peoples, Life Projects, and Globalization.* New York, NY: Zed, 2004.

Borras, Saturnino M. and Jennifer C. Franco. "Global Land Grabbing and Trajectories of Agrarian Change: A Preliminary Analysis." *Journal of Agrarian Change* 12, no. 1 (2012): 34–59.

Borras, Saturnino M., Phillip McMichael, and Ian Scoones. "The Politics of Biofuels, Land and Agrarian Change: Editors' Introduction." *The Journal of Peasant Studies* 37, no. 4 (2010): 575–592.

Braun, Bruce. *The Intemporate Rainforest: Nature, Culture, and Power on Canada's West Coast.* Minneapolis, MN: University of Minneapolis Press, 2002.

Brockington, Dan, and Rosaleen Duffy. "Capitalism and Conservation: The Production and Reproduction of Biodiversity Conservation." *Antipode* 42, no. 3 (2010): 469–484.

Bryan, Joe. "Rethinking Territory: Social Justice and Neoliberalism in Latin America's Territorial Turn." *Geography Compass* 6, no. 4 (2012): 215–226.

Bulkan, Christopher Arif. *The Land Rights of Guyana's Indigenous Peoples.* Unpublished PhD dissertation, York University, Toronto, 2008.

Bulkan, Janette. "Gains and Losses in the Forest Carbon Budget: Carbon in the Forests of Guyana, part 1." *Stabroek News*, 7 August, 2009a.

Bulkan, Janette. "Gains and Losses in the Forest Carbon Budget: Carbon in the Forests of Guyana, part 2." *Stabroek News*, 14 August, 2009b.

Bulkan, Janette, and Arif Bulkan. " 'These Forests Have Always Been Ours': Official and Amerindian Discourses on Guyana's Forest Estate." In *Indigenous Resurgence in the*

Contemporary Caribbean: Amerindian Survival and Revival, edited by Maximillian C. Forte, 135–154. New York, NY: Peter Lang, 2006.

Bulkan, Janette, and John Palmer. "Rentier Nation: Landlordism, Patronage, and Power in Guyana's Gold Mining Sector." *The Extractive Industries in Society* 3, no. 3 (2016): 676–689.

Castleden, Heather, Vanessa S. Morgan, and Christopher Lamb. "'I Spent the First Year Drinking Tea': Exploring Canadian University Researchers' Perspectives on Community-Based Participatory Research Involving Indigenous Peoples." *The Canadian Geographer* 56, no. 2 (2012): 160–179.

Colchester, Marcus. "Maps, Power, and the Defense of Territory: The Upper Mazaruni Land Claim in Guyana." In *Communities and Conservation: Histories and Politics of Community-Based Natural Resource Management*, edited by J. Peter Brosius, Anna L. Tsing, and Charles Zerner, 271–304. New York, NY: Altamira Press, 2005.

Colchester, Marcus, and Jean La Rose. *Our Land, Our Future: Participation and Rights in Mining, Climate Change and Other Natural Resource Decision-making in Guyana.* Final Report of the APA/FPP/NSI project "Indigenous Perspectives on Consultation and Decision-Making about Mining and Other Natural Resources: Toward Community Strengthening, Dialogue and Policy Change," May 31, 2010.

Colchester, Marcus, Jean La Rose, and Kid James. *Mining and Amerindians in Guyana.* Georgetown: The North–South Institute, Ottawa and Amerindian Peoples Association, 2002.

Conservation International. "Kanuku Mountains." *Conservation International Guyana.* www.conservation.org.gy/explore_kanuku.php (accessed January 15, 2013), n.d.

Corson, Catherine, and Kenneth I. MacDonald. "Enclosing the Global Commons: The Convention on Biological Diversity and Green Grabbing." *The Journal of Peasant Studies* 39, no. 2 (2012): 263–283.

Corson, Catherine, Kenneth I. MacDonald, and Benjamin Neimark. "Grabbing 'Green': Markets, Environmental Governance, and the Materialization of Natural Capital." *Human Geography* 6, no. 1 (2013): 1–15.

Cronon, William. "The Trouble with Wilderness; or, Getting Back to the Wrong Nature." In *Uncommon Ground: Rethinking the Human Place in Nature*, edited by William Cronon, 69–90. New York, NY: W. W. Norton, 1995.

David, Beryl, Percival Isaacs, Angelbert Jonny, Larry Johnson, Maxi Pugsley, Claudine Ramacindo, Gavin Winter, and Yolanda Winter. *Wa Wiizi, Wa Kaduzu – Our Territory, Our Custom: Customary Use of Biological Resources and Related Traditional Practices Within Wapichan Territory in Guyana.* An Indigenous Case Study, 2006.

de la Cadena, Marisol. "Indigenous Cosmopolitics in the Andes: Conceptual Reflections Beyond 'Politics.'" *Cultural Anthropology* 25, no. 2 (2010): 334–370.

de la Cadena, Marisol. *Earth Beings: Ecologies of Practice across Andean Worlds.* Durham, NC: Duke University Press, 2015.

Delaney, David. *Territory: A Short Introduction.* Malden, MA: Blackwell, 2005.

De Schutter, O. "The Green Rush: The Global Race for Farmland and the Rights of Land Users." *Harvard International Law Journal* 52 (2011): 503–559.

Dow, Jocelyn, Vanda Radzik, and Duncan MacQueen. *Independent Review of the Stakeholder Consultation Process for Guyana's Low Carbon Development Strategy (LCDS).* Commissioned by the Governments of Norway and Guyana. International Institute for Environment and Development, 2009.

Escobar, Arturo. *Territories of Difference: Place, Movements, Life, Redes.* Durham, NC: Duke University Press, 2008.

Escobar, Arturo. "Latin America at A Crossroads." *Cultural Studies* 24, no. 1 (2010): 1–65.

Fairhead, James, Melissa Leach, and Ian Scoones. "Green Grabbing: A New Appropriation of Nature?" *The Journal of Peasant Studies* 39, no. 2 (2012): 237–261.

Foreman, David. *Confessions of an Eco-Warrior*. New York, NY: Harmony, 1991.

Forest Peoples' Programme. *Guyana: Indigenous Peoples, Forests and Climate Initiatives*. Rights, Forests and Climate Briefing Series – November 2009.

Forte, Janette. *About Guyanese Amerindians*. Georgetown: Guyana, 1996.

Graddy, Garrett T. "Regarding Biocultural Heritage: In Situ Political Ecology of Agricultural Biodiversity in the Peruvian Andes." *Agriculture and Human Values* 30 (2013): 587–604.

Graham, Laura R. "How Should an Indian Speak?: Amazonian Indians and the Symbolic Politics of Language in the Global Public Sphere." In *Indigenous Movements, Self-Representation, and the State in Latin America*, edited by Kay B. Warren and Jean E. Jackson, 181–228. Austin: University of Texas Press, 2002.

Griffiths, Tom, and Lawrence Anselmo. *Indigenous Peoples and Sustainable Livelihoods in Guyana: An Overview of Experiences and Potential Opportunities*. Amerindian Peoples Association, Forest Peoples Programme, and the North–South Institute, 2010.

Hackett, Ryan. " 'Shell Games', Displacement, and the Reordering of Boreal Landscapes in Alberta, Canada." *Area* 48, no. 2 (2016): 153–160.

Hackett, Ryan. "Offsetting Dispossession? Terrestrial Conservation Offsets and First Nation Treaty Rights in Alberta, Canada." *Geoforum* 60 (2015): 62–71.

Hecht, Susanna B. "The New Amazon Geographies: Insurgent Citizenship, 'Amazon Nation', and the Politics of Environmentalisms." *Journal of Cultural Geography* 28, no. 1 (2011): 203–223.

Hylton, John H. *Aboriginal Self-Government in Canada*. Saskatoon: Purich, 1999.

Kanuku Mountains Community Representative Group. KMCRG. *KMCRG*. www.facebook.com/kmcrg/info (accessed January 15, 2013), n.d..

Koster, Rhonda, Kirstine Baccar, and R. Harvey Lemelin. "Moving from Research ON, to Research WITH and FOR Indigenous Communities: A Critical Reflection on Community-Based Participatory Research." *The Canadian Geographer* 56, no. 2 (2012): 195–210.

Kukuigok. "Response by the Amerindian Peoples Association to K. Isles, Kanuku Mountains, Shell Beach Declared Protected Areas." *Demerara Waves*. www.demerarawaves.com/index.php/Latest/2011/10/20/kanuku-mountains-shell-beach-declared-protected-areas.html (accessed January 15, 2013), 2011.

Kuper, Adam. "The Return of the Native." *Current Anthropology* 44, no. 3 (2003): 389–402.

La Rose, Jean. "In Guyana, Indigenous Peoples Fight to Join Conservation Efforts." *Cultural Survival Quarterly* 28, no. 1 (2004). http://209.200.101.189/publications/csq/csqarticle.cfm?id=1737.

La Rose, Jean, Tom Griffiths, and Solveig Fring Lunde. "Taking Stock: Indigenous Peoples and Low Carbon Development Policies in Guyana." In *Indigenous Peoples' Rights, Forests, and Climate Policies in Guyana: A Special Report*, edited by Kate Dooley and Tom Griffiths, 61–92. Amerindian Peoples' Association and the Forest Peoples' Programme, 2014.

Lazarus, Eli D. "Land Grabbing as a Driver of Environmental Change." *Area* 46 (2014): 74–82.

Li, Tania M. *The Will To Improve: Governmentality, Development and the Practice of Politics*. London: Duke University Press, 2007.

Li, Tania M. "Environmental Indigeneity and Transnationalism." In *Liberation Ecologies: Environment, Development, Social Movements*, edited by Richard Peet and Micheal Watts, 339–370. London: Routledge, 2004.

Lowe, Celia. *Wild Profusion: Biodiversity Conservation in an Indonesian Archipelago*. Princeton, NJ: University of Princeton Press, 2006.

Lunstrum, E. "State Rationality, Development, and the Making of State Territory: From Colonial Extraction to Post-colonial Conservation." In *Cultivating the Colony: Colonial States and their Environmental Legacies*, edited by Christina F. Ax, Niels Brimnes, Niklas T. Jensen, and Karen Oslund, 239–274. Athens, OH: Ohio University Press, 2011.

Lunstrum, Elizabeth. "Green Grabs, Land Grabs, and the Spatiality of Displacement: Eviction from Mozambique's Limpopo National Park." *Area* 48, no. 2 (2016): 142–152.

Lunstrum, Elizabeth, Pablo Bose, and Anna Zalik. "Environmental Displacement: The Common Ground of Climate Change, Extraction, and Conservation." *Area* 48, no. 2 (2016): 130–133.

MacDonald, Kenneth. "The Devil Is in the (Bio)diversity: Private Sector 'Engagement' and the Restructuring of Biodiversity Conservation." *Antipode* 42, no. 3 (2010): 513–550.

MacDonald, Kenneth. "Grabbing 'Green': Cynical Reason, Instrumental Ethics, and the Production of 'the Green Economy.'" *Human Geography* 6, no. 1 (2013): 46–63.

Mentore, George. "Guyanese Amerindian Epistemology: The Gift from a Pacifist Insurgence." *Race and Class* 49, no. 2 (2007): 57–70.

Merchant, Carolyn. *Radical Ecology: The Search for a Liveable World*. New York, NY: Routledge, 1992.

Mollett, Sharlene. "Racial Narratives: Miskito and Colono Land Struggles in the Honduran Mosquitia." *Cultural Geographies* 18, no. 1 (2011): 43–62.

Mollett, Sharlene. "Mapping Deception: The Politics of Mapping Miskito and Garifuna Space in Honduras." *Annals of the Association of American Geographers* 103, no. 5 (2013): 1227–1241.

Mollett, Sharlene. "The Power to Plunder: Rethinking Land Grabbing in Latin America." *Antipode* 48, no. 2 (2016): 412–432.

Newman, David. "Boundaries." In *A Companion Guide to Political Geography*, edited by John Agnew, Katharyne Mitchell, and Gerard Toal, 123–137. London: Blackwell, 2008.

Office of the President, Republic of Guyana. *A Low Carbon Development Strategy: Transforming Guyana's Economy While Combating Climate Change*. Policy Document. Georgetown, Guyana, 2010.

Ojeda, Diana. "Green Pretexts: Ecotourism, Neoliberal Conservation, and Land Grabbing in Tayrona National Natural Park, Colombia." *The Journal of Peasant Studies* 39, no. 2 (2012): 357–375.

Oslender, Ulrich. "Fleshing Out the Geographies of Social Movements: Colombia's Pacific Coast Black Communities and the 'Aquatic Space.'" *Political Geography* 23 (2004): 957–985.

Pandian, Anand, and Jake Kosek. "The Cultural Politics of Race and Nature: Terrains of Power and Practice." In *Nature and the Politics of Difference Race*, edited by Donald Moore, Jake Kosek, and Anand Pandian, 1–70. London: Duke University Press, 2003.

Peluso, Nancy Lee, and Christian Lund. "New Frontiers of Land Control." *The Journal of Peasant Studies* 38, no. 4 (2011): 667–681.

Peres, Carlos A. "Indigenous Reserves and Nature Conservation in Amazonian Forests." *Conservation Biology* 8, no. 2 (1994): 586–588.

Peres, Carlos A., and Zimmerman, Barbara. "Perils in Parks or Parks in Peril? Reconciling Conservation in Amazonian Reserves With and Without Use." *Conservation Biology* 15, no. 3 (2001): 793–797.

Reyes, Alvaro. "Revolutions in the Revolutions: A Post-Counterhegemonic Moment for Latin America." *South Atlantic Quarterly* 111, no. 1 (2012): 1–27.

Reyes, Alvaro and Mara Kaufman. "Sovereignty, Indigeneity, Territory: Zapatista Autonomy and the New Practices of Decolonization." *South Atlantic Quarterly* 110, no. 2 (2011): 505–525.

Samers, Micheal. *Migration*. London: Routledge, 2010.

Schwartzman, Stephan, Adriana Moreira, and Daniel Nepstad. "Rethinking Tropical Forest Conservation: Perils in Parks." *Conservation Biology* 14, no. 5 (2000): 1351–1357.

South Central and South Rupununi Districts Toshaos Councils. *Baokopa'o Wa Di'itinpan Wadauninao Ati'o Nii: Thinking Together For Those Coming Behind Us*. South Rupununi: A Document of the Indigenous Peoples of the South Rupununi, 2012.

Sundberg, Juanita. "Conservation Encounters: Transculturation in the 'Contact Zones' of Empire." *Cultural Geographies* 13 (2006): 239–265.

Sundberg, Juanita. "Placing Race in Environmental Justice Research in Latin America." *Society and Natural Resources* 21 (2008): 569–582.

Sundberg, Juanita. "Decolonizing Posthumanist Geographies." *Cultural Geographies* 21, no. 1 (2014): 33–47.

Tobias, Micheal. *After Eden: History, Ecology, and Conscience*. San Diego, CA: Avant, 1985.

Viveiros de Castro, Eduardo. "Perspectivism and Multinaturalism in Indigenous America." In *The Land Within: Indigenous Territory and The Perception of Environment*, edited by Alexandre Surrallés and Pedro G. Hierro, 36–74. Copenhagen: International Work Group for Indigenous Affairs, 2005.

Viveiros de Castro, Eduardo. "Cosmological Deixis and Amerindian Perspectivism." *Journal of the Royal Anthropological Institute* 4, no. 3 (1998): 469–488.

Ybarra, Megan. "Taming the Jungle, Saving the Maya Forest: Sedimented Counterinsurgency Practices in Contemporary Guatemalan Conservation." *The Journal of Peasant Studies*, 39, no. 2 (2012): 479–502.

Zoomers, Annelies. "Globalisation and the Foreignisation of Space: Seven Processes Driving the Current Global Land Grab." *The Journal of Peasant Studies* 37 (2010): 429–47.

10 Science as friend and foe

The "technologies of humility" in the changing relationship to science in community forest debates in Thailand

Vanessa Lamb and Robin Roth

Introduction

At the heart of the "people–park" dilemma are the ways in which scientific forest management regimes have classified forests in ways that restrict access to people who live in and rely on forests, giving rise to frequent tension and contests over the competing claims to access, rights, and knowledge. The populated subtropical forests of northern Thailand are no exception. The upland area is home to a number of Indigenous ethnic minority groups who, over the past century, have continued to experience significant conflict with the state over forest use and protected area establishment. This conflict and the broader debates on the division between forests and people are well-rehearsed in the literature (Hirsch 1997; Roth 2008; Peluso, Vandergeest, and Potter 1995; Forsyth and Walker 2008; Vaddhanaphuti 2003; Wittayapak 2008). Our interest in this chapter is to consider the work by social movements in Thailand, which have been effective in advocating a more central role for communities in forest conservation and management. In particular, we investigate the deliberation over the use and form of "science" by social movements as a means of understanding the changing terms of the contests over people and forests. As allies and as (implicated) researchers, we follow how the communities and movements we work with have come to accept certain aspects of a science they once saw as the domain of oppression and as the opposition. How have social movements advocating a more central role for communities in forest and conservation management in Thailand negotiated a relationship to science? How have they used, neglected, adapted, and dismissed science in their efforts to support access of the rural poor to environmental resources? How is science transformed in this process?

In considering these questions within this chapter, we recognize that none of these categories we invoke—science, people's movements, the state—is homogenous (Agrawal 1995; Agrawal and Gibson 1999). In this vein, the two cases we present reveal the tensions inherent in making and mobilizing knowledge which aims to make claims on behalf of others. The researchers and activists we work with in Thailand did not always engage science the ways they do currently and, in fact, people's movements in Thailand have long resisted science, seen as largely a tool of the state, and scientific management, seen largely as a technology of oppression. In the case of scientific forestry, activists stood against dominant, imperial principles of scientific forest management that require a strict separation of humans from forest and maintained skepticism of scientific methods, such as mapmaking, that decontextualize specific claims in an attempt to make universal claims. As we demonstrate across two cases in northern Thailand, forest-dwelling communities and people's movements are now taking up some of these tools to support their struggles in solidifying land rights and participation in forest governance. This has become potentially even more significant under the post-May 2014 military government. Under this regime, the constitution was destroyed and then imposed, and currently legal mechanisms and access have changed (Rujivanarom 2017), with academics and NGO actors identifying that communities have better access to making arguments and engagements with science than they have in the past (pers. comm., July 2017).

There is more at stake in this examination than intellectual curiosity. These shifts in how science is understood and employed by the community forest movement directly impacts how communities make claims of expertise and legitimacy in Thailand. Here, scientific forest management and the associated implementation of forest policy over the past 100 years facilitated the large-scale displacement of rural people. While precise numbers differ (and are a source of contention), forced displacement from the forest ranges between five and 15 million households (Barney 2005; Vandergeest 1996; Lohmann 1999). More recently, Thailand's *Bangkok Post* reported that, under the current military regime, "more than 1,000 people, mostly poor villagers, have been arrested" in an effort to quell "forest encroachment" (Jitcharoenkul 2015). These alarming numbers point to how forest policy threatens rural peoples' lives and livelihood security in Thailand, but also highlight how the successful and just future of forest conservation is also linked to the relations between people and science.

In our own work, we identify sites in northern Thailand, which in the past experienced this displacement from the forest, particularly as linked to policies leading to displacement of rural forest dwellers who are poor and identify as ethnic minorities. We refer principally to the Karen, an Indigenous ethnic minority group that was also seen at the forefront of Thailand's movement for community rights and community forest management. Here we also see a shifting relationship between science, forests, and social movements, where the stakes are high and the shifts incomplete. We document an increase of deliberation—the work of "humility"—among people's movements and state officials, and, simultaneously, we also identify that issues pertaining to *who* can become an expert with the influence to shape or enact forest governance and decision-making is critical for forest-dwelling communities and for the future of Thailand's forests. Speaking to the core theme of this collection, we consider the social technologies of governance and deliberation, which raise questions of who can become an expert and how that is marked by difference, in that we assert that both governments' and forest-dwelling communities' knowledge production about forests (and who participates in generating this knowledge) is linked to position, racialization of forest residents in northern Thailand, and historical context (Vandergeest 2003; Mollett and Faria 2013).

Humility and solidarity: concepts for science?

As governance becomes less state-centered and more about multi-stakeholder governance, we see the growth of what can be termed "solidarity science" (Diane Rocheleau, pers. comm., May 2014), where Western science and local knowledge work together for more effective management outcomes, which is also arguably linked with the increasing range of actors in environmental and forest governance. This form of knowledge emerges from scientists and researchers working in solidarity with, for instance, rural communities and social movements and thus its production is neither straightforward nor obvious. To frame this chapter, and think about these concepts of "solidarity" and "humility" in relation to forests, science, and governance, we build upon scholarship that identifies a shift in science toward the greater deployment of "technologies of humility" (Jasanoff 2003) to consider the ways knowledge production itself is transformed in northern Thailand. Working together across epistemological differences is not without difficulty or risk, and it can be done most effectively with humility about the limits of scientific knowledge, a high degree of accountability, and engagement with inherent risks (Jasanoff 2003). In Jasanoff's formulation, attention to the technologies of humility "would give combined attention to substance and process, and stress deliberation as well as analysis" (2003, 243). She explains:

> Reversing nearly a century of contrary development, these approaches to decision-making would seek to integrate the "can do" orientation of science and engineering with the "should do" questions of ethical and political analysis. They would engage the human subject as an active, imaginative agent, as well as a source of knowledge, insight, and memory.
>
> (Jasanoff 2003, 243)

In short, rather than overlook analysis of the work to produce science that is more explicitly linked to other ways of knowing, this approach places this work, and the different actors who (can) engage in it, front and center. Further, while participation and transparency are considered "promising" developments, they should not be seen as the answer to problems of governance but "treated as a standard operating procedure of democracy," with their aims "considered as carefully as its mechanisms" (Jasanoff 2003, 243). This also mirrors what Agrawal (1995, 413–414) describes more broadly related to the "local–scientific" knowledge divide, with recent invocations of Indigenous knowledges and local people representing "a shift from the preoccupation with the centralized, technically oriented solutions of the past decade that failed to alter life prospects for a majority of the peasants and small farmers in the world."

Thus, to complement existing approaches to governance and technology, which tend to emphasize prediction, and eliminate risk and "pre-empt political discussion" (Jasanoff, 2003, 239), in this chapter we attend to the "*social* technologies" which "would give combined attention to substance and process, and stress deliberation as well as analysis" (Jasanoff 2003, 243). Through social technological shifts including the redefinition of problems, with the vulnerable and those impacted by change included as agents, such work can produce more meaningful deliberation of both, for instance, the practical challenges of forest governance but also the political and conceptual terrain upon which "forest" and "governance" are constructed.

Recently, our colleagues Forsyth and Walker (2014, 411) have assessed Thailand's community forest movement in relation to the politics of knowledge, with similar interests in how "knowledge and visions of social order co-evolve." However, rather than our focus on "technologies of humility," they surmise the implications differently. They argue that "state and citizens can both actively participate in reifying authoritative expertise about environmental problems; and that this expertise can be based on shared visions of social order, which also exclude alternative perspectives about environmental management" (Forsyth and Walker 2014, 408). Invoking Jasanoff's notions of co-production, the authors focus on how when scientific facts are shared by "both sides" these facts become "real" or legitimate, rather than how those "scientific facts" are negotiated and co-constructed in the first place. We recognize their point and the criticism that the community forest movement in Thailand has accepted certain "scientific facts," which are also linked to the making of authority. Yet, emerging work (King 2017; Huete 2017, among others) also point out that expanding the actors in making knowledge and governing northern Thailand's forests is having impacts on participation, deliberations, and outcomes. Thus, building on our longitudinal research in northern Thailand, to think about the implications for science we push further, to identify that science itself and its practice is also transformed in and through the work and negotiations between foresters, officials, and local, racialized, Indigenous, Karen residents. We assert that this work has led to an unrecognized rapprochement between social movements and science, as well as—in certain instances—between social movements and the state. These transformations are a result, in part, of technologies of humility.

Methods

This chapter represents the co-authors' analysis of several years of fieldwork and their reading and writing about northern Thailand. While the projects were conceived and conducted separately, and during different timeframes, putting them into conversation years later allows us to trace changes in how actors in the community forest movement changed their relationship to science.

Initially, Vanessa Lamb was familiar with Thailand's community forest movement and villager research through her work with environmental NGOs (2003–04, and 2006–08) in the region. This influenced the research conducted in 2009–11, where she focused on long-term doctoral and postdoctoral research in two majority Karen villages along the Lower Salween, where it comprises the political border between Thailand and Myanmar. The dissertation work included participant observation and over 100 semistructured interviews at villages along the Salween River, and at a series of NGO network meetings in Mae Hong Son, Chiang Mai, and Bangkok. She conducted research in the Thai, Karen, and English languages, with the help of a Thai- and Karen-speaking research assistant. Linked to Lamb's postdoctoral research, she carried out two follow-up trips in 2012 and 2013 and, again, follow-up interviews in July 2017.

Robin Roth conducted doctoral research (2000–02) and subsequent research in northern Thailand periodically between 2004 and 2011. Her doctoral work consisted of in-depth ethnographic research including participant observation, community-based mapping and over 100 semistructured interviews and household surveys in two Karen communities located in what became Mae Tho National Park. She also interviewed forestry officials and NGO employees and observed their interactions at meetings in the region. From 2004 to 2011 she conducted follow-up household surveys and life history interviews and extended her research to Karen communities in other national parks in northern Thailand.

Collectively, our field experiences allow for reflection on the changing terms of the contests over forest resources in Thailand from the early 2000s to present. Despite our different goals with individual research projects, we both paid attention to the production of knowledge, the role of scientific management, and the actions of the community forest movement in our field sites. We are thus able, through the remainder of this chapter, to identify a trajectory of change in the ways social movements engaged science to argue for greater rights for forest-dwelling communities.

To present this work, we first lay out a brief history of how science came to be associated with the Thai state, subsequently moving on to a discussion of social movements, particularly the community forest movement, to illustrate changes in the use/mobilization of science over time. We examine the debates and discourses of science alongside debates on the role of local people in management and decision-making of natural resources. We argue that this history illustrates key shifts or transformations in the relationship between science and local knowledges and local movements, which are also present in the two case studies we discuss below. A movement that was once largely seen as "anti-science" has emerged as drawing part of its legitimacy from science, exposing how science has changed, how people's movements have been a significant part of that, and how attitudes toward and engagements with science have changed. We then move to present and reflect on our own efforts at solidarity science and the ways that this work constitutes "technologies of humility" as a critical component of successful collaborations. In focusing on "technologies" in this chapter, we do draw out examples of mapping of forests as it emerged across both of the research sites in northern Thailand. However, building on Jasanoff (2003), we highlight that, in addition to mapping as a more conventional technology, we consider the *social* technologies of environmental governance as related to the work of local knowledge and mapping. In particular, it is this work of deliberation that we wish to draw out and consider in tracing the emergence of "forest science" and people's movements engagement with and role in forest governance.

State science/local knowledge: the origins of a science-based state

Established in 1896, the Royal Forestry Department (RFD) emerged during a period when Siam (present-day Thailand) attempted to prove its ability to establish bureaucratic order comparable with colonial powers throughout the region (Peluso et al. 1995). Initially led by a British forestry officer (Usher 2009, 5), the RFD later developed its forest management classifications with the help of US-based consultants. It was through these processes, for instance, that the American notion of uninhabited wilderness preserved in national parks came to be central to the RFD's mission, and that state-led watershed management included classifications outlawing human habitation. But this history of science and the Thai state has a much longer record.

Science, in its classic positivist incarnation, played a significant, if controversial, role not only in forestry but in the development of Siam into the modern Thai state. Prior to establishment of the RFD, King Mongkut (1851–68) attempted to use Western science to "prove" that Siam was a civilized state and worthy of respect from its European colonial suitors. To do this, he publicly and correctly predicted a solar eclipse through the "science" of astronomy and mathematics, and not Thai astrology (Winichakul 1994; Rigg 2004, 49). His successor, King Chulalongkorn, is similarly noted for "thwarting European colonization" by modernizing the Thai state, including the adoption of cartography to consolidate the Siamese territory as a key feature in this modernization strategy (Winichakul 1994). The use of Western science, and the dismissal of other ways of knowing in order to establish legitimacy was not inconsequential. It became the foundation of the modern authority of the Thai bureaucracy.

King Chulalongkorn's declaration of all uncultivated land as forest land belonging to the kingdom, and the establishment of the RFD in 1895, marked the beginning of the line between "forest land" and "land inhabitable by people" (Laungaramsri 2001; Peluso and Vandergeest 2001; Peluso et al. 1995; Ganjanapan 2000). This line was formalized, and scientific management promoted, during a post-monarchy Siamese state that passed a number of pieces of forest legislation: the Forest Protection and Reservation Act (1938), the Wildlife Conservation and Protection Act (1960), and the National Park Act (1961). Consultants and bureaucrats carefully modeled these pieces of legislation on British colonial legislation in Burma and India, as well as domestic legislation in the United States (Roth 2004; Vandergeest 1996).

State policies, and the work on the ground by state authorities to separate forests and people, are linked to discourses that have long inscribed difference onto Thailand's physical landscape. In Thailand, this meant the mapping of upland ethnic minorities as "non-Thai" tribal others who are considered/classified as less civilized than their lowland Thai counterparts (Vandergeest

2003; see also Li 2001; Tsing 1999). The Siamese elite, at least as far back as the turn of the nineteenth century, did not only draw lines separating people from forests but also delineated and produced difference among non-elite rural peoples. Rural peoples' relative position was designated on a scale between civilized (e.g., the elite) to the uncivilizable (e.g., forest, tribal peoples) (Winichakul 2000; see also Stott 1991; Vandergeest 2003). The Thai elite saw villagers living in the lowland as on their way to becoming civilized. Subsequently, Siamese and Thai rulers and governments put in place guidelines and policies intended to guide villagers on the path to being more civilized, such as dictating what to wear and how to act (Winichakul 2000, 536).

These lines between forests–people and modern–uncivilized are continually reinscribed in modern Thailand forestry. For instance, academic work, perhaps unintentionally, affirmed upland minorities as distinct from lowland Thais in religion, custom, dress, language, and, most importantly, farming technique (Peluso et al. 1995). Upland minorities were thus seen not only as less than Thai, but, owing to swidden farming practices, as a threat to forests and thus became targets of civilizing missions that would have them removed from the forest (Peluso et al. 1995). Assertions of wildness and incivility from the late 1800s and early 1900s continue to be translated to a more recent context, with active efforts to physically remove "farmers from the forest" (Forsyth and Walker 2008). This enduring view of "forest dwellers" as forest destroyers persisted even in the face of scientific evidence to the contrary. As Puginier explains, in the case of a group of northern Thailand villages in Mae Hong Son Province,

> Eighty percent of the Tambon [district] was classified as Class 1A, which implies that the area is protected forest and no settlement is allowed.... However, since the villagers preserve their forests so well, the satellite images that were used for surveying showed a dense forest cover for the area. This is a paradox situation, in that Karen farmers who practise a sustainable system of forest and land management are threatened with eviction [by National Park officers], while those in areas of permanent forest removal are allowed to remain there.
>
> (Puginier 2004, 197)

Commentators continue to note that the history of the Thai forest bureaucracy is in part a history of struggling against the presence of people in forests (Usher 2009) and using policy to reify spatially the separation of nature from people. These policies made rural populations the subject of scientific management regimes that, in many instances, effectively sought to eliminate their presence. In this context it is perhaps not surprising that "science" and "scientific management" were made targets by social movements working to support rural, resource-dependent communities and were often juxtaposed with "local" knowledge and management. Yet, we might ask if this alone explains the emergence of an "anti-state" local knowledge. As Martello (2004, 301–302; see also Agrawal 1995) notes, "Fundamentally, both local knowledge and science should be seen as emerging and developing through historically located practices, in particular social and institutional contexts, subverting any fundamental theoretical divide between them." We start to "locate these practices" in the next section.

Community forests and local knowledge: science and scientific management as foe?

> The organization that in ancient times put up the most powerful resistance to the state was the community.
>
> (Prawet Wasi, cited in Nartsupha 1991, 124)

The quotation above encapsulates some of the thinking of the "community culture" work in Thai scholarship and activism, which largely characterized the community as working "in resistance to the state." The contrast to science, largely envisioned as the domain of the Thai state, was not coincidence. Advocates for local knowledge in resource management in Thailand in the 1980s and 1990s, particularly those ascribing to the community culture school, like Wasi, quoted above, generally referred to community work in Thailand as "anti-state" (Nartsupha 1991, 140). While there are multiple strands of the community culture approach, key tenets identified early on include the notions that community- or village-based knowledge and culture was to be prized, upheld, and preserved. Villager knowledge and culture was seen as the "original" knowledge base, pre-existing not only the modern Thai nation-state but also global capitalism and the influence of a "global culture" (Nartsupha 1991, 140).

This work resonated with the increasing tensions around forest-based livelihoods that were the subject of scientific conservation management, setting the stage for a full-fledged debate on the long-simmering issues relating to the role of people in forests and, by implication, the role of state science in management. The emergence of the community forest movement at a national scale can be traced back to this time, which saw not only the community culture critique emerge but also a shift in management of Thailand's forests. Specifically, the 1989 logging ban ended legal logging in the country, shifting the RFD toward a conservation mandate, which placed it at odds with a long history of community use and management of the forests.

Thus, throughout the 1990s and 2000s, the community forest movement in Thailand continued to capture national and international attention, particularly as seen in the landmark submission of the People's Community Forest Bill to Thailand's parliament in 1999 (Usher 2009). Over this period, which we explore in the case of Mae Chaem, presented in the next section, the community forest movement could still be characterized as broadly antagonistic to the RFD and the practice of scientific forestry. Yet, there was also an emerging acceptance of scientific methods and mapping technologies like GIS within the movement.

Making the people–park boundary: uneven engagements with mapping and science

Mapping was and continues to be part of the Thai state's arsenal for creating and clarifying resource rights and for preparing large areas for inclusion into national parks. In the early 2000s, communities targeted for this mapping had a great deal of fear about what it meant to be "on the map" and, more importantly, what it meant to be "in a park." That fear was driven, in part, by stories from far-flung friends and family who told of the strict division between people and national park land, encapsulated in the colloquialism that "you can't take a single stone from the park," which was a cause of concern for villages that relied on the forest for food and livelihood (Roth fieldnotes, 1999). At the same time that community members expressed these fears, they also identified that the act of mapping people *as part of the forest* could offer a potential challenge to the key tenets of scientific forestry.

In Mae Chaem District, northern Thailand, the RFD started to establish Mae Tho National Park in the mid-1990s. The RFD was met with significant resistance from communities concerned about what the park's establishment would mean for their land claims, resource access, and governance of the forest. The RFD officials responded by creating exclusion zones around each village to delineate "people" from the "park." This move effectively created a boundary between village land and the "forested" park land, which had not previously existed. It also ignited negotiations with the RFD and communities of this area, the majority of which identified as the Karen ethnic Indigenous minority group. These processes were differentiated not only within communities—where it helped produce winners and losers (see also Roth 2009)—but among communities in terms of which communities would participate in mapping their villages in negotiation with the RFD and which would refuse.

In participating villages, forestry officials and their partner NGO used mapping technologies to negotiate with communities vis-à-vis the boundary between park and people. The intent of these negotiations, from the RFD's perspective, was to reduce the amount of land used for agriculture to free up land for inclusion into the national park. Communities subject to this mapping felt conflicted about the process. They were concerned about what it would mean for their livelihood; for instance, it could mean that, with smaller areas of land, shifting cultivation requiring larger areas of land for rotation would no longer be possible, and that traditional land management would be increasingly difficult. However, NGO staff impressed upon community residents that the RFD's mapping technology, which included GPS and GIS, was precise and that it would clarify exactly what their rights are, avoiding the ambiguities that had led to conflict in the past. Furthermore, the RFD's partner NGO created a watershed network (similar to a committee of watershed users) and they educated community members on the importance of maintaining a forested watershed as the rationale for the park. In sum, the RFD and its allies promoted the science of mapping and linked this with watershed science and the foundational idea that people and park are separate, as the best solution for forest conservation in the area.

While some villages worked with the RFD and their partner NGO, other communities resisted this project and had other ideas and plans for the villages in the area. Supported by a grassroots organization that advocated for community-based management, they saw the generation and use of local knowledge as the preferred solution in the area. In the late 1990s and early 2000s, community members would routinely ask any outsider coming into the village, "Do you believe people can live in forests?" (Roth fieldnotes, 1999). They posed the question as a means of differentiating those who supported state solutions from those who supported or might support the community forest movement. These communities were skeptical of a science that claimed that their local practices of forest management, specifically the use of swidden agriculture, was destroying the forest and a science that insisted on the strict separation of people from the forest. They also resisted the process of negotiation described above, refusing to map their territory with forest officials, and invoking local knowledge as a preferred way to address and understand forest and forest management.

At the same time as resistance to mapping as a "state tool" persisted, there was also a growing familiarity with mapping and its benefits and pitfalls, and there was an acceptance that mapping needed to have scientific accuracy and that this was necessary to be able to communicate claims to the Thai state. While villagers used with some frequency terminology like "GPS" and seemed familiar with this technology, owing to continued marginalization of many ethnic communities in Thailand there also existed a lack of electricity and infrastructure, as well as inadequate access to formal education. Together, this meant that, as these communities faced such challenges, they turned to outside expertise to lead the mapping process (see also Roth 2008, 2009).

When employing participatory mapping techniques in creating a land use map, it soon became clear that many community leaders understood the problems of creating clear boundaries where there were none before. A common concern was that new boundaries delineating one community from the next indicated the authority of ownership, which was reflected in comments including "it is not their land or our land, it is nature" (Roth fieldnotes, 2001). But, even with such concerns, rather than opt for a map where boundaries were "fuzzy" or graduated, what community members wanted was a conventional map using GPS technology to ensure clarity, legibility, and accuracy. The resistance to the RFD-led mapping, then, was more a resistance to the role of the state leading the mapping endeavor than a resistance to the science or tools of mapping.

By 2002, NGOs and allies had shifted from resisting the state and its mapping tools as indicative of an oppressive way of viewing their traditional land management, to embracing the ability of mapping technology to help protect their traditional management while still resisting the authority of the state. However, this was not a case of simply co-opting science for their own ends, since they continued to resist mapping norms that the state promoted. They refused to map individual fields and instead mapped communal land, which supported their traditional land management strategies. Highlighting the subversive aspects of the process, community members often played on conventional representational strategies in mapping. For instance, community members discussed the possibility of using light green rather than the more conventional brown to denote agricultural fields. Jokingly, one village leader suggested we use red to denote protected forest and green to denote agricultural land as a way of destabilizing the state's perception of park being green and agriculture being brown. In the end, however, the map used publicly displayed a more conventional color palette. The map was front and center whenever the RFD came into the village to discuss park boundaries or extent of agricultural lands; the map had become a tool of the community to resist the state.

This case of park establishment in northern Thailand and the response is linked with the shifting role of the RFD and allied NGOs used mapping as a means of firmly delineating park land from village land and how communities who resisted the process saw mapping as a tool of the state to be resisted. The case demonstrates that in the early 2000s, those resisting the RFD began to see mapping as a tool that could be used, with a critical eye and assistance from allies, to support community struggles and aims to make claims to forest management and authority over land.

Villager research and engagements with "citizen science"

In nearby Mae Hong Son Province, the existing forest protection policies and legislation have meant that the "people–park divide" is actively managed and contested. This second site of our ongoing research is where the Ministry and RFD have evicted record numbers of forest-dwelling residents from the forest. Indigenous Karen communities who continue to reside in Mae Hong Son along the Salween River border, and in the general proximity of the Salween National Park, are threatened not only with removal from "forest lands" but also with displacement by a series of hydroelectric dams proposed both upstream and downstream on the Salween (Lamb 2014). To appreciate this situation fully, the history of resource use and local governance in Thailand that we note above, where the "state" and RFD control much of "forest lands," is particularly significant. The Royal Forest Department *2011 Statistics* book lists Mae Hong Song Province as 88.85 percent "forest land." This essentially means that many established villages and towns have not and cannot receive or apply for land title documents, putting residents in a particularly precarious situation at the heart of the "people–park" dilemma (see also Lamb 2014).

While significant challenges persist, here we also see here a novel example of engagement with locally situated science and resource management called "villager research" (*Thai Baan*). As a methodology, it builds on previous experiences with the community forestry movement, NGOs, and government officials in Thailand from the 1990s onwards. It is a villager-centered approach to local knowledge, where "the main focus is that the villagers themselves are the researchers" (Lamb interview transcript, June 2011). Research assistants (RAs) in the villager research project are allied NGO staff with some experience of community-based research who help to systematize the research findings. Some scholars have differentiated villager research from "local knowledge" and associated it with the now–globally recognized term "citizen science" (Herbertson 2012).

Nay, a self-identified "Thai-Karen" resident of Mae Hong Son and former NGO worker who participated in villager research, explained this history of activism and "villager research" (*Thai Baan*) in terms of linking the work on dam displacement and the community forest issue. Nay, along with other community residents, worked on a range of issues, "such as community forests, community development, and community organizing" (Lamb interview transcript, June 2011). He detailed how they worked on local resource governance: "It started with the forest issues – establishing village committees [which worked to organize the communities around water and forest management]." Villagers also worked to develop a broader network across Thailand. Taking up villager research was a strategic shift. Nay explains:

> [L]ater, the Salween water diversion project and the Salween dam projects came along. We discussed this because we wanted to know how to fight the dams … we met with groups who had experience … and went to see those projects and their Thai Baan research which helped to explain to or make the public know about various issues. Villagers in the network came back and discussed this, they decided that they wanted to do this Thai Baan Research.
>
> (Lamb interview transcript, June 2011)

That the villagers decided to move forward with research, and that they wanted to position themselves as the researchers in this process, was repeated in several different interviews and discussions. Conducting their own research was described as both pragmatic and strategic, similar to the ways that communities in the case above engaged with mapmaking tools and processes. While the villagers did engage outside expertise (RAs) in creating a methodology for collecting and recording their own knowledge about forests, the river, and related livelihoods, the local researchers were not asking outsiders to make maps. In fact, during fieldwork, the maps of villages and farm lands/agricultural areas had already been made locally in villager research books (e.g., SEARIN 2005) and in the Salween study (Chantavong and Longcharoen 2005).

The existence of community-based land use maps did not mean that communities did not have complicated relationships with that process, even as they recognized it as important or even necessary. In discussing the difficulties and challenges of mapping in villager research, participants often said that, while useful, the process of mapping "missed out" on important parts of the research. For instance, Mary noted,

> We made the map of the entire Salween River basin, all of the path of Salween Thai-Burma.… If you talk with villagers they will tell you about

> the *wong* [whirls, or literally circles in the river]; what is that? They will tell you, that is where the water comes up from below and most fish like to be there, big ones. Is it Dangerous? [In addition to danger, there is] … lots of beauty too [as seen in the research], but we cannot "collect" it all [*kep may mot*].
>
> (Lamb interview transcript, May 2011)

While she identified "danger," Mary also believed that the local researchers could overcome this. Instead, the challenge was in documenting and making legible these important qualities using representational methods and standards available. Along with the maps, the villager research project also saw cultural and natural histories of the communities compiled and presented, both in books and when presented orally within the villager research network.

Technologies of humility and the state

Our work thus far outlines how forest residents and allies in the community forest movement in Thailand engaged science, both in opposition to it and in their engagements with and reliance on it. However, the various state actors engaging in forestry and forest science also continue to shift their approach as it pertains to both the strict separation of people from forest and the value of local knowledge and management. In the sites we work, we have witnessed an easing of conflict between villagers and foresters alongside an increased recognition and respect for local knowledge.

One shift in this relationship was most evident during the 2000s. While resistance to the RFD's official mapping and establishment of the national parks continued, some members of the forest service shifted their views of scientific forestry and started making changes to conservation practice. As one assistant park director in Mae Tho National Park expressed as early as 2000, there was a need for patience because "those of us who went to university recently have a better understanding of social forestry" than the generation of foresters that was currently in charge (Roth fieldnotes, 2000). The official explained that the main forestry university in Thailand had only recently introduced courses on social forestry and this new generation of foresters had yet to obtain positions of power. By 2004, pilot projects allowing for income-generation projects, NTFP marketing, market-oriented agriculture, and ecotourism opportunities were promoted by different agencies within the state (Roth fieldnotes, 2005). For instance, in Mae Thao National Park, Denmark's aid agency sponsored a pilot project on "Joint Management of Protected Areas" on community participation in park management, and the Department of National Parks started the "Development of Community Participation in Sustainable Parks Management" project in 11 communities (Roth fieldnotes, 2009).

We also saw this shift expressed in interviews with the RFD officials in the Mae Hong Son district office in June 2011. The office includes in its jurisdiction the Salween Wildlife Sanctuary and one of the villages in the villager research project. The head of the RFD office and head of the wildlife sanctuary had been based in the village "for many years" prior to being based in the district town office. The head described those early years, in the 1980s and 1990s, as difficult, with the relationship between him and the community strained at best. He had "watched people steal teak, that's what it's like there," emphasizing the lack of trust between villagers and the RFD in charge of "protecting" the forest (Lamb fieldnotes, June 2011). When asked about the current circumstances his tone changed. Today, there is no longer a state officer based in the village; instead, they hire a "community helper," emphasizing a shift in trust and understanding. The forestry official also identified their office and the district governor's participation in one of the citizen science books, describing it as a "worthwhile book," another significant change in tone.

Even as anecdotes, these conversations with forest officials indicate an evolving understanding of knowledge/science and represent a shift from the proclamations and narratives of earlier decades which described forest residents as "backwards" or that positioned local people as "the nemesis" of state forestry (Usher 2009, 187) or, further, an obstacle that forestry science needed to remove. This matters, we argue, because it is in these shifts of officials' viewpoints that we see an emergence of a greater degree of mutual understanding between local and scientific knowledge, community members, and forestry officials. While this relationship has been complicated by renewed interest in forest evictions under the present military government, with public protest increasingly putting residents at risk (risk for individuals and NGOs is seen as too high, not an effective strategy), engagements with science are being openly discussed as increasingly more important (pers. comm., July 2017).

Beyond our two study sites, in a separate series of cases in northern Thailand currently under study there is a range of new engagements in forest conservation, not limited to community, NGOs, and forestry officials but expanded to also include private companies (King 2017, 16; Huete 2017, 13) and celebrities (Na Nan 2017). In one northern Thailand case (Huete 2017, 13), the author surmises a shift in the community's engagement with "science as proof," noting that

> these same communities have now been able to use this same scientific discourse [which was previously "used to justify oppressive measures against small communities"] against the government. Scientifically proving to them that they in fact live sustainably within their natural surroundings.

In this case, science provides a seemingly less political or less adversarial way of engaging the state, but is at the same time used to mobilize the community's claims to governance and management of forest resources.

Discussion: still rethinking parks and people?

Taking a step back, we argue that the history and contemporary work by local communities to rethink the "people–park" divide is producing more deliberative science, governance, and decision-making, and that it is part of a much larger shift in the way "science" is understood. As governance becomes less state-centered and more about multi-stakeholder governance, there is a need to examine the ways different stakeholders engage and leverage science as a means of negotiating management of the forests. Jasanoff argues that there is a need for "technologies of humility," which "requires not only the formal mechanisms of participation but also an intellectual environment in which citizens are encouraged to bring their knowledge and skills to bear on the resolution of common problems" (2003, 227).

It is this work which we demonstrate in this chapter—the work of individual residents, whole communities, state agencies like the RFD, nonstate organizations, and others to deliberate and forge relationships to reframe science, mapping, and decision-making for forests. It is this work that forges pragmatic and strategic links between villages and state agencies in and through the deployment of technologies like GIS/GPS mapping but also in and through the ways that this is "negotiated" and conventional norms subverted.

In these two cases, not only did we identify that the strict tenet separating people from forests was destabilized in scientific forestry but we also traced how some of the successes of community forest movements in this regard came through the adoption of mapping science. The strict line between what counts as science and "not-science" (and who operates in those categories) was also destabilized. Thus, in these sites in Thailand's northern hills we show how the lines between and legitimacy of "science" and "local knowledge" also shifted, building on the work of residents, activists, scholars, and state officials. In our analysis, we also see implications for how we understand the contemporary engagements with science in Thailand under the military government after May 2014. As some well-used strategies, including the courts and direct action/protest, are currently seen as less effective and less feasible under the current military regime, communities and their advocates' engagements with science become more important (pers. comm., July 2017).

However, as also seen in the people–forest debates in Thailand, serious questions of accountability have been raised in connection with these mapping and citizen science endeavors regarding what counts as forest and who was best suited to manage it, with a divide set up between local communities and forest officials (Laungaramsri 2001; Usher 2009). In both cases it is also of note that, even with increased use of science, the communities and their NGO advocates insisted on their own mapping. In other words, these normative questions of accountability became part of the discussion of what constitutes a forest. This is a shift worthy of note both within the specific context of Thailand and within discussions of the wider public accountabilities and responsibilities of science. It is this set of questions that we argue emerged through these negotiations over science, over multiple groups and individuals, and just *who* these actors are matters/mattered to the ways that forests and forestry develops. In both cases, this acceptance is partial and still requires work and appraisal. Participation within and among forest-dwelling communities is uneven, and the question of who participates matters not only in its potential to locate people differently, to impact claims, and as part of speaking back to science, but it also matters for the continued work in diversifying and democratizing science.

Moreover, while work interrogating the differentiation between urban, civilized Thais and the forest-dwelling "others" has also shown how racialized identities matter to resource management (Vandergeest 2003), there a need for more work on gender, other markers of difference, and the intersections between multiple notions of difference, particularly in relation to just who participates in these knowledge-making processes and the uneven distribution of impacts. As forest and conservation governance changes away from a state-only mode of governance toward one that requires the participation of numerous user groups, local communities, and private enterprise, these social technologies will become more central. These new networks of actors in governance are even now, through their interaction, providing opportunities to create a diversity of "sciences" that are understood to be partially complete and in progress. Without acknowledgment of partiality, risk, and accountability, however, exclusions from expertise will continue along various axis of difference as new traditions emerge. These traditions, old and new, require attention and assessment from within and without.

Conclusion

In Thailand, through a range of scientific forest management regimes, upland forests have notoriously been classified in ways that restrict access to people who live in those forests, giving rise to significant debate and protest over the role of people in forests. These debates continue into the present day, where there continues to be politically motivated oppression of forest-dwelling ethnic minorities in Thailand (Areerat 2014; Prachatai 2014). What we show in this chapter are that histories of these contests for control (and claims to that control) in deliberations over land and forests in Thailand represent an important transformation in deliberations over science. In this chapter, the short history of Thailand's engagements demonstrates the work of producing these deliberations, where both the state and social movements participate and work to reframe the debate throughout the 2000s, to have moved toward greater acknowledge of accountability and engagement when it comes to the techniques of forest management. Not only did a key tenet of scientific forestry—the separation of forests from people—become destabilized and undermined, but some of the credit for the successes of community forest movements in this regard came through the adoption of mapping science. In certain locations in northern Thailand, building on the work of residents, activists, scholars, and state officials, we show how the lines between and the legitimacy of "science" and "local knowledge" also shifted.

References

Agrawal, A. 1995. Dismantling the Divide between Indigenous and Scientific Knowledge. *Development and Change* 26(3): 413–439.

Agrawal, A. and C. Gibson. 1999. Enchantment and Disenchantment: The Role of Community in Natural Resource Conservation. *World Development* 27(4): 629–649.

Areerat, K. 2014. Junta's Attempt to "Return Forest" Hurts the Poor. *Prachatai*, October 24.

Barney, K. 2005. *At the Supply Edge: Thailand's Forest Policies, Plantation Sector and Commodity Export Links with China.* Washington, DC: Forest Trends.

Chantavong, M. and L. Longcharoen (eds) 2005. *Salween: River of Life and Livelihoods.* Bangkok: Foundation for Ecological Recovery.

Forsyth, T. and A. Walker. 2008. *Forest Guardians, Forest Destroyers: The Politics of Environmental Knowledge in Northern Thailand.* Seattle, WA: University of Washington Press.

Forsyth, T. and A. Walker. 2014. Hidden Alliances: Rethinking Environmentality and the Politics of Knowledge in Thailand's Campaign for Community Forestry. *Conservation and Society* 12: 408–17.

Ganjanapan, A. 2000. *Local Control of Land and Forest: Cultural Dimensions of Resource Management in Northern Thailand.* Chiang Mai: Regional Center for Social Science and Sustainable Development, Faculty of Social Sciences, Chiang Mai University.

Herbertson, Kirk. 2012. Citizen Science Supports a Healthy Mekong. *World Rivers Review* 28(4): 1–7.

Hirsch, P. (ed.) 1997. *Seeing Forests for Trees: Environment and Environmentalism in Thailand.* Chiang Mai: Silkworm.

Huete, A. A. 2017. *Climate Mitigation Initiatives: Perspectives on the Forest and Global Warming in Two Karen Communities.* Paper for the 13th International Conference on Thai Studies, July 2017, Thailand. www.icts13.chiangmai.cmu.ac.th.

Jasanoff, S. 2003. Technologies of Humility: Citizen Participation in Governing Science. *Minerva* 41: 223–244.

Jitcharoenkul, P. 2015. Poor Villagers "Targeted" by Forestry Laws. *Bangkok Post*, 20 June. www.bangkokpost.com/archive/poor-villagers-targeted-by-forestry-laws/598004.

King, E. 2017. *Operational Process of a Non-State Initiated: Payment for Environmental Service Pilot Project in Pong Khrai Village, Mae Sa Watershed, Northern Thailand.* Paper for the 13th International Conference on Thai Studies, July 2017, Thailand. www.icts13.chiangmai.cmu.ac.th.

Lamb, V. 2014. Ecologies of Rule and Resistance: Making Knowledge, Borders, and Environmental Governance at the River. PhD dissertation, Department of Geography, York University, Toronto, Canada.

Laungaramsri, Pinkaew. 2001. *Redefining Nature Karen Ecological Knowledge and the Challenge to the Modern Conservation Paradigm.* Chennai: Earthworm.

Lohmann, L. 1999. Forest Cleansing Racial Oppression in Scientific Nature Conservation. *Corner House Briefing* 13. www.thecornerhouse.org.uk/resource/forest-cleansing.

Martello, M. 2004. Global Change Science and the Arctic Citizen. *Science and Public Policy* 31(2): 107–115.

Mollett, S. and Faria, C. 2013. Messing with Gender in Feminist Political Ecology. *Geoforum 45*: 116–125.

Na Nan, S. 2017. *Problematizing the Military Regime in the Politics of Hyper-Royalist Conservation and Rural Development in Nan Province.* Paper for the 13th International Conference on Thai Studies, July 2017, Thailand. www.icts13.chiangmai.cmu.ac.th.

Nartsupha, Chatthip. 1991. The "Community Culture" School of Thought. In *Thai Constructions of Knowledge*, edited by M. Chitakasem and A. Turton, 118–141. London: School of Oriental and African Studies.

Peluso, N. and P. Vandergeest. 2001. Genealogies of the Political Forest and Customary Rights in Indonesia, Malaysia, and Thailand. *The Journal of Asian Studies* 60(3): 761–812.

Peluso, N. L., Vandergeest, P., and Potter, L. 1995. Social Aspects of Forestry in Southeast Asia. *Journal of Southeast Asian Studies* 26(1): 196–216.

Prachatai. 2014, Karen Minority Complains on Junta's "Return Forest" Policy. *Prachatai*, 15 October. https://prachatai.com/english/node/4408.

Puginier, O. 2004. The Karen in Transition from Shifting Cultivation to Permanent Farming. In *Living at the Edge of Thai Society: The Karen in the Highlands of Northern Thailand*, edited by C. Delang, 183–209. London: Routledge.

Rigg, J. 2004. *Southeast Asia: The Human Landscape of Modernization and Development*. London: Routledge.

Roth, R. 2009. The Challenges of Mapping Complex Indigenous Spatiality: from Abstract Space to Dwelling Space. *Cultural Geographies* 16: 207–227.

Roth, R. 2008. "Fixing" the Forest: The Spatiality of Conservation Conflict in Thailand. *Annals of the Association of American Geographers*. 98(2): 373–391.

Roth, R. 2004. Spatial Organization of Environmental Knowledge: Conservation Conflicts in the Inhabited Forest of Northern Thailand. *Ecology and Society* 9(3): 5.

Rujivanarom, P. 2017. When Freedom of Speech is SLAPPED by Law Enforcement. *The Nation*, 6 August. www.nationmultimedia.com/detail/politics/30322931.

SEARIN (Southeast Asia Rivers Network-Living Rivers Siam). 2005. *Thai Baan Research in the Salween River: Villager's research by the Thai-Karen Communities* [in Thai with English summary]. www.livingriversiam.org/pub/print.html.

Stott, P. 1991. Mu'ang and Pa: Elite View on Nature in a Changing Thailand. In *Thai Constructions of Knowledge*, edited by M. Chitakasem and A. Turton. London: School of Oriental and African Studies.

Tsing, A.L., 1999. Becoming a Tribal Elder, and Other Green Development Fantasies. In *Transforming the Indonesian uplands: Marginality, Power and Production*, edited by Tania Li, 159–202.

Usher, A. Danaiya. 2009. *Thai Forestry: A Critical History*. Bangkok: Silkworm Books.

Vaddhanaphuti, C. 2003. The Role of the Social Sciences in Emerging Civil Society in Thailand. *Asian Journal of Social Science* 31(2): 155–161.

Vandergeest, P. 1996. Mapping Nature: Territorialization of Forest Rights in Thailand. *Society and Natural Resources* 9: 159–175.

Vandergeest, P. 2003. Racialization and Citizenship in Thai Forest Politics. *Society & Natural Resources* 16(1): 19–37.

Winichakul, T. 1994. *Siam Mapped: A History of the Geobody of a Nation*. Honolulu: University of Hawaii Press.

Winichakul, T. 2000. The Quest for "Siwilai": A Geographical Discourse of Civilizational Thinking in the Late Nineteenth and Early Twentieth-Century Siam. *The Journal of Asian Studies* 59(3): 528–549.

Wittayapak, C. 2008. History and Geography of Identifications Related to Resource Conflicts and Ethnic Violence in Northern Thailand. *Asia Pacific Viewpoint* 49(1): 111–127.

11 The Río Plátano Biosphere Reserve

A postcolonial feminist political ecological reading of violence and territorial struggles in Honduras

Sharlene Mollett

In the early morning hours of May 11, 2012, Honduran security forces, with assistance from the United States Drug Enforcement Agency (DEA), mobilized four helicopters over the Patuca River, a major waterway inside the Honduran Mosquitia. At the same time, a passenger boat conducting what was later confirmed to be *legal* commercial business was traveling on the Patuca in close proximity to the Miskito village of Paptalaya, Ahuas. During a search for suspects supposedly traveling in a boat filled with contraband, officers mistakenly shot at the Miskito passenger boat. Using high-caliber weaponry, the officers killed four people including two pregnant women and a 14-year-old boy. Four others were seriously wounded. In the aftermath of this event, the Honduran military and the DEA attempted to legitimize the shooting by describing the murders as retaliation; military officers claimed that they were protecting themselves after having been fired upon by the boat's occupants. But six years later there is still no evidence that Miskito passengers ever had weapons. And, what is worse, there has been no accountability for the lost lives and profound struggles endured by the Miskito survivors and their families since that fateful morning. As a joint investigation by the Center for Economic Policy and Research and Rights Action maintains, the ongoing impunity for killing four innocent people and seriously wounding four others reflects a failed policy of using "militarization and military-style tactics applied to drug interdiction efforts" inside Miskito peoples' territories (Mollett 2012; Bird and Main 2012, 6). While the post-coup terrain in Honduras is certainly more violent, elite, military and state-sanctioned violence against Indigenous and Afro-indigenous peoples in Honduras is longstanding and predates both the 2009 coup and the intensification of narco-violence throughout the country.

State intervention and Miskito sacrifice has a long history inside the Mosquitia. Such histories are enclosed inside the Río Plátano Biosphere Reserve (RPBR). The Reserve, established under the UNESCO Man and the Biosphere Program in 1980, is the largest protected area in Honduras and measures more than 800,000 hectares. Named a UNESCO World Heritage Site in 1982, the Reserve, often referred to as *el pulmon del mundo* (the lungs of the world), holds significance for both the Honduran government and for international conservation movements working on behalf of the MesoAmerican Biological Corridor. The Reserve's creation and its ongoing policies are designed to curb the intense deforestation of Mosquitia forests. Both the state and the UN's Man and the Biosphere Program partially link this ongoing deforestation to *colono* land invasions. In the early 2000s, owing to the ongoing encroachments, the UN placed the Reserve on the endangered list. In 2007, the Reserve was taken off this list *only* because the ICF (National Institute for Conservation and Forestry Development, Protected Areas and Wildlife) agreed to a militarized presence designed to curb *colono* incursions inside the Reserve (Mollett 2013). These invasions justified increased militarization as a method to stem *colono* encroachments, and yet *colono* land incursions remain profound.

Within the Reserve, the Miskito peoples share the "cultural zone" with other Indigenous and Afro-descendant groups (Pech, Creole, Tawahka, Garifuna, Creole) and a small native *ladino* community. Together they officially number roughly 20,000 people (AFE-COHDEFOR 2000). According to the Reserve's *Plan de Manejo* (Management Plan), the "cultural zone" is designed for the protection of "traditional peoples" and their habitats. But, according to Indigenous residents, their lives and land use practices are subjugated to the interests and needs of *colonos* (Mollett 2011). Struggles against *colono* encroachments punctuate everyday life for Honduras's *Originarios* (first peoples) in the Reserve.

In Latin America, national governments and international conservation organizations have increased their reliance on violent forms of "green security" inside protected areas (Kelly and Ybarra 2016; Devine 2014). It would seem that the militarization of biodiversity conservation and an acceptance of "waging war to save biodiversity" is global (Duffy 2014, 819). In Honduras, militarization as a way to protect *el pulmon del mundo* and the resulting violence it invokes are underpinned and justified through enduring colonial racial ideologies that dehumanize Indigenous peoples. As Weheliye describes, "racialization figures as a master code within the genre of the human represented by Western Man, because its law-like operations are yoked to species sustaining physiological mechanisms in the form of a global color line" (2014, 27). In Honduras, racial ideologies are deeply imbued in both mundane and spectacular violence inside and outside the Reserve and shape the ways in which the Reserve policies are designed and (un) enforced through racialized and dehumanizing logics.

State-sanctioned violence against Indigenous peoples is not always as spectacular as the events of May 11, 2012. In this chapter, Miskito dispossession also unfolds through what Robert Nixon calls "slow violence," "a violence that is neither spectacular nor instantaneous, but rather incremental and accretive, its calamitous repercussions playing out across a range of temporal scales" (Nixon 2011, 2). I would also add that such slow violence is not linear, but discontinuities are part of its composition (Stoler 2013). Attentive to the sensibilities of a postcolonial intersectional thinking and feminist political ecology, I illustrate Miskito land struggles inside the RPBR by demonstrating how "patriarchy and racialized processes are consistently bound in a postcolonial genealogy that embeds race and gender ideologies within nation building and international development processes" (Mollett and Faria 2013, 120). Thus, in this chapter I rethink "parks and people" by linking the violence of biodiversity conservation inside the Reserve with the growing violence and repression against Indigenous land and territorial defenders mobilized against an extractivist Honduran state.

In September 2013, the Honduran government awarded collective territorial legislation to the Miskito peoples inside the Mosquitia (Malkin 2013). Led by the national Miskito organization MASTA (Unified Peoples of the Mosquitia), the Miskito currently possess over one million hectares of land. Drawing from ongoing research in Honduras (Mollett 2006, 2011, 2010, 2016), this chapter blends unpublished ethnographic data (two months in 2012) with news media, archival documents and development reports to examine the violent challenges to Miskito territorial autonomy. Such violence extends beyond the Reserve and is emplaced on the bodies of land and territorial defenders as they protest against the state's extractivist development agenda. To demonstrate, I briefly highlight the contributions of critical political ecologists and scholars of green grabbing to illustrate some of the ways protected area management reproduces inequalities and is complicit in anti-Indigenous violence. Next, I build on the critiques of neoliberal conservation but shift attention away from critiques of capitalism alone to illuminate the racial, cultural and gendered histories and logics bound up inside the Reserve and throughout the region of Latin America. I then show how these histories are contemporaneous and illustrated through the persistent flux of *colonos* land invasions. I then demonstrate how such violence and repression extend beyond the Reserve and specifically on Indigenous and Afro-descendant women's bodies as they conduct their activist work in defense of land and territory. I argue that biodiversity conservation and extractive development are linked, imbued with intersecting logics of race and gender from the past, operationalized in the dehumanization of Indigenous and Afro-descendant peoples in the present. In Honduras, Indigenous peoples' struggles over land and territory are simultaneously historical contests that work to disrupt state and elite practices of Indigenous peoples' dehumanization, conducted in the name of modernity and development.

Protected areas as "sacrifice zones"

Protected area enclosures are contested spaces often understood through the concept of green grabbing. Namely, green grabbing refers to "the appropriation of land and resources for environmental ends" (Fairhead et al. 2012, 238; Cárdenas 2012; Ojeda 2011; Wily 2014). In this process, states and elites operationalize "green" discourses and practices to justify land displacement in ways that undermine access and control of land for local citizens (Peluso and Lund 2011; Cárdenas 2012). A trend in this literature tends to highlight the discontinuities of the past to emphasize the novel ways "agrarian social relations, rights and authority [are] being restructured and *in whose interests such restructurings benefit*" (Fairhead et al. 2012, 237, emphasis added, as cited in Mollett 2016, 416).

Neoliberal conservation is a common focus within critiques of green grabbing. Centered is the inherent contradiction that within capitalism, "where profit motives are the driving force in relationships between people and natures: the demand for profit will tend to trump positive social and environmental outcomes whenever it is at odds with them" (Büscher et al. 2012, 13). Such contradictions are ever more salient when they become entangled with an enduring ideological loyalty to biodiversity conservation dogmas. This entanglement renders it unthinkable to move away from biodiversity protection enclosures: protected areas, biodiversity offsetting and carbon markets. Within this realm, violence and land displacement, as outcomes, become biodiversity conservation commonsense (Brockington et al. 2008; Apostolopoulou and Adams 2017). In fact, as Büscher et al. (2012, 23) maintain,

> Neoliberal conservation intervenes in diverse biocultural systems around the world, displacing, enclosing, commodifying, and spectacularizing these into the idealized natures that are to be saved. In neoliberal conservation, then, globally diverse actors produce proliferating and profitable commodities that rely on surprisingly similar packages of ideologies and practices, premised on constructed distinctions between human and non-human natures, while ironically promising the opposite to (normally non-local) consumers in the form of closer contact and intimacy with nature.

Political ecologists and geographers also highlight that land tensions are at the heart of struggles over biodiversity conservation (Redclift and Springett 2015; Zimmerer 2015; Ybarra 2012). A common critique illuminates the simultaneous advance of capitalist markets, green governance and environmental protections that aim to align Indigenous peoples' tenure vulnerabilities with highly valued natures as a way to mitigate the degrading effects of markets, ignoring how Indigenous peoples envision forests and farmlands as mutually constituted (Anthias and Radcliffe 2015; Altamirano-Jimenez 2017; Mollett 2011).

Indigenous peoples' displacement from rainforest regions, like the Reserve, is further illuminated by eco-feminist Maria Mies's analogy of the iceberg. For Mies, the tip of an iceberg represents the global political economy (2007).The iceberg's tip, like the formal economy, is underpinned and supported by a majority of people (of ice), emplaced within the informal economy but *rendered invisible*. The informal economy lies below the waterline and is characterized by exploited laborers and the value that comes from their devalued and unpaid work (Mies 2007). The bodies below the water line, namely women, racial and ethnic minorities, Indigenous peoples, the working poor, and the landless, are what Mies calls "subsistence producers," those whose labor

> do[es] not count, namely labour of small scale subsistence farmers, who mainly produce for their sustenance, then the work done in all colonies

> where people work almost for nothing for the colonial masters, and finally, the production of nature. Does nature also not produce year after year almost for free?
>
> (Mies and Shiva, 1993, cited in Mies 2007, 269)

For Dempsey and Collard, environmental critiques must "make visible this simultaneous exploitation of and dependence on the invisible contributions of nature", which serve as "a mode of organizing society that also relies on this exploitation" (2017, 35). While there are few cases where communities have successfully (defined on their own terms) adapted a variety of neoliberal enclosures, many others are simply evicted, compelled to make their lives elsewhere. The violence of being made to sacrifice on behalf and at the behest of a global affluent community is unevenly placed on the bodies and places deemed "sacrifice zones" (Klein 2014, cited in Dempsey and Collard 2017, 36). In such zones exist people whose labor and relations to nature, in Mies's words, "don't count" (2007).

Mies's accounting, like much of political ecological critiques of protected areas and biodiversity conservation, rightly attend to capitalism and capitalist logics. Still, I seek to extend political economic critiques of protected areas and make visible the ways in which the global unevenness of protected area expansion does not simply reflect political economic inequalities but global racial disparities and logics. In particular, rural Indigenous and Afro-descendant peoples are imagined and expected to be environmental "traditional" stewards, while the whiter elites from the Global North and transnational corporations continue to destroy the earth through "modern" capitalist production; indeed, there are more than class dynamics at work here. As I argue elsewhere, "grabbing"—green or otherwise—"is part of a long racial-cultural project with specific targets for change and in some cases *erasure*" (Mollett 2016). Furthermore, such racial-cultural projects define humanness through its exclusions. As Butler writes,

> Sometimes the very terms that confer "humanness" on some individuals are those that deprive certain other individuals of the possibility of achieving that status, producing a differential between the human and the less-than-human.... The human is understood differently depending on its race, the legibility of that race.... Certain humans are recognised as less than human, and that a form of qualified recognition does not lead to a viable life. Certain humans are not recognized as human at all, and that leads to yet another order of unliveable life.
>
> (Butler 2004, 2, cited in Marhia 2013, 23)

For those people and places deemed less than human, their places "can be poisoned, drained or destroyed for the supposed greater good of progress" (Dempsey and Collard 2017, 36), rendered open to erasure in both mundane and spectacular ways. The murders of Miskito people inside the Reserve and the struggle over natural resources therein, I will show, substantiate how Miskito struggles to defend ancestral territories are simultaneously a rejection of their historical "misrecognition" as less than human (see Gilroy 2018).

Colonial continuities and Miskito territorial insecurities in the Mosquitia

After receiving collective territorialization for lands located outside the Reserve in 2013, Miskito communities inside the Reserve also began to receive formal territorial demarcation. This marked the end of more than a decade-long stalemate between the state (first under AFE-COHDEFOR and then ICF) and the Miskito over a proposed land registration program, *El Catastro y Regularizacion* (C&R), which set off myriad land conflicts in the Reserve due to the state's plan to individuate Miskito collective territories (Mollett 2011; 2013). In contrast, recent territorial legislation was operationalized through World Bank development funding under the *Programa Administracion de Tierras Hondurena* II (PATH II), which honored Miskito customary collective territorial arrangements. Still, Miskito organizing and social protest at the national level and inside the Reserve was essential to current legislation (Mollett 2013; Bryan 2009). The Honduran government did not just hand over "national" territory to the Miskito; it was won.

The struggle to win formal rights to Mosquitia territories extends long before contemporary *colono* land invasions began almost 40 years ago. In 1859, the Honduran state signed the Wyke–Cruz Treaty (Mollett 2011, 2016). This treaty, an agreement between the former British officials and the new Republic of Honduras, granted Miskito people "possession" rights to their ancestral territories. (Republic of Honduras [1859] 1957, Art. 111, cited in Mollett 2011). Despite this treaty, the Miskito never received any formal legislation; rather, they have endured centuries of challenges to their autonomy, whereby successive state narratives and practices rendered inferior black, Indian and *zambo* populations and their nonsedentary land use practices. Nation-building narratives were concerned about "nature" in the Mosquitia and sought to save it from the "idle" and "ignorant" "hordes" (*El Cronista* 1930; cf. Mollett 2011; for a fuller discussion see Mollett 2011, 2016).

Making visible the colonial racial continuities in the making of Mosquitia-state relations illustrates how "such struggles [over natural resources in the Reserve] are racialized in their *historical and contemporary constitution*" (Mollett 2016, 416; see also Sundberg 2008). Understanding power and violence in conservation as the extension of only political economic histories of the colonial and postcolonial Latin America ignores that "what arrived in the Americas (from 1492 on) was a broader and wider entangled power structure that an economic reductionist perspective of the world-system is unable to account for" (Grosfoguel 2007, 215–216, cited in Mollett 2016). Furthermore, as Anibal Quijano insists, racial and cultural classifications and hierarchies that supported the "conquest" shape exploitation in step with the accompanying exigencies and struggles of capitalist accumulation. Latin America is constituted through both modernity and coloniality, where white supremacy (operationalized through *mestizaje* and *blanqueamiento*) and Indigenous and Afro-descendant subjugation (among other groups) are materialized through simultaneous processes: land dispossession, the exploitation of indigenous and black bodies and religious conversion, all of which are underpinned by various forms of mundane and spectacular violence (Quijano 2000; Mignolo 2007).

Silent incursions inside the Reserve

Miskito territories are comprised of layered forms of governance. Inside the Mosquitia, the Miskito Territory is divided into 12 territorial councils, with one tripartite area that reflects overlapping communal lands shared by three communities (Mollett fieldnotes, 2012; Forest Trends 2015). Under MASTA governance, the majority of these zones were delineated in 1998 to facilitate zoning and management in line with respective Indigenous territorial councils, incorporated as part of MASTA's organization. Territorial councils are customarily divided into community lands, which are also subdivided by families. Family lands extend from coastal and river based communities to upriver locations often far from primary residences. Inside the Reserve, Miskito family lands reflect a series of socioeconomic relationships among members (Helms 1971; Perez Chiriboga 2002, 81; Mollett 2010). Traditionally, land is distributed through matrilineal inheritance. Indeed,

> [t]he proliferation of Miskito residential arrangements is sustained by an enduring practice of matrilocal residence patterns or matrilocality where a couple (along with the bride's female siblings and their families) lives in close proximity to the mother of the bride and often her siblings where families share kitchens, water pumps, boat docks, food and childcare. However, many men (approximately one-third) also live with their parents inside the original family settlement, receiving wives and girlfriends from other villages to share in family lands. Within family land units and often between them, a system of *pana pana* (one another) or reciprocity shapes access to natural resources. This local cooperative work system involves different kin groups who call upon each other to assist primarily in agricultural activities and food exchanges.
>
> (Mollett 2010, 361)

Commonly, Miskito peoples plant crops in house gardens on the coast and cultivate larger parcels in farming communities up river. They grow a variety of foods including fruit trees, plantain, malanga, sweet potatoes and a diverse range of medicinal plants, herbs and spices. Yuca is a regional staple. As swidden agriculturalists, Miskito farmers rotate cultivation among many small parcels located in different ecological zones and leave two or three parcels in fallow at a time.

Cultivation takes place in multiple locales in part as a way to take advantage of the Mosquitia's various microclimates, but also to protect food security against climate fluctuations. Communal lands and waterways are shared by villagers for cattle grazing, fishing and hunting activities. Both adults and children participate in farming and many men, women and older children work in both formal and informal employment on the coast and in and outside the Mosquitia (Mollett 2010, 2011).

Miskito customary land use practices and relations to nature are threatened by state forest management practices. The Reserve is monitored and managed by the National Institute for Conservation and Forestry Development, Protected Areas and Wildlife (ICF) (and former owners under AFE-COHDEFOR). Inside the Reserve, militarization is operationalized to reduce the large-scale trade in illegal timber and *colono* land encroachments (Global Witness 2009). However, Indigenous residents insist it is they who experience the restrictions and the violence of enforcement. Indigenous villagers must seek permits to use timber to build homes and canoes, to hunt and for access rights to fish within ancestral territories (Mollett 2006). For all Indigenous residents, these policies not only ignore the spiritual and economic relations to nature but also challenge their territorial autonomy as the Mosquitia's *originarios*. Miskito peoples report being stranded upriver when military officials burned their canoes after they were suspected of felling prohibited mahogany. Soldiers have also, at the insistence of Reserve officials, removed fresh fish from a fisher's boat confiscated in a "prohibited" zone inside Miskito territories (Mollett fieldnotes, Brus Laguna, 2012). Miskito unease with the use of the military to enforce what they see as "cruel" protected area policies aligns with Garifuna (an Afro-Indigenous group) fisher peoples' complaints inside the Cayos Cochinos Marine Protected Area (MPA), located on the Honduran north coast. In the MPA, naval officials are implicated in abusive patrols against Garifuna residents. Such violence, framed by the navy as enforcement, prohibits lobster diving and fishing for conch, key ancestral subsistence practices for the residents of Chachahuate fishing village (Brondo 2013).

In addition to aggressive state enforcement, state impunity with regards to *colono* land invasions remains a source of collective Miskito disdain. According to the management plan, *colonos* who arrived before 1997 are permitted to live in the cultural zone. But *colono* land invasions have intensified since the late 1990s and are experienced by Miskito villagers as "everyday" occurrences (Mollett fieldnotes, 2012). *Colono* presence is reflected in the "repetitive cycle of extensive farming, clear cutting, fencing, privatization, *milpa* production, pasture expansion, cattle production and the transformation of the forests for the advance of monocultures" (Mollett 2016). These practices are in violation of protected area regulation and have not been erased by recent territorial legislation (Galeana and Pantoja 2013; Forest Trends 2015). Prevailing *colono* testimonies of "poor," "landless" and "displaced" farmers looking for a fresh start inside the Reserve are salient narratives that have shaped decades of state impunity vis-à-vis *colono* land invasions after 1997. Below, I complicate these narratives and illuminate the multiple kinds of threats that remain embedded within *colono* land invasions inside the Mosquitia, even after territorial legislation.

The late 2000s saw a changing coastal landscape. Previously, *ladino colono* families had selected to settle above upriver and coastal Indigenous communities spread across the Reserve's north coast, presumably "hidden" from Reserve officials and Miskito villagers. However, by 2010 single *ladino* men came directly to the coast, renting rooms and working as *mozos* for both wealthier Miskito and native *ladino* residents. Others expressed that they came to "find Miskito women" (Mollett fieldnotes, 2012). With the promise of collective land rights coming to the Reserve, RAYAKA leadership was once again demanding answers from INA and ICF about what to do about *colono* settlements and the continuous invasions. But many Miskito read the changing landscape on the coast as a "sign" to leave; as one Miskito woman expressed, "the coast doesn't feel the same … it doesn't feel as secure [*sana*]." Another was more explicit: "young *colono* men are here for women and for land, they are *bravo*, I'm leaving to live with my sister in La Ceiba" (Mollett fieldnotes, 2012). This growing insecurity regarding *colono* invasions was also punctuated by reports of increased narcotraficking inside the Mosquitia. Many Miskito chose to leave coastal villages temporarily in the face of growing narco violence. Others saw growing violence linked to continuing *colono* land invasions upriver. A Rayaka member invited me to join him and another Miskito farmer to verify rumors about a new *colono* settlement upriver. I illustrate this encounter through ethnographic fieldnotes below.

> One day, Mani, Jilo and I took a motorboat across the Lagoon and walked upriver through forest for what seemed close to two hours. During our long walk we chatted about forest animals and the supernatural beings that emerge during the night. I was amazed about how both Jilo and Mani were also impressed by the trees. But as I was focussed on their size, they were astonished that members from a neighboring community of *colonos* had not yet "*robado todo el bosque*" (stolen the entire forest). As we started to wonder about turning back, Jilo noticed a clearing in the trees. As we slowed our pace and approached, we acknowledged the smoking embers. We carefully walked through the partially burnt ground where the *milpa* had begun to push through the soil. Along a barely visible path that extended through long grass from the forest line, we saw a short row of wooden homes and two cows tied to an incomplete fence. In a shed like structure with three walls and a roof we counted twelve-50 lb bags of beans and even more bags of rice. Further along the path we saw two horses and a generator, piles of wood that Jilo estimated would last six months. I counted 10 kerosene canisters off to the side. I also counted five hens and a rooster. As we approached the houses, the sun beamed off the roofs of the shiny new *lamina*. At the largest house we saw five men and two women sitting under a deck, presumably seeking shade. Upon seeing us they all quickly stood in

a line in front of the house. As Mani and Jilo slowed down, I took a step to introduce us. About six feet away, coming from the entrance of another house, a large man with a cowboy hat told me to "grab your monkeys and run". As we turned to leave I apologized for the intrusion and that I was "a professor from Canada hoping to ask a few questions". Hoping that my Anglo-accented Spanish would confirm my story, the man in the cowboy hat seemed to soften but still insisted that we leave and reasoned "women shouldn't be on the trail alone". Another man shouts "go back to your country". As we quickly returned to the clearing and past the smoking embers, we heard the hooves of a horse hit the forest trail headed our way. Jilo pushed me quickly off the trail. From the ground, I saw the man in the cowboy hat on horseback. As he came down off his horse, he, while laughing, told me to "relax" (calmarse) and that he would "accompany [me] to the *cayuco*". While Mani and Jilo walked ahead of us, Hubert, the man in the cowboy hat, walked his horse with me back to the river.

On the way he asked whether I was *really* from Canada, questioning it because he didn't know there were "*morenos*" there. He asked about the cold and whether there were Hondurans in Canada. After finding the courage to ask Hubert about the settlement, he explained that he had founded the community, "San Hubert" after leaving Colon two years ago to work for a rancher close to Lempira. He says, "I first came here to work as a *mozo*, I heard of *indios humilde*s (poor *ladinos*) coming to live here to work as *mozos* and doing better than in Colon". He said that he met a Miskito girl from Cocobila and that she invited him to move to the coast with her. Hubert said his wife grew up on the coast and he was excited to start a life with her but that her family didn't want them to live together because he explains "*los zambos* don't like *los indios*". So Ria and he moved to a plot of land that had belonged to her maternal grandmother. Later, they agreed that she would live on and off with him up river travelling back and forth to the coast. Hubert invited his brothers and their wives from Colon to join them. He continued, "we live peacefully, we don't bother anyone, … we are poor. There was no land for us in Colon, life was really hard there, it's a struggle. But here we have a better life". Finally back at the canoe, Hubert's demeanor changed once again. After he and I said goodbye, for the first time he directly spoke to Jilo and Mani, "you shouldn't be in the forest without a gun, it's not safe", then turned his horse, jumped up and left. Jilo untied the canoe and Mani pushed us from the river's edge.

While we sat in silence during the trip down river, once we entered the lagoon, Mani and Jilo started speaking quickly. They insisted, "we know him, he's a Narco". Mani continued, "and they are not poor; they have come to find land for the *Colombiano*. We know him, he is the *indio hijo puta* (ladino son-of-a-bitch) who stole (*robado*) Ria from her parents last year. When her father found her living with him in Barra Patuca (a Miskito community up the coast), Hubert threatened to kill Ria's father if he ever returned. After months of worry and a severe beating that Ria's brother

> endured by one of Huberts *mozos*, Ria's dad offered Hubert a small parcel of land upriver (St. Hubert) so that Ria could move home with her parents.... "The Colombiano pays them to find land for cattle. All that food, no *poor* person has that much food, or they wouldn't be poor [laughing]". Jilo interrupts, "We saw the smoke [slash and burn agriculture], the houses, the *lamina*, [this means that] they have just arrived."
>
> (Mollett fieldnotes, 2012)

That narcos and *colonos* are not mutually exclusive is a common refrain among Miskito leaders. Scholars too have begun to trace narco-led deforestation and their investments in rural lands based on "time series satellite images [that]reveal new biodiverse patchworks of field and fallow forest—characteristics of native landscapes—are giving away to a *narco* landscape" (McSweeney and Pearson 2013, 9). However, narco-funded small-scale farmers have been invading Miskito lands at least since the early 1990s. This practice notably intensified in 2006 when Mexican drug trafficking organizations relocated operations to Honduras and Guatemala (McSweeney et al. 2014; Mollett fieldnotes, 2012). In fact, " 'hot spots' of deforestation often overlap spatially with trafficking nodes" (McSweeney et al. 2014, 489). However true, I want to emphasize how the visibility of narco–*colono* entanglements is evidence of failed state protected area operations in the Reserve. Worse still, the state's unwillingness to protect both humans and more-than-human natures is ever more glaring by villager complaints of military abuses in the form of illegal raids, death threats, torture and sexual violence often on behalf of narcos (Cuffe 2014; Mollett fieldnotes, 2012). While these correlations are intellectually interesting, they also lend credence to the fact that narcos, like the state and *colonos*, believe that their rights to be in the Reserve are superior to the rights of Indigenous peoples. During our encounter in St. Hubert, no one directly addressed Jilo and Mani except via a particularly animalized (dehumanizing) racial slur, "monkeys." And later, when they were addressed by Hubert, it was through a not-so-subtle show of *ladino machismo*, warning against coming unarmed to the forest, making the point that if we returned we would undoubtedly be met with violence.

Embodied violence: land and human rights defenders in Latin America

Miskito land struggles in the Reserve are entangled with forms of patriarchal and racialized violence perpetrated by the state (or on behalf of the state) against Indigenous land and human rights defenders. Land and human rights defenders seek to challenge extractive state practices that are destroying Indigenous and Afro-descendant landscapes and leaving poisoned natures and displaced peoples in their wake. According to Global Witness, "nowhere on earth are you more likely to be killed for protesting the theft of land and destruction of the natural world *than Honduras*" (2017, 5; emphasis added). Since the 2009 coup, 123 land

and environmental activists have been assassinated and hundreds of others continue to live with threats, physical attacks and false imprisonment (Global Witness 2017). A flow of right-wing governments have prioritized mining, agribusiness and energy projects in a deliberate aim to attract foreign direct investment (Republica de Honduras 2010; Loperena 2016).

In 2011, under the Porfirio Lobo government, Honduras hosted a conference termed "Open for Business." This led to the expansion of mining concessions and water privatization schemes. Indeed, the "Open for Business" campaign continues to directly threaten the lives of land and territorial defenders through a "systematic campaign to terrorise local communities into accept[ing] the theft and industrialization of their land, and a profound failure to realize peoples' rights to be consulted on the use of their natural resources" (Global Witness 2017, 5). Intensified since the coup, natural resource struggles in Honduras occur in a world of state impunity and where "people's human rights—particularly those of its 1.27 million strong indigenous population—have been *sacrificed* in the name of 'development'" (Global Witness 2017, 8). Such invasions do not only violate Indigenous and Afro-Indigenous rights under the International Labor Organization Convention 169 and the United Nations Convention for the Rights of Indigenous Peoples; such "invasions" are also neocolonial acts that

> rel[y] on racist attitudes against indigenous and other tribal peoples (i.e. Afro-descendants) providing governments and companies with an excuse to behave as though the resources they encounter belong to them, regardless of the inhabitants of the area or the social environmental consequences.
>
> (Birss 2017, 316)

Similar struggles occur throughout Latin America. Such contests are not simply material but ontological. For example, a mining activist from La Toma, an Afro-descendant community in Colombia's Southwest region, argues that "it is patently clear to us that we are confronting monsters such as transnational corporations and the State. Yet nobody is willing to leave his/her territory; I might get killed here but I am not leaving" (cited in Escobar 2016, 19). This example of "ancestrality" emerges from a "living memory that orients itself to the ability to envision a different future—a sort of 'futurality' that imagines and struggles for, the conditions that will allow them to persevere as a distinct world" (Escobar 2016, 19). Indigenous and Afro-descendant peoples draw upon their cosmologies to confront a coloniality of power and myriad processes of dehumanization.

Coloniality of gender power and feminicide in Honduras

In March 2016, Berta Caceres, mother, Lenca feminist and land and environmental defender, was assassinated in her home in La Esperanza, Intibucá, an Indigenous municipality in western Honduras. As the leader of the Council of

Popular and Indigenous Organizations of Honduras (COPINH), Caceres was the 2015 recipient of the Goldman Environmental Prize for her leadership in COPINH's mobilizations against the Agua Zarca Dam and its construction on the Gualcarque River. As the dam and the proposed hydroelectric project threatened to change the river ecology and displace the Lenca from both land and water, Lenca leaders were violently targeted by DESA, the *Desarrollos Energeticos Sociedad Anonima* power company, the owners of the dam project. According to a report by GAIPE, an international advisory group of experts in international human rights law, "strategies used by DESA's shareholders, executives, managers and employees" included "surveillance, threats, contract killing, [the]sabotage of COPINH's communication equipment; cooptation of justice officials and security forces" (CNN 2017). In 2017, the project was cancelled as the major funders withdrew their support owing to international outrage over not only the Caceres assassination but the killing of Nelson Garcia, Caceres's colleague at COPINH, who was also assassinated just 12 days after Berta. The murders mark a trend in violence aimed at Indigenous land and territorial defenders throughout the region.

The ways in which such violence targets women in specifically gendered ways illuminates how a coloniality of power also shapes gender hierarchies both past and present. Extending Quijano's "coloniality of power" framework, feminist decolonial scholar Maria Lugones argues that gender too is a historically produced category of rule whereby:

> [o]nly white bourgeois women have consistently counted as women as so described by the West. Females excluded from that description were not just their subordinates. They were also understood to be animals in a sense that went further than the identification of white women with nature, infants, and small animals. They were understood as animals in the deep sense "without gender" sexually marked as female, but without the characteristics of femininity.
>
> (Lugones 2007, 202, 203)

A coloniality of gender power is concretized in the ways in which feminicide (*feminicidio*), a violent form of women's dehumanization, cannot be easily separated from anti-extraction activism led by Indigenous and Afro-descendant community leaders. According to Fregoso and Bejarano (2010), feminicide grants attention to how intersectional forms of power underpin violence around notions of race, gender and sexuality, taking on local contingencies when understanding women's vulnerability to violence. Feminicide is grounded in political economic, cultural and social inequities that include processes of racialization and racial hierarchies. As feminicide is more than a "tool of patriarchal control but also serves as tool of racism, economic oppression and colonialism" (Smith 2006, 417), "the scale and range of the violence in general and the specific brutality and severity of rape, sexual torture, and mutilation suggests high levels of misogyny and dehumanization of [racialized] women" (Fregoso and Bejarano

2010, 7). Understanding *feminicidio* acknowledges state impunity and complicity in women's lived experience with violence both in private and public space.

While the visibility of feminicide surged before the coup, the fact is that Honduras is experiencing a worsening trend for new forms of violence against women (Ronderos 2011; IM-Defensoras 2015). From 2005 through 2013, women's violent deaths increased by 263.4 percent (IM-Defensoras 2015). According to the MesoAmerican Initiative of Women Human Rights Defenders, "increased rates of feminicide/femicide" are "worsened by acts that are particularly cruel in nature, have been carefully planned, and are carried out in the presence of children" (IM-Defensoras 2015, 24). Significant for thinking through the relationships between "parks and people," it is important to note that in 2012 and 2014 "women defenders of land and territory" in Central America experienced the highest instance of attacks, including murder, assassination attempts, intimidation, psychological harassment and threats (IM-Defensoras 2015, 36).

The kinds of violence currently brought to light by the MesoAmerican Initiative of Women Human Rights and Global Witness reports reflect a time, prior to the 1990s, when security brigades and death gangs used the worst kinds of violence to repress and terrorize civilians. Victims of state terrorism were commonly "vulnerable civilian participants in movements or sectors which challenged the military's goals or doctrines" (Brysk 2000, 243). States commonly tortured Indigenous, Afro-descendant and poor *mestizos*, and particularly women. Dehumanization was operationalized through degrading, cruel and inhumane treatment that also targeted female sexuality and feminine bodies: gang rape, sexual slavery and forced pregnancy (Fregoso and Bejarano 2010). For Fregoso and Bejarano (2010, 13), "the unbridled misogynist practices of military regimes illuminate the intersections of political repression and 'patriarchal culture' as mutually constituting forces."

Land and territorial defenders work on behalf of their communities against state and transnational interests in extractivist development. The violence wielded against them rarely starts with murder, but in fact assassinations are the last of a long line of strategies used to silence state and elite opponents (Birss 2017). According to IM-Defensoras (2015), the expansion of extractivist development agendas is having a specific impact on women activists in Central America. Chavez Ixcaquia, a Maya K'iches leader and land rights activist from Guatemala, argues that "as women we aren't affected by criminalization in the same way as men"; "when they threaten me with going to jail, they tell me that ugly things will happen to me there. They tell me they will rape me, both on the way to jail and once I am there" (Birss 2017, 320). In addition, women land and territory defenders are often questioned about their dedication to their families and particularly their children given the time spent on organizing and planning protests and for their public visibility. In interactions with law enforcement, threats of rape and name-calling (*puta*) are common. As one woman leader from Honduras reports, "the smear campaigns are focussed on calling her a prostitute, a bad mother and other derogatory terms" (IM-Defensoras 2015, 40).

Criminalization through the filing of false charges is another tactic by transnational elites facilitated by state and municipal officials. For example, Honduran Garifuna land activists from the village of Guadalupe, Colon, who accuse foreign tourism operators and real estate executives of land theft, experience multiple legal challenges by these same elites who counter community complaints by accusing community members of slander (Trucchi 2017). Medalime David, a young woman and Garifuna activist (along with other community members) faces court charges for "defaming his reputation and the company he represents" when they accused Patrick Daniel Forseth, the CEO of CARVIDA, a real estate and tourism consortium, of stealing community lands. Medalime and her colleagues were incarcerated for "land invasions" when they occupied a portion of their own ancestral community lands that they claim were illegally sold to CARVIDA by the Trujillo municipality. Extra-legal land sales facilitated by municipal officials are common on the Honduran north coast, lending credibility to David's claims (Brondo 2013; Mollett 2014; Loperena 2016). For David, the disparities in justice among the Garifuna community, Canadian tourists and real estate developers is telling: "once again we see how the money moves all and as in this country being an *advocate, woman and member of indigenous peoples* is a reason for criminalization and persecution" (Trucchi 2017).

Indigenous and Afro-Indigenous land defenders likely face more violent challenges to their freedoms. On September 19, 2017, the Honduran Congress approved Article 590 of the Penal Code. With this law, a group of two or more people whose aim is to "gravely subvert … the constitutional order or provoke … a state of terror in the population or part of it" is now considered a "terrorist association" (Gies 2017). Within the law, a group can be classified as a "terrorist association" "even if its established purpose is a lawful one." Moreover, according to the law "leadership, promoters or financial supporters of [such an] association should be punished with prison terms of 15 to 20 years", subject to the discretion of a single judge (Haugaard 2017). According to Eugenio Sosa, a sociology professor at the National Autonomous University in Honduras, Article 590 "seeks to anticipate—to suffocate at times and above all anticipate—possible popular overflows … in the face of a general public that is very jaded by impunity, corruption and very severe social inequality" (Gies 2017). Garifuna, and OFRANEH leader Miriam Miranda similarly denounces Article 590 as the latest in a systematic erasure of social protest and silencing of a freedom of expression. She maintains that "the current government administration has done everything possible to restrict dissent as part of the re-election strategy laid out by the Juan Orlando Hernandez regime." She insists that the "re-composition of political forces" permits "the approval of countless neoliberal and undemocratic laws" to come into operation in the country (Gies 2017). The new penal code reflects what Radcliffe refers to as "[t]he presumed association between ethnic mobilization and terrorism resulting in particular material outcomes for indigenous individuals, as well as crafting a generalized attribution of subversion to ethnic populations" (2007, 387). In the face of a remilitarized state that seeks to remove indigenous bodies imagined to be "in the way" of neoliberal development projects, it seems that extraction and conservation and their concomitant practices are deeply similar.

Back at the Reserve: menacing continuities

In the aftermath of the aforementioned botched DEA/Honduran military raid in Ahuas, Honduran and US officials legitimized the violence by blaming the victims. Former DEA chief James Kennedy questions "why *innocent* civilians would be on the water in the middle of the night":

> these people out in Gracias a Dios or other departments, they aren't doing what they used to do, they aren't growing corn, and *pina* or pineapple and other products, they are waiting for a narcotics plane or boat to come in.
>
> (Cited in Mollett 2012)

Such an explanation discloses how processes of racialization dehumanize the Miskito, making killing them justifiable because officials, both foreign and national, misread the cultural landscape. Boat travel is key to the Mosquitia's socioeconomy, where traveling during the night ensures an early arrival to agricultural fields and markets and avoids travel during the heat of the day. Official narratives however are part of a longstanding racial discourse that problematizes Miskito land uses through narratives of civilization and savagery and through constructions of *terras nullius* in places populated by Indigenous peoples.

To be sure, the growing emphasis on extractive investments throughout the country has resonance inside the Mosquitia. According to MASTA president Normal Goff, without "full legal titles to our land, the government is able to give concessions to foreign companies, without any kind of consultation with us. The government is obsessed with bringing external investment into the country" but "now with the backing of titles we can stop this agenda"; "the Miskito people can protect [the forest] but only [when] we have title to those lands" (Cultural Survival 2013). Notwithstanding Goff's enthusiasm, for ordinary Miskito villagers threats to territorial autonomy remain. *Colono* land invasions new and old continue to challenge the legitimacy of Miskito territorial security. Prior to Miskito territorial legislation in 2013, a new land law was passed as part of the first Honduran Land Administration Program, known as PATH I (Republica de Honduras 2004). In short, the Honduran Property Law is ambiguous. While reaffirming the inalienabilty of Indigenous peoples' communal land rights, the law established a legal opportunity to *erase* or *dissolve* ethnic communal land titles (Republica de Honduras 2004). In fact, "the law permits *terceros* (third parties) already settled inside indigenous lands the rights to remain in these lands even when by law their initial land invasion was illegal" (Mollett 2016, 423). The Honduran Property Law legitimizes *colono* land invasions and exposes the fragility of recent territorial legislation, as does the state's commitment to extraction.

In January 2014, barely five months after titling, the state awarded contracts for oil exploration to a British oil and gas company (BG Group) for offshore sites along the Mosquitia's Atlantic Coast. The state allotted the BG Group a 35,000-square kilometer concession for an initial period of four years for exploration, but with the rights to drill for up to 25 years (Palencia 2014). While most people learned about these offshore concessions when they were announced in 2014, the contracts had already been granted in May 2013—four months *prior* to Miskito territorial legislation. The chronology is significant. In fact, as the late Berta Caceres noted, "What a coincidence. They authorize land titles just as they are to begin asking the Miskito people to approve oil and gas exploration by the English company British Gas Group" (*El Heraldo* 2014). And she was correct. According to Rigoberto Cuellear, the minister of natural resources and the environment, "in order to [legally] award the environmental licence to the English company, a process of consultation with the Miskito peoples must be completed" (*El Heraldo* 2014). Territorial legislation paved the way for a more amenable Miskito leadership vis-à-vis consultation and BP concessions. Furthermore, the Honduran government violated international law in offering exploration rights to the BG Group before consulting with Miskito communities. According to a recent decision handed down by the Inter-American Court of Human Rights in a different case brought by the Garifuna against the Honduran state, "[r]egarding the right to consultation and cultural identity, the Court considered that the consultation must be applied *prior to* any exploration project that may affect the traditional lands of the indigenous and tribal communities" (Cultural Survival 2016).

The enduring tenure insecurities faced by Miskito peoples, despite territorial legislation, may pose different challenges for Miskito women. Miskito territorial legislation was awarded to Miskito Territorial Councils (TCs). With few exceptions, most TCs are led by men and Miskito men comprise the majority of official members. On its face this does not necessarily undermine Miskito women's tenure security. But, as I write extensively elsewhere, during debates over *Catastro y Regularizacion*, gendered struggles over land became increasingly visible as Miskito tenure insecurity grew more salient and Miskito men strategized how to maintain control over community lands (Mollett 2010). While, currently, collective territorial control is legally sanctioned, threats to Miskito women's access to land still remain. Matrilineal inheritance and matrifocal family arrangements are changing as men, through both customary and statutory systems, increasingly control the lands of the Mosquitia. But, while Miskito male dominance is truncated by *colono* invasions, militarized conservation and a lack of state protections against transnational and third party interests (i.e., illegal logging) inside the Reserve may mean that, '[f]or indigenous women, the systematic violation of their collective rights as Indigenous Peoples is a major risk factor for gender based violence, including the violence perpetrated in their own communities" (FIMI 2006, 15).

Final thoughts

In the context of a constitutional assembly for Indigenous and Afro-Honduran women, the late Berta Caceres argued that in a time of extraction the fight is "to support the struggle not only against capitalism but also against racism and patriarchy" (Thompson 2011).

In this chapter, I rethink "parks and people" to show how a history of Indigenous peoples' dehumanization links biodiversity conservation and the country's extractive development agenda through racial and gender based violence. A coloniality of racial and gender power characterizes Honduras's "colonial present" (Gregory 2004). Extraction and protected area management are on the same side of the coin, linked by a persistent colonial proclivity to subjugate and erase Indigenous and Afro-Indigenous peoples and displace them from ancestral relations to land. Through militarization, protected area policies, land legislation, murder, criminalization, state impunity and extra-legal extractive practices, the country's Indigenous peoples are deemed "in the way" of progress and as a result face spectacular and mundane forms of violence. This violence that unfolds on human bodies and on more-than-human natures render clear the durability of a colonial history and logic that dictate whose bodies and whose landscapes have value and whose "don't count" (Razack 2016; Mies 2007). Such dehumanizing destruction demands intervention.

References

AFE-COHDEFOR. 2000. *Plan de Manejo, Reserva del Hombre y La Biosfera del Río Plátano*. Tegucigalpa: Proyecto Manejo y Proteccio´n de la Biosfera Río Plátano.

Altamirano-Jimenez, Isabel. 2017. How Do Real Indigenous Forest Dwellers Live? Neoliberal Conservation in Oaxaca, Mexico. *Atlantis*, 38(1): 207–219.

Anthias, Penelope and Sarah Radcliffe. 2015. The Ethno-Environmental Fix and its Limits: Indigenous land titling and the production of not-quite-neoliberal natures in Bolivia. *Geoforum*, 64: 257–269.

Apostolopoulou, Evangelia and William Adams. 2017. Biodiversity Offsetting and Conservation: Reframing Nature to Save It. *Onyx*, 51(1): 23–31.

Bird, Annie and Alexander Main. 2012. *Collateral Damage of a Drug War: The May 11 Killings in Ahuas and the Impact of the US War on Drugs in La Moskitia, Honduras*. Washington, DC: Center for Economic and Policy Research and Rights Action.

Birss, Moira. 2017. Criminalizing Environmental Activism. *NACLA Report on the Americas*, 49(3): 315–322.

Brockington, Dan, Rosaleen Duffy and Jim Igoe. 2008. *Nature Unbound: Conservation, Capitalism and the Future of Protected Areas*. London: Routledge.

Brondo, Keri Vacanti. 2013. *Land Grab: Green Neoliberalism, Gender, and Garifuna Resistance in Honduras*. Tucson, AZ: University of Arizona Press.

Bryan, Joe. 2009. Where Would We Be without Them? Knowledge, Space and Power in Indigenous Politics. *Futures*, 41(1): 24–32.

Brysk, Alison. 2000. *From Tribal Village to Global Village: Indian Rights and International Relations in Latin America*. Stanford, CA: Stanford University Press.

Büscher, Bram, Sian Sullivan, Katja Neves, Jim Igoe and Dan Brockington. 2012. Towards a Synthesized Critique of Neoliberal Biodiversity Conservation. *Capitialism Nature Socialism*, 23(2): 4–30.

Butler J (2004) *Undoing Gender*. New York, NY, and London: Routledge.

Cárdenas, Roosbelinda. 2012. Green Multiculturalism: Articulations of Ethnic and Environmental Politics in a Colombian "black community." *Journal of Peasant Studies*, 39(2): 309–333.

CNN. 2017. *Environmentalist Murder, a Criminal plot, a New Report Says*. www.cnn.com/2017/11/02/americas/honduras-cceres-killling-report/index.html

Cuffe, Sandra. 2014. Drilling the Caribbean: Indigenous Communities Speak Out Against Oil and Gas Exploration in Honduras. *Upside Down World*. http://upsidedownworld.org/archives/international/drilling-the-caribbean-indigenous-communities-speak-out-against-oil-and-gas-exploration-in-honduras. Accessed November 1, 2017.

Cultural Survival. 2016. *Indigenous Rights Win Major Step Forward in Honduras*. www.culturalsurvival.org/news/indigenous-rights-win-major-steps-forward-honduras. Accessed February 14, 2018.

Cultural Survival. 2013. *Campaign Update: Honduras Gives Title to Lands to Miskito People*. www.culturalsurvival.org/news/campaign-update-honduras-gives-title-lands-miskito-people. Accessed February 2, 2018.

Dempsey, Jessica and Rosemary-Claire Collard. 2017. If Biodiversity Offsets Are a Dead End for Conservation, What Is the Live Wire? A Response to Apostolopoulou and Adams. *Onyx*, 51(1): 35–39.

Devine, Jennifer. 2014. Counterinsurgency Ecotourism in Guatemala's Maya Biosphere Reserve. *Environment Planning D: Society and Space*, 32(6): 984–1001.

Duffy, Rosaleen. 2014. Waging a War to Save Biodiversity: The Rise of Militarized Conservation. *International Affairs*, 90(4): 819–834.

El Cronista. 1930. La Importancia seimpre creciente y siempre de acutalidad de extenso y fértil territorio de la Mosquitia Hondurena. April 15, 19, 21, 22.

El Heraldo. 2014. Entregan tierras a comunidades indigenas de la Mosquitia. www.elheraldo.hn/pais/583152-214/entregan-tierras-a-comunidades-indigenas-de-la-mosquitia. Accessed February 2, 2018.

Escobar, Arturo. 2016. Thinking-Feeling with the Earth: Territorial Struggles and the Ontological Dimension of the Epistemologies of the South. *AIBR. Revista de Antropología IberoAmericana*, 11(1): 11–32.

Fairhead, James, Melissa Leach and Iain Scoones. 2012. Green Grabbing: A New Appropriation of Nature? *Journal of Peasant Studies*, 39(2): 237–261.

FIMI. 2006. Mairin Iwanka Raya: Mujeres Indigenas confrontan la violencia. www.fimi-iiwf.org/archivos/8162f56478b843333dc95a1f5f381ab1.pdf. Accessed November 1, 2017.

Forest Trends. 2015. Titling Ancestral Territories in the Hondurans Muskitia. www.forest-trends.org/documents/files/doc_4974.pdf. Accessed February 2, 2018.

Fregoso, Rosa-Linda and Cynthia Bejarano, eds. 2010. Terrorizing Women: Feminicide in the Americas. Durham, NC: Duke University Press.

Galeana, Fernando and Enrique Pantoja. 2013. Strengthening Indigenous Peoples' Land Tenure Governance: The Case of the Miskito People in Honduras. *Annual World Bank Conference on Land and Poverty 2013*. Washington, DC: The World Bank.

Gies, Heather. 2017. Honduras, the Deadliest Country in the World for Environmental Defender, Is About to Get Deadlier. *Upside Down World*. http://upsidedownworld.org/archives/honduras/honduras-deadliest-country-world-environmental-defenders-get-deadlier. Accessed February 14, 2018.

Gilroy, P. 2018. "Where Every Breeze Speaks of Courage and Liberty": Offshore Humanism and Marine Xenology, or, Racism and the Problem of Critique at Sea Level. *Antipode*, 50(1): 3–22.

Global Witness. 2009. *Illegal Logging in the Río Plátano Biosphere: A Farce in Three Acts*. Washington, DC: Global Witness.

Global Witness. 2017. *Honduras: The Deadliest Place to Defend the Planet*. London: Global Witness.

Gregory, Derek. 2004. *The Colonial Present*. Malden, MA, and Oxford: Blackwell.

Grosfoguel, Ramon. 2007. The Epistemic Decolonial Turn: Beyond Political-Economy Paradigms. *Cultural Studies*, 21(2/3): 211–223.

Haugaard, Lisa. Under Attack but Undeterred: Human Rights Defenders in Honduras. *Latin America Working Group (LAWG.ORG)*, December 6, 2017.

Helms, M. W. 1971. Asang: Adaptations to Culture Contact in a Miskito Community. Gainesville, FL: University of Florida Press.

Honduras Culture and Politics. "Miskito Land Councils Receive Land Titles," September 13, 2013. http://hondurasculturepolitics.blogspot.ca/2013/09/miskito-land-councils-receive- land.html. Accessed November 1, 2017.

IM-Defensoras. 2015. Violence Against Women Human Rights Defenders in Mesoamerica: 2012–2014 Report. *MesoAmerican Initiative of Women Human Rights Defenders*, Mexico.

Kelly, Alice B. and Megan Ybarra. 2016. Introduction to Themed Issue: "Green Security in Protected Areas." *Geoforum*, 69: 17–175.

Klein, Naomi. 2014. *Capitalism vs. the Climate*. Alternative Radio.

Li, Tania Murray. 2010. Indigeneity, Capitalism, and the Management of Dispossession. *Current Anthropology*, 51(3): 385–414.

Loperena, Christopher Anthony. 2016. Conservation by Racialized Dispossession: The Making of an Eco-destination on Honduras' North Coast. *Geoforum*, 69: 184–193.

Lugones, María. 2007. Heterosexualism and the Colonial/Modern Gebder System. *Hypatia*, 22(1): 186–219.

Malkin, E. 2013. Honduras Grants Land to Indigenous Group, in Bid to Help It Protect Forests. *New York Times*, September 12. www.nytimes.com/2013/09/13/world/americas/honduras-grants-land-to-indigenous-group-in-bid-to-help-it-protect-forests.html. Accessed February 2, 2018.

Marhia, Natasha. 2013. Some Humans Are More Human than Others: Troubling the "Human" in Human Security from a Critical Feminist Perspective. *Security Dialogue*, 44(1): 19–35.

McSweeney, Kendra and Zoe Pearson. 2013. Prying Native People from Native Lands: Narco Business in Honduras. *NACLA Report on the Americas*, 46(4): 7–12.

McSweeney, Kendra, Erik A. Nielsen, Matthew J. Taylor, David J. Wrathall, Zoe Pearson, Ophelia Wang and Spencer T. Plumb. 2014. Drug Policy as Conservation Policy: Narco-deforestation. *Science*, 343(31): 489–490.

Mies, Maria. Patriarchy and Accumulation on a World Scale – Revisited. 2007. Lecture, Green Economics Institute, October 29, 2005. Published in *International Journal of Green Economics*, 1(3/4): 268–275.

Mies, M. and Shiva, V. 1993. *Ecofeminism*. London: Zed.

Mignolo, Walter. 2007. Delinking the Rhetoric of Modernity, the Logic of Coloniality and the Grammar of De-coloniality. *Cultural Studies*, 21(2–3): 449–514.

Mollett, Sharlene. 2006. Race and Natural Resource Conflicts in Honduras: The Miskito and Garifuna Struggle for Lasa Pulan. *Latin American Research Review*, 41(1): 76–101.

Mollett, Sharlene. 2010. Está listo (Are You Ready)? Gender, Race and Land Registration in the Río Plátano Biosphere Reserve. *Gender, Place & Culture*, 17(3): 357–375.

Mollett, Sharlene. 2011. Racial Narratives: Miskito and *colono* Land Struggles in the Honduran Mosquitia. *Cultural Geographies*, 18(1): 43–62.

Mollett, Sharlene. 2012. *Honduras Caught in the Middle: Militarization and Narco Traffickers Threaten Indigenous Culture*. Alter Net. www.alternet.org/world/hondurans-caught-middle-us-militarization-and-narco-traffickers-threaten-indigenous-culture

Mollett, Sharlene. 2013. Mapping Deception: The Politics of Mapping Miskito and Garifuna Space in Honduras. *Annals of the Association of American Geographers*, 103(5): 1227–1241.

Mollett, Sharlene. 2014. A "Modern" Paradise: Land, Labor, and Displacement-in-Place on the Honduran North Coast. *Latin American Perspectives*, 41(6): 27–45.

Mollett, Sharlene. 2016. The Power of Plunder: Rethinking Land Grabbing in Latin America. *Antipode*, 48(2): 412–432.

Mollett, Sharlene and Caroline Faria. 2013. Messing with Gender in Feminist Political Ecology. *Geoforum*, 45: 116–125.

Nixon, Robert. 2011. *Slow Violence and the Environmentalism of the Poor*. Cambridge, MA: Harvard University Press.

Ojeda, Diana. 2011. Whose Paradise? Conservation, Tourism, and Land Grabbing in Tayrona Natural Park, Columbia. *International Conference Global Land Grabbing*, January 1, 2011.

Palencia, Gustavo. 2014. BG Group to Begin Honduras Oil, Gas Exploration with $20 mln Investment. *Reuters*. www.reuters.com/article/honduras-oil/bg-group-to-begin-honduras-oil-gas-exploration-with-20-mln-investment-idUSL2N0KR06220140117. Accessed February 13, 2018.

Peluso, Nancy Lee and Christian Lund. 2011. New Frontiers of Land Control: Introduction. *The Journal of Peasant Studies*, 38(4): 667–681.

Perez Chiriboga, Isabel. 2002. *Espiritus de Vida y Muerte: Los Miskitu Hondurenos en Opoca de Guerra*. Tegucigalpa, Honduras: Guaymuras Editorial.

PRISMA. 2016. Conservation and Community Rights: Lessons from Mesoamerica. *PRISMA*. www.prisma.org.sv/uploads/media/Conservation_and_Community_Rights.pdf

Quijano, Anibal. 2000. Coloniality of Power and Eurocentrism in Latin America. *International Sociology*, 15(2): 215–232.

Radcliffe, Sarah. 2007. Latin American Indigenous Geographies of Fear: Living in the Shadow of Racism, Lack of Development, and Antiterror Measures. *Annals of the Association of American Geographers*, 97(2): 385–397.

Razack, Sherene. 2016. Gendering Disposability. *Canadian Journal of Women and the Law*, 28(2): 285–307.

Redclift, Michael and Delyse Springett. 2015. *International Handbook of Sustainable Development*. New York, NY: Routledge.

Republica de Honduras. 2004. Ley de Propiedad; 12,5000 millones de dolares se incorporan a la economia con la entrega de titutols de propiedad [The Property Law; 12.5 Millon Dollars Will Be Incorporated into the Economy with the Award of Property Titles]. *Poblacion y Territorio*, 3(6): 28–34.

Republica de Honduras. 2010. *Plan de Nacion*. https://eeas.europa.eu/sites/eeas/files/lc_10.pdf

Ronderos, Katherine. 2011. Poverty Reduction, Political Violence and Women's Rights in Honduras. *Community Development Journal*, 46(3): 315–326.

Smith, Andrea. 2006. Looking to the Future: Domestic Violence, Women of Color, the State and Social Change. In *Domestic Violence at the Margins: Readings on Race,*

Class, Gender and Culture, edited by Natalie J. Sokoloff and Christina Pratt. New Jersey: Rutgers University Press.

Stoler, Laura Ann. 2013. *Imperial Debris: On Ruins and Ruination*. Durham, NC: Duke University Press.

Sundberg, Juanita. 2008. Placing Race in Environmental Justice Research in Latin America. *Society and Natural Resources*, 21: 569–582.

Thompson, Margaret. 2011. Indigenous and Afro-Honduran Women's Constitutional Assembly. *Upside Down World*. http://upsidedownworld.org/archives/honduras/indigenous-and-afro-womens-constitutional-assembly-in-honduras/. Accessed November 1, 2017.

Trucchi, Giorgio. 2017. Honduras: vientos de persecución en tierra Garífuna. *Albasud*. www.albasud.org/noticia/989/honduras-vientos-de-persecuci-n-en-tierra-gar-funa. Accessed November 13, 2017.

Weheliye, Alexander. 2014. *Habeas Viscus: Racializing Assemblages, Biopolitics and Black Feminist Theories of the Human*. Durham, NC: Duke University Press.

Wily, Liz Alden. 2014. The Law and Land Grabbing: Friends or Foe? *Law and Development Review*, 7(2): 207–242.

Ybarra, Megan. 2012. Taming the Jungle, Saving the Maya Forest: Sedimented Counterinsurgency Practices in Contemporary Guatemalan Conservation. *Journal of Peasant Studies*, 39(2): 479–502.

Zimmerer, Karl. 2015. Understanding Agrobiodiversity and the Rise of Resilience: Analytic Category, Conceptual Boundary Object of Meta-Level Transition? *Resilience*, 3(3): 183–198.

Index

For Product Safety Concerns and Information please contact our EU representative GPSR@taylorandfrancis.com
Taylor & Francis Verlag GmbH, Kaufingerstraße 24, 80331 München, Germany

www.ingramcontent.com/pod-product-compliance
Ingram Content Group UK Ltd.
Pitfield, Milton Keynes, MK11 3LW, UK
UKHW021303190926
475701UK00009B/644
9780367820862